A DUBIOUS CODICIL

By the same author

The Missing Will: An Autobiography

fiction
Sheldrake

A DUBIOUS CODICIL

Michael Wharton

Chatto & Windus
LONDON

Published in 1991 by
Chatto & Windus
20 Vauxhall Bridge Road
London SW1V 2SA

A CIP catalogue record for this book is available from
the British Library

ISBN 0 7011 3064 4

Phototypeset by Input Typesetting Ltd, London
Printed in Great Britain by
Mackays of Chatham plc,
Chatham, Kent

To Jane

Contents

I
Beyond the Lodge

The marble entrance-hall and, the part standing for the whole, the mahogany reception desk of the *Daily Telegraph*'s neo-Egyptian building in Fleet Street – slab-faced, solid and lofty for those times before the London skyscrapers overtopped St Paul's and proclaimed the empire of imaginary money – was known to all the staff, of whatever degree, as 'the Lodge'. It was so called because it was the entry to the domain of the dynasty of newspaper magnates who had founded and still owned the newspaper, the Berry Family, originally from South Wales, the head of which had borne, since 1941, the title of Viscount Camrose.

The second son of the first Viscount was the Hon. Michael Berry, who now ruled as Editor-in-Chief in a suite of panelled, finely furnished rooms on the fifth floor (known to all as 'The Fifth Floor'), complete with office, study, library, dining-room, kitchen, bedrooms and everything else needed for a miniature gentleman's seat. There was even a narrow strip of garden, with real flower-beds, real shrubs and a real lawn, below the parapet outside the tall French windows, and a real gardener to tend it. If it had been possible (and there were times, later on, when I believed it was), there would have been an avenue, terraces, fountains, statues, a walled garden producing peaches and nectarines as fine as any in Fleet Street for the master's table, a lake, a deer park, pheasant coverts, a home-farm and a prospect of rolling, fertile countryside, most of it in the possession of the family.

Mr Berry (or 'Michael', as some of his employees liked to call him, not necessarily to his face) was a worthy proprietor of this establishment. He had two others, one in the Home Counties and one in Cowley Street, Westminster, where his wife, Lady Pamela Berry, presided over a famous salon. She was a highly fashionable and sociable person, daughter of the first Lord Birkenhead, whose supposed part-gypsy descent (he was a Smith, or Petulengro) was evident, so some thought, in her dark good looks, flashing eyes and animated manner. It was possible, certainly, to imagine her dancing by a gypsy campfire or sitting, dressed in the bright colours favoured by gypsy womenfolk, on the steps of a gaily-painted hooped wagon of the traditional kind, making clothes-pegs which she would later offer for sale to mesmerised, even terrified, village housewives, with curses if they did not buy, and a promise of cut-price fortune-telling if they did.

Mr Berry evoked no such old-fashioned fantasies. It was impossible to imagine him in the complementary role of a Romany *Chal* or even a Gypsy Gentleman. He seemed in every way the opposite of his wife. He was, at the time I entered his service, a tall, handsome man of middle age without a trace of grey in his jet-black hair, with pleasant good manners and an air of extreme reserve. His shyness was notorious. It was said that once, when as a young man he had to make a public speech, he fainted clean away. But by my day he had learned, by admirable application, to master his shyness and even turn it to an advantage, making his hesitant manner serve a special kind of edged and ironical humour, most enjoyable for those who could appreciate such nuances, provided they were not its victims.

For myself, I never was. But then, petrified with class-conscious dread of both Michael Berry and Lady Pamela, I scarcely exchanged more than a few words with either of them during my whole thirty years of service. Michael Berry, whose shyness might in theory have made a bond between us (there is an Irish proverb, 'One beetle knows another beetle'), once invited me, along with other selected members of staff, to one of his regular small luncheon-parties; I was so nervous I could not lift a glass to my mouth, and had to explain to him that my doctor had forbidden me alcohol, a thing so obviously untrue that he must have smiled inwardly. About the same time, Lady Pamela invited me to one of her evening parties in Cowley Street; I was so nervous I drank too many champagne cocktails, encouraged by a sympathetic butler, himself apparently drunk, and becoming unstable, I trod clumsily and heavily on her foot. Neither invitation was ever repeated.

No such anguished thoughts as these, of course, were in my mind when, on the cold grey New Year's Day of 1957 I passed, for the first time as an employee, through the mahogany-framed revolving door of Peterborough Court, as the Berrys' domain was called. Vaguely, I noted the racks of newspapers round the walls and the bronze tablet with its roll of honour commemorating employees killed in the two wars. Vaguely I returned the greetings of the men at the reception desk and took one of the three slow, ancient lifts to the 'Way of the World' room on the fourth floor to present myself to my friend of two years' standing, and now my colleague, Colin Welch.

Did I have any coherent thoughts at all? I had had scarcely any sleep; I had passed the night in a drunken phantasmagoria, partly with my wife Kate, partly with others mostly unremembered, in pubs, clubs and other places barely identifiable at the time, now a confused blur. My head throbbed; and such was the force of this superlative hangover that it did not even throb in a regular rhythm, but with unpredictable, jerking agony. Stale

3

alcohol pumped through my veins and seethed in every joint and ganglion. Through eyes three-quarters closed I peered at the pale grey world as though trapped at the back of a splintered mirror. My hands and feet seemed to disengage from my body as the great clock which hung over Fleet Street, below the window, began to strike the hour of eleven.

It was Monday, the first day of the columnar week. A column would have to be ready for the 'deadline' of six o'clock that evening for the following day's paper. It must have been obvious to Colin, a man well able to recognise the symptoms of hang-overs, but of robust constitution and resilient temper, that he could expect no writing from me. He must have wondered, on that first morning, if he had done the right thing in rescuing me from the BBC and bringing me on to the paper as a regular, salaried collaborator on his column, which at the time used many occasional contributions from various hands, previously including mine. But he showed no uneasiness, giving me a few 'files' to look over, explaining the organisation and timetable of the column and introducing me to those who worked on it.

He had started the column on 18 October 1955 (it is impor-tant to get dates right), with a staff of two editorial assistants and a secretary, Miss Thompson, a dark, well-built woman in her thirties, an expert at typing, filing correspondence and constructing card indexes of formal beauty whose scanty remains lingered in the filing-cabinets for years afterwards, hopelessly pleading reminders of a lost efficiency which came to seem pointless and meaningless and perhaps had always been so.

The duties of the two editorial assistants, Michael Hogg and John Herbert, consisted mainly of reading the day's newspapers and occasionally extracting possible subjects for us to write about. John Herbert, son of A. P. Herbert, the MP and comic writer, was a tall, agreeable man in his late twenties; he left, soon after I arrived, to better himself in the world of the higher auctioneering. Michael Hogg, about the same age, was equally agreeable, but already somewhat inclined to world-weariness and a fairly low view of people in general. He had an enchanting wife, Elizabeth, always known as Liz, daughter of an eccentric Herefordshire baronet. She was an accomplished musician and further endeared to me by her knowledge of those 'Celtic' legends and Dark Age Affairs ('the Matter of Britain') on which I have always doted.

When I first joined the staff, and before he left to take a job elsewhere on the paper, it was Michael Hogg's daily duty to 'put the column to bed' on the 'stone' down below in the basement, where the printers and compositors worked and where, every day, at about half past three in the afternoon, the great presses began to roll with a distant roar which pervaded and gently shook the whole massive building. There was a slight vibration, like a ship's engines; the promise of a voyage never fulfilled, let alone begun, but always mysterious and pleasurable to anyone as addicted to illusions as I was.

An indispensable part of the columnar 'team', as it would have repulsively been called if it had existed later on when journalists began to write about each other and become familiar figures on the television screen, was Michael ffolkes, whose real name was Brian Davis. He drew the one or two stylish little drawings which had appeared every day in the four-days-a-week column from its earliest days. Already a successful comic artist, with aspirations and talents for something more, he worked from a studio high up in Shaftesbury Avenue, a strange room of narrow triangular shape crammed with an astounding assortment of treasures, as well as with his artist's paraphernalia – masks, crystals, brass jugs and trays, completed or half-

5

completed drawings and paintings, screens stuck with exotic odds and ends. A huge photograph of a painting by the nineteenth-century French Salon painter Bouguereau was pasted on one wall, showing a crowd of naked nymphs, all identical, perfectly shaped, white-skinned, and of ideal nubility. This stupefying work of painstaking bad taste and technical skill amused Michael greatly; but it would be hypocritical to say that he – or any other man – did not enjoy looking at it.

From this junk-shop of a studio he telephoned every day at lunchtime to discuss what he should draw, and showed remarkable rapport and skill in providing what was needed, often producing little masterpieces of elegance and wit which, when reduced to microscopic proportions on the printed page, might easily escape the readers' notice. It was an affectation of his to maintain that he had never met any people like the 'characters' who subsequently appeared in the column. Yet somehow he contrived to realise them in a few lines with remarkable accuracy. He would sometimes drop into the *Telegraph* office in the evening with the day's drawings: a stocky, dark-haired man of about thirty when I first knew him, some twelve years younger than myself, a man of complicated origins, jaunty and charming, with a good opinion of himself. And why not? He was a friendly, amusing man, good company, and a very talented artist.

In some ways he was more like my BBC acquaintances than the Fleet Street people I was now getting to know. He was fond of a drink and his studio was never without a good supply of it, including champagne, for he believed in a 'high standard of living'. In his liking for drink he was, of course, no different from the Fleet Street journalists or anyone else I could get on with; but he was what might be called raffish, an old-fashioned 'Bohemian' artist with a distinctly irregular private life made

6

possible by a respectable, domestically efficient Jewish wife who looked after their flat in Pimlico and their two young children.

Colin Welch, the man who had rescued me so providentially from the BBC, though I did not realise how providential this was to prove, now regarded me, on that first day of my new career, with what must have been dubious eyes, as he and his assistants went through the process of producing a column while I gradually surfaced from my hangover. He was a lively, learned man of about the same age as Michael ffolkes; he had served in the army towards the end of the war and was wounded in the Normandy campaign. After the war he went up to Peterhouse, Cambridge, along with his friend and coeval Peregrine Worsthorne, and read history and economics.

He was at this time a compact, strongly-built man with thick dark curly hair and an exceptionally fine set of teeth, enabling him to smile more often and convincingly than I, though he would almost certainly have done so whatever his teeth had been like. He wore spectacles and his face belonged to a certain unmistakably English type which can be found in all classes anywhere, any day of the week.

But *this* man could not be found any day of the week in any class. He had 'a first-class mind', and imagination and literary talent to go with it. He was a magnificent talker on many subjects and one of the finest mimics I have met, able to set me in fits of laughter even when doing imitations of people I did not know, such as the aged father of Desmond Williams, a legendary Irishman who had just failed to get a fellowship at Peterhouse and now taught history at the National University of Ireland.

Colin had a prodigious knowledge and memory of music, and should some favourite musical work come to mind, he was capable of whistling, note-perfect, long extracts, even, it

seemed, whole operas, persisting until even the most passion-
ately musical begged him to stop. Fond of drinking as he was
and with certain traits of fascinating eccentricity (he had a
habit, for example, of picking his nose, occasionally tasting the
extracted mucus or 'bogey', without any attempt to conceal
himself, as most people would, behind a newspaper), we could
hardly fail to get on, even though this merry, energetic, public
school man (like Worsthorne, he had been at Stowe) with his
easy, agreeable manners and incipient fondness for powerful
motorcyles, was a very different person from myself.

On that first day and for the succeeding few days, when I
had got over my initial panic and began writing my share of the
column, at first hesitatingly then with growing confidence, I felt
slightly homesick for the BBC. I had expected to find a world
of dynamic, shirt-sleeved journalists in Fleet Street, with green
eye-shades, always working madly against the clock and continually talking on several telephones at once with their feet on
the desk.

In fact the office of the *Daily Telegraph* seemed rather like a
shabbier version of 'B. H.', with older, less comfortable furniture and inferior washrooms and lavatories, without carpets on
the floors or tastefully arranged flowers in the foyer. I had
exchanged 'programme', 'cue', 'script' and 'studio' for 'copy',
'deadline' and 'stone', and for 'the Corp' (as the BBC was
called by its employees before it became 'the Beeb') 'the office',
one of the many different newspaper offices which made up
Fleet Street, 'the Street of Shame', as some of its denizens
called it even in those days, long before it came to deserve the
name so thoroughly – and, in its later days, after the Great
Diaspora, a name worse than shame and almost beyond words.

I had exchanged the George and the Stag, and its ancillary
afternoon drinking club – the 'M. L.', with its agreeable ming-

8

ling of BBC people and members of the 'mantle trade' from neighbouring Great Portland Street – for the Kings and Keys, a long, narrow pub next door to the *Telegraph* and part of the Berry domains, where the company was made up of journalists and printers. Although I did not know it, I was to spend a good deal of the next thirty years in this pub and to elaborate, in these rather unpromising surroundings, much of what might be called the mature 'Peter Simple' column. So I must fix it in memory and describe it. When I first went there it was very much a 'basic pub': a rough, almost primitive place with a few old cane chairs arranged along the bar; if it did not have sawdust on the floor it should have done.

The greater part of it was an L-shaped saloon bar, with a small 'snug' in one corner near the door which was traditionally used only by the blue-overalled printers when they grew tired, on fine evenings, of leaning against the front of the building between shifts, gazing sardonically at all that went on in the street, hoping, perhaps, for an accident to happen. Observant, self-confident and well-paid, they were able, as they well knew, to enforce their will over the management at any time by bringing the presses to a standstill, and so thought themselves, not without reason, greatly superior to the journalists. About these, I felt, they knew much more than the journalists knew about them, stolidly sinking their pints of beer and listening with half an ear as the objects of their observation became more and more noisy, ribald, excited and recklessly indiscreet towards closing time.

The landlord, in those early days, was a middle-aged Irish-man, Sean Macnamara, who was reputed not only to have fought with distinction in the Troubles and the Civil War, reaching the rank of Commandant, but to have been one of General O'Duffy's Blueshirts, one of those who volunteered to

9

fight for Franco and were therefore on the right side in the Spanish Civil War as far as I was concerned. His tales of ambushing British soldiers during the Troubles went down much better then than they would now. He was a pleasant enough man of strong will-power, and a born landlord. He demonstrated both his military authority and his power of command, as well as his right-wing opinions, to notable effect one evening when I was in the bar and the bulbous, drunken face of Brendan Behan, then at the height of his fame, appeared round the door. 'Out! I'll not serve your sort here!' barked Macnamara, repeating the words in Irish for good measure, and the man who in any other circumstances would have begun flailing his fists, vomiting and breaking up the furniture – all perhaps at the same time (for he was a highly talented man in this department) – instantly disappeared.

I had exchanged the 'grey men' of the BBC administrative machine and the endless conferences of the Talks Department for the far from grey editor of the *Daily Telegraph*, Sir Colin Coote, to whom alone the column was responsible. He was inclined to distrust it. It had been the brainchild, in the first place, of his deputy editor, Donald McLachlan, a clever but highly eccentric man, formerly in Naval Intelligence, with a cryptographer's mind and a habit of making tangential remarks which sometimes made him difficult to follow. 'I've got an idea for you,' he would say when I encountered him somewhere in the building. 'Come into my room and I'll tell you all about it.' But by the time I had followed him into his room he had to admit, with a rueful look, that he had forgotten what his idea was. Sir Colin's opinion of him was obviously low. He showed this by a practice of referring to him in the presence of subordinates as 'Macglashan', 'MacCorquodale' or anything of that sort which took his fancy, always with a look of complicity for whoever else was present. (As I still had a vestige of Army feeling about what was and was not done, I found this disagreeable, even shocking.) He gave similar treatment to H. D. Ziman (always known as 'Zed'), the literary editor, who had been at Rugby with him but had earned him contempt for not being able to bowl overarm; a garrulous Jewish intellectual, he lived in Belsize Park and gave wine and cheese parties: none of these things can have endeared him to the editor.

Sir Colin was a portentous figure in his late sixties, large, rubicund and upright, very healthy-looking but with a hint of the sardonic and choleric in his expression. Later on, when Michael Hogg had left and, for a time, Colin and I took turns to 'put the column to bed', I had to face him across the imposing editorial desk in his panelled room where conventional portraits of previous owners and editors looked down from the walls. I found it quite an ordeal. Here was a man who had 'done everything' – fought gallantly in the Great War, sat in Parliament, raced at Brooklands, flown solo to Le Touquet and back. He had also had three wives and was, I had been told, a figure of high romance.

In hospital after being wounded in France, he had fallen in love with a beautiful French nurse, and she with him. But through the chances of war they completely lost touch with each other. Back in England and picking up the threads of his career, he married an Englishwoman of his own class and had several children. Then one day in the Thirties he was sitting in Brown's Hotel, having tea with his wife and family when, suddenly looking up, he saw his French beloved, older but still just as beautiful, crossing the room and making for the lift.

Without a moment's hesitation he excused himself, got to his feet and followed her into the lift. Between floors (I cannot say how many – they may have gone up and down the whole way several times for all I know) he pleaded with her to stop whatever she was doing – she may have been married herself – and run away with him. She agreed, they fell into each other's arms, descended to the ground floor by another way and disappeared. Divorced, they married. But their happiness was brief. She died soon afterwards, leaving him broken-hearted. For his third wife he took, in due course, a sensible Dutch lady, a magnificent cook and above-average bridge player.

The last part of this story was undoubtedly true, whatever might be said of the rest. I could not help thinking of it on evenings when it was my turn for the painful duty of sitting on the other side of his desk and watching him read the day's offerings: it helped me in a situation which was not unlike my encounters with my unfortunate tutors at Oxford twenty years before. But at least I was usually sober and did not have to read the stuff aloud; I was paid for it and on the whole it was of a higher quality than my Oxford essays. Not that this necessarily helped. Sir Colin's attitude was not encouraging (perhaps his suspicion of anything connected with 'MacGillivray' persisted) and never once did I notice even a hint of a smile. 'Not too many skits please, Wharton,' he would say when some fantasy of mine seemed to him to have got out of hand. 'I don't quite see the point of this bit about Alderman Foodbotham being too big to get into the tram terminus.' On these occasions he had something in common with the overpowering alderman himself. And once he asked of ffolkes and his drawings: 'Does he get paid for these sketches?'

For obvious reasons, he was a great francophile (his stamp-collection was said to consist only of French stamps), and excessively anti-German. Inclined to be pro-German myself for atavistic and other reasons, I now learnt to apply a trick I had acquired in the army: if you had not shaved very convincingly before going on parade, you would leave a button undone. When the inspecting officer came round this diverted his attention from the more serious fault, and could immediately be put right. So when I wanted to make sure of slipping some item into the column, perhaps a 'skit' too fantastical for Sir Colin's taste, I would write another item full of praise for the Germans. The decoy always worked. 'Can't have this!' he would say, good-humouredly enough, as he read something extolling German virtue. 'Can't have the Hun getting above himself, you know!' And so some new aspect of Alderman Foodbotham or Mrs Dutt-Pauker got into print.

For my knowledge of Sir Colin's private life, particularly the romantic side of it, I was indebted to Claude Worsthorne, wife of 'Perry' Worsthorne (I had met both of them occasionally in the FitzGibbon circle when the Welches were our neighbours at Much Hadham). After Miss Thompson left, Claude became columnar secretary. Known as Claudie, she was a skilled story-teller with a talent for scandalous embroidery which may some-times have got her into trouble. A very small, attractive, blonde Frenchwoman born in Egypt (her father was a director of the Suez Canal Company), she had a fine command of English apart from a few Gallicisms and personal idiomatic eccentricities. But although some believed she did not have to do this, she always spoke English with a strong French accent.

She had been married when very young, just before the outbreak of the Second World War, to a young scion of the Welsh squirearchy who promptly joined the RAF and vanished, leaving her pregnant in a large dark house in Carmarthenshire to be cared for by two aunts, among people who scarcely spoke English, let alone French. She escaped and made her way to London where she joined the Free French and was said to have been photographed at the side of General de Gaulle ('Titch

and Lofty'). Totally fearless, with marked scatological tendencies and, on the whole, a poor opinion of the English (her
description of the smell inside a crowded London bus was a
tour de force) she was now married, with a daughter of about the
same age as mine, to one of those upper-class cosmopolitan
Englishmen whose relations all have confusingly different
names.

Perry Worsthorne was the younger son of Lady Norman
(later married to the notorious Governor of the Bank of England
and *bête noire* of my old comrades the Greenshirts) by the
Belgian Baron Kok de Gooreynd. Lady Norman, herself part
Belgian, came from an ancient Lancastrian family, the
Towneleys, whose estates once included the town of Burnley
(their house, Towneley Hall, is now the municipal museum).
Adopted as Conservative Candidate for Burnley, the Baron
shrewdly reasoned that the name Kok de Gooreynd might not
appeal to the general run of the electors. So he took the name
of Worsthorne from a small village on what remained of the
Towneley estates. For all that, he was not elected. He then
reverted to his original name. But of his two sons, the elder,
Simon, took the name Towneley on inheriting the property,
while the younger, Peregrine, who retained the name Worsthorne, inherited nothing.

Claudie, whether mistakenly or on purpose – I could never
make out which – was addicted to getting English phrases
slightly wrong ('Claudieisms'); later she used to say pityingly of
her husband, 'Poor boy, 'e 'as not a pea to 'is name'. She also
said ''e is as poor as a church rat'. Neither statement, to judge
from the Worsthornes' manner of life, was strictly true; they
moved in higher social circles than other journalists on the
Telegraph, including the editor, and Perry's lofty, flamboyant
manner was not popular with all of them.

When I joined the paper and secured, for the first time in my life, at the age of forty-three, a regular salaried job, I dropped, with relief, all the odd and disparate freelance activities – writing for *Punch*, editing the Football Association Yearbook, ghosting memoirs, rewriting other people's books and so on – which had furnished me with a meagre and precarious livelihood. I now had a contract and a salary of £1,600 a year, plus 'expenses'. This was more than I had ever dreamed of; indeed it was quite a long time before I stopped being surprised at being paid anything at all for what I was doing.

Cunningly, I kept one link with the BBC. I retained the part of my job there which entailed reading the manuscripts of about a hundred short stories a week – the work of amateur writers – and selecting about half a dozen of them for various actors to read on the then popular radio programme 'Morning Story', produced by my sad but lovable friend and drinking companion James Langham, one of the last gentlemen of the BBC. So innocent were those short stories; their plots seldom involved anything more exciting than a poor but deserving person unexpectedly coming into a fortune or the late-won love of some lonely widow or widower; innocent, indeed, was the BBC itself in those days, innocent and secure!

Yet at that very moment – the year 1957 was almost the precise turning-point, if there was such a thing – a movement was beginning, not only in the BBC but all over England, which in a few years was first to shake, and then bring down, that innocent security in ruins. It was the beginning of what became known, whether in approval or condemnation, as 'the permissive age'. I and most of my friends had always been 'permissive'; but here was a new kind of permissiveness, the low permissiveness of democracy; sexual freedom, once taken for granted by a few, was claimed by the too-many, and not

15

only claimed but openly preached as a 'right', a principle and before long, a duty. Reticence and modesty became matters for public ridicule. A certain amount of hypocrisy is necessary in any civilised society. Now it was shoved aside. The new reformers, who often had financial or political motives, or both, for hastening this process, had the way clear. Ironically, they might themselves have been shocked and horrified if they could have foreseen the outcome in England thirty years later.

In those days we saw only the first, feeble intimations of the horrors of today. 'Espresso bars' appeared, populated by dim young nihilists who had never heard the term; 'teddy boys'; 'guitars and skiffle-boards'; 'rock 'n roll'; and 'angry young men'. They jeered at stuffy old class-ridden England, sometimes, indeed, amusingly and justifiably. How far away it all seems now, and, considering all that has happened since, how innocent!

One small sign of decay I had noted some years before when a couple of intellectual Australians, he a physicist, she a would-be novelist with whom I had a brief, sad and remorse-ridden love affair, told me they regarded jazz as an important 'art form'. I had always enjoyed this kind of music as a background to getting drunk in night-clubs on the rare occasions I went to night-clubs with Constantine FitzGibbon, the only person I knew who frequented them. I was amazed and incredulous to come across intelligent people who took jazz seriously; and not merely that, but were themselves amazed and incredulous to find I didn't. It was the first time I had come across this phenomenon, later familiar in the writings of Kingsley Amis and Philip Larkin.

In the wider world other greater phenomena were becoming noticeable, and now that I was obliged to read the newspapers, unavoidable: the headlong advance of that science and technology I had always feared and detested, manifesting itself in such things as scientific farming; nuclear power stations; military rocket-ranges in, of all places, the Hebrides; chemical contraception (the application of technology to sexual love) and artificial insemination for human beings; the 'conquest of space', in which the Soviet Communists with their 'sputnik' took the lead and were the first to spout boastful nonsense about such technological conjuring tricks, 'signs and wonders' to delude simple-minded people.

Those were the days when the last remnants of the British Empire in Africa were liquidated and replaced by pseudo-states under 'black majority rule'; and, by a strange process of reversal, when the first batches of immigrants were arriving in England. Those were the days also, when television began to take a hold on minds and habits, stealthily growing from an ingenious toy into one of the greatest influences – and certainly the most evil – in the life of England. Bogus art and every sort of impudent imposture began to flourish as never before. Such was the rich and abundant material 'Peter Simple' had to work on. Like Juvenal who had written in the decadence of Imperial Rome, I found it impossible not to write satire. The difficulty was to find a way to do it: a column with fictitious 'characters' epitomising various types of detestable humbug seemed the best way.

Mrs Dutt-Pauker, the 'Hampstead thinker', the rich fellow-traveller and specialist in every kind of left-wing prejudice from adulation of the Soviet Union to virulent hatred of white South Africa, was, I think, the only important columnar 'character' who had appeared, in a rudimentary form, before I joined the column. Her name, invented by Colin, was, of course, an ingenious combination of Palme Dutt, the Suedo-Bengali theoretician of the Communist Party of Great Britain, and Anna Pauker, the post-war Romanian Communist leader who once complained that 'not nearly enough middle-class people were committing suicide'. This stereotype I contrived to flesh out, in the course of time, with details derived from some of the well-off left-wing ladies of our part of Hampstead.

It was not long before other 'characters' began to take shape. It was understood in the first place that for the most part Colin would write the 'serious' and polemical items of the four or five which made up the daily column (my knowledge of politics was slight in those days, and of economics, nil, as it has remained) and I the 'funny' and fantastical items. For these, in my early days on the column while I was still trying to adjust to my new life, Colin sometimes provided the germ (for example, he suggested the name of the fatuous soldier General Nidgett, who spoke like Montgomery, only more so); I had originally called the prodigious Bradford alderman (a version of one of my giant archetypal figures, along with Sir Marsden Braithwaite in my novel *Sheldrake* and, in real life, Lord Hothfield, the perpetual mayor of Appleby, and Sir Stanley Rous, the overpowering head of the Football Association) by the inadequate though authentically West Riding name of 'Alderman Sugden'. 'Foodbotham' was Colin's suggestion, a better comic name and one which would avert any trouble from the real-life Sugdens of the region. It was a curious thing that I was at first careless of possible libel; yet I still retained, from my training at the BBC, an instinctive horror of advertising; it was many years before I could write the words 'Guinness' or even 'Rolls-Royce' without profound misgiving.

By nature passive and lacking in initiative, and morbidly afraid, through inordinate pride, of failure, I could not, I think, have started the column myself from scratch, even if it had been purely humorous and fantastical, though I had found my gifts in that direction exploitable in *Punch* and *Sheldrake*. This was a pity because there was no reason, in principle, why I should not have secured myself a newspaper column long before, perhaps on leaving the army, and become reasonably rich and famous (though not in the way I originally hoped) and saved myself those years of self-indulgent obscurity in the BBC with all the troubles they led to. Such thoughts are of course utterly profitless.

However, given the impetus and example of a more vigorous personality, himself with no small comic talent, I soon began to discover a capacity for developing my inventions on my own lines. For a man lazy and apathetic by nature the routine of working four days a week to a newspaper deadline was salvation; capable of very hard work when given an incentive and with a very strong sense of duty and honesty springing from self-suspicion of being fundamentally irresponsible and dishonest, combined with guilt at the waste of my earlier years, I found myself, for the first time in my life, in a job I could actually do well and – a thing entirely new to me – get well paid for. Or so it seemed, with my low expectations at that time.

Colin had rescued me not only from the dead-end of the BBC but from my own sense of futility, my only too conscious failure to make use of whatever talent I may have had. For this I was deeply grateful. But needless to say, as with all my endeavours, a morbid doubt lurked. Could my work be regarded as a structure, however elaborate, luxuriant and transformed by my own personal idiosyncrasies and talents it later became, raised on another man's foundations? And if so, was this an aspect of the Jewish side of my nature, the vestigial, thinned-out yet still troubling legacy of my part-Jewish paternal grandparents?

In his book *Sex and Character*, published at the beginning of this century, the German Jewish writer Otto Weininger builds a great edifice of mad logic to show that all human beings partake, on a graduated scale which he demonstrates mathematically, of the masculine and feminine nature, the active and passive, the creative and derivative, and that only the most masculine people can possess original genius, the highest human quality. The Jewish nature, he holds, is essentially feminine, which is why there are no Jewish artists, writers or composers of original genius, only adapters and developers, however talented, of the ideas and insights of others. Knowing that as a Jew (and also a homosexual) he could not be a man of genius for all the fame his book had brought him, the wretched and despairing Weininger, epitome of Jewish self-hatred, shot himself at the age of twenty-three in Bonn, birthplace of Beethoven, the greatest genius and therefore the greatest man who ever lived. In one of his few jokes Hitler is reported to have said of Weininger that he was the only good Jew whom he had ever heard of and a fine example for all the others to follow.

Because of the book's supposed 'anti-semitism' – an objection which rests on the assumption that the Jews as a race are above criticism, an assumption reactively derived from Hitler's persecution – and also because of its 'sexism' and opposition to homosexuality, both attitudes unacceptable to present fashion (probably for the same reactive, anti-Hitlerian reason) – *Sex and Character* is now very difficult to find. There is an English translation, but the only copy I have ever come across is in the London Library, heavily annotated in the margins with many a 'true!' and 'excellent!' as well as stronger and more tasteless comments. It is one of the great 'forbidden' books of this century, along with Whittaker Chamber's *Witness*, and like that great testimony against 'liberalism', should be reprinted by some enterprising publisher, if only to tease and annoy established opinion and be dismissed as evil nonsense by pipsqueak reviewers in the Sunday press. I have read that Wittgenstein, who was three-quarters Jewish, had the same misgivings as I (and in crude statistical terms, with about three times as much reason) about Weininger's theories, which made him doubt whether he could be a truly original thinker. Sensibly, this undoubted hero of the mind decided that he would try to be as original as he was able to be. And that, I think, will have to do for my unheroic and comparatively mindless self.

Seen across the level prairie-fields of our denuded England thirty years later, by an old man beset both by the terrors of his own approaching death and by the multiplying terrors whose shadows are deepening over his country and the world, that distant time can sometimes seem like a lost dream of richness and happiness. It certainly should have been rich and happy in reality. My wife Kate and I had a pleasant furnished house – or rather half-house – in Downshire Hill in Hampstead, rented from the painter Fred Uhlman and his wife, who lived next door. It was one of the prettiest streets in London. We had our daughter Jane, a child of remarkable beauty and intelligence. We had our old friends from the BBC and new friends from the world of journalism; the FitzGibbons still held court at Sacomb's Ash, still gave their weekend parties for a strange assortment of people, some high in Constantine's social league-tables, some low, but all equally welcome. Among them were an agreeable couple, neighbours of theirs, Andrew and Elizabeth Foster-Melliar and their daughter Belinda, a year younger than Jane; they became lifelong friends. Elizabeth, née O'Kelly, from the County Kildare, was Catholic and helped to ensure that Jane was christened, somewhat late in life at the age of four, at the pretty Catholic church in Hampstead.

One of her godmothers was Theodora FitzGibbon and her

godfather Peregrine Worsthorne. The service was, of course, in noble Latin, and the sight of the small girl gravely holding her candle and promising to forswear the Devil and all his works might well have moved even a less facile heart than mine – that is to say, almost anybody's – to tears. Afterwards there was a party at our house. Kate was good at giving parties. Unlike myself, she was good at making friends, even if she did not always keep them (who, for that matter, does?). I sometimes felt that I depended on her for making contact with other people, and that this dependency was growing, distinctly to my disadvantage. Later on, when things had gone wrong, perhaps irremediably wrong, between us, she would remind me how one evening in the early days of our marriage, when we were in London on a visit from Manchester at the time the BBC employed me there, she had suggested looking up some old friends – René Cutforth and his wife Marguerite, perhaps. But I, looking dismally out of the window at the sun setting over the rooftops, had said, 'Oh, who on earth would want to see us?' Of course, when we met our friends, I was glad and so were they. Rightly, Kate had no patience with this miserable attitude. Not that it was anything more than intermittent, but it was always there under the surface like an evil spirit, blighting life and hope, needing only the least encouragement, such as any imagined slight, to reveal its dull and squinting face.

Were we happy? The thought is like a cloud stealing over the sun. We ought to have been supremely happy; certainly I ought to have been – possessor of this fine young girl, eighteen years younger than myself, intelligent, imaginative, humorous, responsive, on whom, I could not fail to notice, the glances of other men sometimes rested with unmistakable speculation. It may be that we should not have married; I am not the only man who has found, after living with a woman, that marriage subtly changed his feelings, however free of conventional morality he may have thought himself, making what was illicit into what was permitted and killing desire stone dead. How, even if I had fully realised this myself, which I did not, could I have explained it to my young, loving and eager wife, who had promised to 'make my life pure gold', this Nordic blonde who, when I 'confessed' to having Jewish blood, immediately claimed to have Jewish blood herself, a manifest absurdity?

It is true that she was wilful, egotistical, wild and dangerous. 'Jack' Dillon, one of the great BBC 'characters', had warned me not to have anything to do with her; he explained, in his best storytelling form, that she was a prime specimen of a teredo, the dreaded shipworm of old days which, once attached, would bore away until the timbers rotted and the vessel became unseaworthy and sank, preferably with all hands aboard. She was also extremely eccentric in many ways and this she remained after our marriage, though her proto-hippie get-up of pullover and corduroy slacks, supplemented by a personal shabby mackintosh, which she had worn when we first met in the Stag's Head in Hallam Street, gave way to smarter but still unusual clothes. But her fingernails remained movingly dirty.

This eccentricity had captivated me in BBC days, when, after eating mussel soup in the local Italian restaurant, we hastened to my attic room high above Portland Place to discard any clothes, eccentric or otherwise, we may have been wearing – and how these things tear at my heart with a terrible pang of regret! – to roll about on the floor or on the bed or anywhere else available.

Those days were long past. We had a marriage and no marriage – not, if the truth were told, a thing uncommon among the people we knew. We had the tie of affection and intermittent lust, and of a shared love of books, poetry, music, drinking and

23

walking in the country. We were not faithful to each other; which of us was the first to be unfaithful I cannot say. We went our own ways, with occasional affairs of little consequence, so it seemed; we behaved as we had always done before we were married. But Kate was growing stronger. She was no longer the 'child bride' or 'beauty of the future' of the FitzGibbons' fantasy; nor the ephebic 'sonny boy' that Manchester shopkeepers, seeing only her top half over their counters, had sometimes called her to our amusement. She was turning into a mature young woman, outwardly self-confident (for all those inward doubts about herself which never left her) with an assertive voice and manner which some people came to regard, a thing by no means unpleasing to her, as 'posh' or even 'upper-class'.

She seemed somehow to have acquired a family background which did not belong to other members of her family I had met. Dominated by me in our early days, she now began to dominate. This is not, of course, an unusual role reversal; indeed it may happen more often than not. But I resented it, wincing at her overbearing ways and, perhaps, envying them. The FitzGibbons, who still had much influence over me, were inclined to laugh at her. Over a *tête-à-tête* supper in a Soho restaurant, Theodora confided to me, in one of her favourite amusing catch-phrases, that she had 'taken an instant dislike' to Kate and advised me to divorce her on the grounds of adultery as soon as possible. I said I would think it over and let her know what I decided. On the way home to Hampstead in the tube I picked up a pretty Welsh girl called Glenys and gave her coffee at an espresso, but though she invited me to her neighbouring bedsitter, I declined the offer. Regretting this the next day, I rang her but found her decidedly less friendly. All this was thoroughly in character, or, as Theodora would have said, 'typical of you'. Such was the absurd frivolity we all affected, thinking ourselves invulnerable to time and chance.

When we spent a month's holiday that summer at the Uhlmans' cottage in North Wales, Beudy Newydd, a lonely converted barn in the hills a few miles from Penrhyndeudraeth, taking with us the delightful, rather melancholy Elizabeth Foster-Melliar and her daughter Belinda (Andrew, jokingly believed by the FitzGibbons to be a spy, was not available), it was Kate who arranged matters with Fred Uhlman, dubious though he was about us, and not without reason, considering our frequently drunken and rowdy behaviour. She had grown masterful; and it was she who organised the slow journey by the old Cambrian Express from Paddington through Welshpool and along the coast of Wales, glorious in the old June weather which – perhaps Kate had organised this too – lasted without a break for almost all our holiday. It was she who organised supplies of food and drink from the local grocer, an old-fashioned Welsh archetype who, gratified by the long list, asked subserviently when she had finished: 'And will that be all, madam?' in a tone which suggested that, had she said 'And your immortal soul', he would have written that down too.

Perhaps because I was interested in the Welsh language and could understand it to some extent, though unable to speak it, and was sympathetic to Welsh nationalism, she expressed a hearty English contempt for the Welsh. 'He seems to be half-witted,' she complained, in tones that may have owed something to Theodora, of the elderly farmer across the *cwm* who supplied our milk. In fact, to my extreme pleasure, I found he could hardly understand a word of English.

It was Kate, too, who made friends with some of the neighbours, not usually those the Uhlmans had recommended who were inclined to be too respectable and not fond enough of drinking, but an assortment of youngish English people who forgathered at the pub they ignorantly called 'the Ring' (*yr Inn*, i.e. the Inn) at Garreg on the edge of the Traeth Mawr, and who were often adversely commented on, as I secretly knew, by the affably-smiling Welsh-speaking regulars. This was the domain of the celebrated architect Clough Williams-Ellis, creator of the fantastic Italianate village of Portmeirion; an eccentric old figure in knee breeches and yellow stockings. Many of the people we met were summer tenants of his cottages, all painted peacock blue, scattered over the rocky, bracken-covered hills.

Many of these English people, who formed a little community, very typical of that period in that they adhered to the 'left-wing package-deal', were would-be writers or painters or both. Though they were not without money, some, particularly those of the upper class, lived in studied squalor. One called 'John Jones the Englishman' who had a strikingly beautiful pre-Raphaelite wife with long auburn hair and a string of beautiful children to match, was convenor of the Communist Party in Harlech, evidently not an onerous post. He seemed to spend most of his time asleep on a bench outside his house.

Another one, distinguished by having rather more 'reactionary' views than the others and an admirer of the 'Peter Simple' column, had a small sheep farm in the mountains near Manod, the hollow hill where the Crown Jewels and treasures from the national collections had been kept during the war; a tarmac road led to it, ending abruptly in a great steel door. But he spent most of his time looking after his powerful sports cars, which he drove expertly and terrifyingly at breakneck speed along the winding roads. He sometimes stayed in bed late, leaving his sheep to fend for themselves on the mountain or, dashing impulsively to London, ignored them altogether. They tended to dwindle in number: after one period of absence he found, to his evident surprise, that they had all been slyly incorporated into the flocks of his neighbours. 'I suppose I'd better go to market and buy some more,' he said cheerfully, at which his long-suffering wife, another pre-Raphaelite but pale-haired, sad and lily-white, hung her head over the kitchen sink.

All these part-time settlers, who would be going back to London when summer ended, expressed great dislike of their landlord, accusing him of meanness in demanding their rent and not looking after his properties; it was typical that although they had made them into pigsties they still expected him to keep them in good order. They scoffed when we hired a car to take us to dinner at Portmeirion. The driver, Mr Jones, would take us only a hundred yards short of the entrance, explaining that it was 'the gate of hell', an opinion confirmed when we staggered out in the small hours to his enrichment.

We took the children to the sea, walked over the hills to Maentwrog or Beddgelert, where at the Royal Goat Hotel we ate delicious Welsh mutton and, asking for brandy from a young temporary barman, possibly monoglot, were given half-pint glasses full to the brim. It was a carefree time, or should have been, when the sun shone every day on the green world of Wales. We spent a good deal of time drinking beer on the crudely-built terrace and admiring the mountains. The Uhlmans, who had wisely locked up most of their possessions, had left out a portable gramophone of the kind I had had as an undergraduate, but only one record with it, an LP of Dvořák's Seventh Symphony. So whenever I hear this tuneful yet slightly sombre work it unfailingly calls up the memory of those weeks of summer, my first visit to Wales since my time at the army camp at Transfynydd in 1942, not far away over the mountains of Ardudwy, and soon to be the site of an abhorred nuclear power station. But before this, though I might strive to ignore it, our lives had been irrevocably altered.

I had realised that Kate was having an affair in London, but thought little of it. It was nothing new; and, nothing new either, I was having an affair myself. My friend was a small fair-haired woman in her early thirties with a neat, pleasing body; not pretty but with fine grey eyes, and one irresistible attraction for me, slightly protruding, 'goofy' teeth. She was the English wife of a Sephardic Jewish anarchist bookseller, a friend of David Thomson, who was then still working at the BBC and still, in spite of having standard 'liberal' opinions for a particularly good reason – the natural generosity and kindness of his nature – on reasonably friendly terms with me. Both Penny and her husband were said to be Reichians. Perhaps that was why she was so good in bed; or perhaps that is simply a matter of a man and woman liking each other.

There was something mysteriously familiar about her anyhow; I felt I had come across her somewhere before, but could not tell where. Here is a good opportunity for implied sexual boasting ('He's had so many women he can't keep count') to which I am not entitled. In fact it was only after our brief affair was over that I suddenly realised where I had come across her before. It was ten years ago, and she had been standing two or three places in front of my BBC girl friend Anne and myself as we queued up outside the Everyman Cinema in Hampstead one summer evening. I was instantly captivated by this unknown girl, who was wearing a beret, the only attractive kind of female headgear, and had an air of interesting artiness as well as sexual appeal. I was vaguely annoyed and frustrated because there was no chance of speaking to her; and although I looked for her after the film I could not see her. I soon forgot

28

her consciously. But without my being aware of it she had become one of those 'women I might have loved', glimpsed for an instant in the street, then lost, one of those phantoms which all men, I suppose, carry around in their minds as unattainable love-objects, so that any real woman can only seem second-best. That is all very well. But to have got to know her after all, to have made love to her, and not to know it! This is really carrying idiocy too far.

Thus preoccupied, I may not have realised for some time that Kate was not merely having an affair but was seriously in love. Yet a certain physical change in her, a blooming and softening which made her more physically attractive to me as well as to others, should have told me unmistakably that this was something more important than our casual affairs. Jealousy, which clinched the matter, did not arrive till later.

Not far from the Daily Telegraph, a few doors from the Kings and Keys, there was a rather sleazy café called 'Mick's' where Colin, I and others sometimes had lunch or, more usually, tea. It was frequented by partisans of CND, then beginning to make a name in the world, who provided ironical material for the column, notably old Peggy Duff and Pat Arrowsmith, famous in their day as leaders of the growing movement. For all their fanaticism we were amused to note that these CND people were capable of making jokes about their preoccupation ('Pass the Caesium-90, please!' I heard one bearded fellow say when he wanted sugar for his tea). It was here, on a winter's afternoon, that Kate's lover, as he now revealed himself, arranged to meet me. Kenneth, who was married, was a well-known journalist, a man I liked and admired, an honourable man whose behaviour and code of morals I knew to be very different from our own. He told me how things were, and said: 'I will ask you a question. If you answer "yes", this affair will go no further. Do you love Kate?'

I thought for a time, peering at the CND workers chatting about their plan of campaign, their leaflets, their demonstrations; at the cakes and sandwiches in the smeared glass cabinet; at the card hanging on the door which said 'closed', which for those outside, of course, meant 'open'. Then I said, 'No'. Would it have made any difference if I had said 'Yes'? Considering Kate's wilful and determined character, considering that all her impulses of life, although I did not fully realise it then, and all her wild energies (even the FitzGibbons admitted they were enough, if harnessed, to supply a large town with electrical power), were already diverted into a new course, I do not think so. I had answered 'No.' '. . . Like the base Indian, threw a pearl away,' he murmured, 'richer than all his tribe'. Stiffly I acknowledged the possible aptness of the quotation, but repeated 'No'. When I had left him I began to wonder whether this was a true answer, as I have wondered ever since from time to time, though less and less often, but without coming to any definite conclusion for all my delving into our beginnings.

2
A Kind of Idyll

I shall try to write down everything I can remember about that early time. In the year 1953 I was working for the BBC in Manchester, writing scripts for programmes on all kinds of 'regional' subjects, from the history of the Duchy of Lancaster to the centenary of the Manchester Ship Canal; and at the end of my posting, as though in desperation, on medical subjects which enabled me, later on, to pose at dinner parties as an oto-rhino-laryngologist until at last I met a genuine one. At that time Kate and I, at the beginning of our marriage, used to spend weekends and any other days we could at my mother's cottage at Amswick, a tiny hamlet in one of the smaller Yorkshire Dales.

There we had scarcely any company but ourselves and our year-old daughter. My mother was then seventy-four according to her own account – she had, I think, already got into the habit old people have of adding a few years to their ages and, when questioned, declared she had lost her birth certificate. She had moved there from my elder brother's farm in the Lake District, finding she got on no better with her daughter-in-law after my father died, and possibly worse. Her cottage at Amswick was quite roomy but fairly primitive, though there were one or two pieces of anomalous furniture she had salvaged from the wreck of what she thought of, more and more, as days of wealth and grandeur, becoming richer and grander with every day that passed. There was a fine chest-of-drawers, corner-cupboards, some pieces of Dresden china, a historic barometer which my

31

paternal grandfather must have tapped daily in the sombre hallway of his mansion, Oaklea, in the Manningham district of Bradford, hard by the gates of Lister Park. There were two round German plates of the same provenance, always said to be of incalculable value, hanging on the wall of the sitting-room, and an expensive folding card table with chromium rings at the corners in which to hold glasses.

We had no glasses to put in them. There was nothing but tea to drink, but on wet evenings we used the card table to play 'Solo' whist. My father had had a passion for cards and in the days of his prosperity, when we lived in Harrogate, he often played bridge with the few friends he had. My mother, though willing, was so bad at the game that she induced almost apoplectic rages in my father. So, increasingly, they must have compromised with 'Solo', a simpler game which rated much lower on the social scale and was generally associated with commercial travellers or small businessmen who played it on trains on the way to work ('Why don't you join our Solo School on the 8.35?').

But even this humble relation of bridge, at which my mother's more sophisticated in-laws had been skilled, taking every opportunity it afforded of humiliating her, was now a link with the great days of the past. I am fond of cards myself, as of all games which, as closed systems with inflexible rules, are an excellent refuge from reality. So it was no hardship for me to play these nightly games of Solo after tea (it was still Yorkshire tea at six or seven o'clock in those days) with my mother, with Kate, for whom it must have been a novel experience, engendering some of the various fancies we shared, and with a widow in the village who was always called by the single name 'Berner', a name whose origin was never explained. When I asked my mother about it, she either repeated the question or seemed not to understand why anybody should ask it.

Berner was a sad-faced but quite animated woman of about fifty with a submerged, unused intelligence. She was the only person in the village whom my mother would allow into her house. Why this was so I cannot say. Berner, like my mother herself, spoke with a fairly strong West Riding accent and was in no way socially superior to the other village people, whether Mr Metcalfe the farmer or Mrs Askew, another widow, or Joe Bates, the elderly retired shopkeeper who spoke so slowly that it was possible to leave the room for a minute or so and be back in time to hear the end of a sentence.

Yet as my mother's idea of her past became grander, so her neighbours became more and more unworthy; she would even say of the rich man who had bought the largest house in the village but visited it only occasionally, 'I've heard his father used to work in your grandfather's mill'. In this way the neighbours, who liked my mother and perhaps felt sorry for her, for she was likeable and amiable enough beneath her stereotyped Yorkshire rudeness, were excluded by her obstinate clinging to delusions of grandeur. So it was that we found ourselves some evenings, always the four of us, at the card table under the hanging 'Aladdin' oil-lamp whose mantle periodically went black because of the draught and had to be adjusted until it burned clear again. There was no electricity in the dale then (it must have been one of the last places in England without it) and when a year or two later the 'electric' arrived my mother said she did not want it. They installed it in spite of her grumbles and, perhaps to annoy her, put the switches in awkward, even inaccessible places. This made her grumble anew: 'I can't abide waste in any shape or form,' she said in one of her stock phrases, unfailingly used in certain contexts; others were 'scrupulously

33

clean'; 'hermetically sealed' and 'I have a rooted objection' to whatever it was.

My father had been a pathological gambler, and this, according to my mother, had been one of the main causes of our descent in the world. Yet she remained perversely true to his memory by insisting (not that anybody opposed her) that we always played for money however small the stakes, using my father's old poker-chips. These were well-worn cowry shells kept in a bag which had, I think, been made by 'Aunt', my mother's unmarried younger sister, who had been what was called 'simple' – that is, on the verge of half-wittedness – and played the part of a domestic slave. The bag was very badly made, lopsided and with a patch underneath where the stitches had gone wrong, the subject of frequent and unvarying comment ('she never could learn to sew').

When the shells had been counted and divided up between the players, the game proceeded. It went on for several hours with interruptions caused by shouting outside and thunderous knocks at the door, disturbing yet entirely predictable, for there were no shops in the village or anywhere near it and every evening of the week a different tradesman arrived in his van from Cassington, the nearest town. On Mondays it was the 'bread man', on Tuesdays the 'meat man', on Wednesdays the 'fish man', on Thursdays the 'vegetable man', and on Fridays 'Fred Williamson'. Faced with ironmongery and hardware my mother had run out of categories.

The card-playing scene – with its shuffling and dealing, its long silences ending with cries of exultation or despair when some player succeeded or failed in his bid at 'Solo', 'Abundance' or, most exciting of all, 'Misère', where the bidder can win only by losing all the tricks – would have made an excellent genre painting in the style of Karl Spitzweg, and had I been able to

34

paint or to persuade any painters I knew to paint it, I would certainly have done so. What would it have been called? Simply 'The Card Players'? Or there might have been a whole series, suitable, but for the fact that I would have preferred dark colours, purple and brown (in thick impasto), for hanging on the walls of some ideal saloon bar: 'Cardplayers Interrupted by the Fish Man', 'Cardplayers Interrupted by the Meat Man', 'Cardplayers Interrupted by Fred Williamson' and so on.

By the end of the game there were no sensational wins or losses, for the stakes were small. One evening Berner won 4*s* 2*d*, bringing a suspicious look, instantly suppressed, to my mother's face; and on another evening Kate, by an amazing run of luck with the cards and what was agreed to be superlative play ('What is he laughing at?' my mother asked. 'Ee, I don't know what your father would have said') won two 'Abundances' in successive hands and scooped the board for 6*s* 9*d*. There were none of the dramatic scenes of my father's time when sums which grew ever more vast in memory changed hands at a continually accelerated speed as in a fast-motion cinema film. But as we settled down to tea and biscuits between Berner's departure and bedtime we all felt agreeably satisfied. Kate and I lit our candles in those cheap round enamelled tin holders once manufactured in hundreds of millions (where have they all got to now?), and went upstairs to bed, where we always lay naked. Hearing my mother stirring in the next room, we tried to muffle our noises of pleasure and amusement. Entwined, we slept soundly.

On evenings when the weather was fine, we used to go down to the one flat field in the valley bottom; it was long and narrow, and by the riverside, where in some places the clear water ran swiftly over rocks, in other places slowly in deep ale-brown pools under the boughs of ash and sycamore. There, using a flat piece of wood about the size of a cricket bat but thinner, and a tennis ball, which we stored, when not in use, in a crevice in the dry stone wall which bounded the field, we played a game we had invented. I called it, in my affected way, the Minoan Ball Game, not because it resembled any game played in Minoan times but partly because everything had to have a fancy name and partly because Kate was not unlike a Minoan woman bullfighter to look at. The game was a combination of French cricket and rounders and tended to become more complicated with new rules as time went on; we took turns to bat and scored by innings, which sometimes accumulated such high scores that a game might have to be held over until the next evening.

It was there, on the smooth greensward where we ran about, pitching, hitting or catching as though our lives depended on it, that Kate showed her true Atalanta-nature. She liked the story and the comparison, and who would not? She was not graceful in the ordinary way, in fact she had in those days a clumsy, almost staggering gait acquired through having tried to minimise her height – as a young growing girl she had thought herself too tall – by a kind of half-stoop which held a certain pathos for me who knew, or thought I knew, its origin.

But when we were playing the ball game all this disappeared in her unselfconscious swiftness and skill. It was a delight to watch her and a delight to play. What I lacked in speed I made up for in tactics, bowling with varied spin on the ball or placing it in difficult positions; so we were evenly matched; often it was twilight, with a few stars beginning to glimmer, before we stopped play and took the homeward path. We always paused at the bridge over the river to peer down into the clear water and look for trout darting between the stones. Our northern streams were new to her; I liked to show her these things which had been familiar to me for so long. I showed her the obvious summer stars I knew: Vega, Deneb, Altair, Arcturus. She was very quick and intelligent. Because she had left school at the earliest possible age, out of rebelliousness and a wish to get out into the world, she 'had a mind uncorrupted by knowledge'; but it was receptive and retentive and rapidly filling up with what she thought worth knowing.

The village people knew of the game we played by the river-side and passers-by occasionally stopped to lean over the wall by the road high above our field to watch us for a moment in a puzzled way. But although they may have tapped their fore-heads in private, they made no comment. Nor did my mother, though when we prolonged the game almost until dark she was always waiting anxiously at the front door, as though we were errant children. Had some wandering psychologist seen us, making his way on foot through the Yorkshire Dales in the hope of finding patients (he would have had to be a very optimistic or very crazy psychologist: another subject for a genre painting in the manner of Spitzweg, 'The Wandering Psychol-ogist', perhaps) – had some such person seen us, he might have directed us peremptorily, even banging our heads together, to games more suitable for a newly-married couple on a summer evening, when even in this austere limestone country the scent of the earth was heavy and the leaves and tall grasses rustled seductively as the light slowly faded into embracing darkness.

Behind her cottage my mother had a small, narrow garden which sloped steeply up the hill and was overhung by the great rocks of the lowest of the limestone scars which rose in series out of the dale up to the moorland and rough sheep-runs of the 'tops'. She had some fine rose bushes, another vestige of her greater days, which she tended and defended against pests – particularly slugs – with the Yorkshire ferocity that was a dormant part of her nature. Here, on a seat among the winding

37

paths, we used to sit on fine days, talking of this and that and playing with the baby, who took her first steps and said her first words about this time. I used to amuse her by bouncing a ball on the sloping lichened stone roof of the outhouse and catching it; one morning early Kate and my mother surprised me as I dipped my finger in the dew which collected copiously in the folds of the alchemilla, an ugly, aggressive plant which has this sole redeeming quality of collecting dew, and feeding it to the child's lips. The two women laughed at this foolishness. Perhaps I was thinking of Edward Thomas's poem in which he finds his child sniffing the bitter herb, Old Man, which grows by his doorway and wonders if she will remember it; I may have wondered if Jane would remember her grandmother's garden.

Like my mother, we had scarcely anything to do with our neighbours, though for different reasons. Our friends were nearly all in London and but for occasional visits we might easily have forgotten about them altogether during our remote life in the North. We occasionally passed the time of day with an odd middle-aged couple, Louis and Winifred Hotchkiss, who had settled down together in a bungalow on the outskirts of Amswick and made a living mainly by running a small nursery garden. Winifred had worked at the BBC in Manchester, as I was then doing, but had given up 'all for love' by running off with Louis, a man of aggressively working-class mining stock whom she had met on one of her broadcasting assignments (he had written a 'working-class' novel and was a local literary celebrity). She was a middle-class woman and a Cambridge graduate and, what was more, *they were not married*, at least at that time, so they were not popular in the neighbourhood. Unknown but suspected hands were said to have thrown bricks through their windows. They did not become any more popular by being declared socialists (Winifred must have been one of

few 'Hampstead thinkers' in the Yorkshire Dales at that time
– though she was without the essential quality of having a lot
of money). My mother contented herself with saying in a special
tone of voice: 'Silly woman! Just imagine, at *her* age!' But
nobody was particularly interested in imagining anything about
a pair who seemed happy enough with themselves.

We spent a good deal of time on the other bank of the river,
opposite our Minoan Ball Ground, at a place where a small
spring welled out, forming a tiny tributary among the rocks
which by means of dams and other engineering devices could
be made into a miniature valley with an imaginary city for the
entertainment both of the baby and ourselves. Kate was as fond
of makebelieve as I was, or maybe even fonder. One of her
favourite games was 'the resistance game', played at night
among rocky fields which took the place of the French Maquis.
It was all part of what I called her 'infamous war on reality'; it
was characteristic of her that far from being offended by the
phrase she thought it an excellent joke.

We made long expeditions on foot across the hills to places
like Malham Cove, then quite unfrequented (now, like so many
places in the neighbourhood, a weekend traffic jam). Once,
leaving the baby in my mother's keeping, we went on foot, then
by bus and train, all the way to Appleby, where we stayed in
the Tufton Arms, scene of so many stirring events in the days
when I lived with my first wife Pepi and our son Nicholas a
few miles away at Hoff, last seen on the summer day in 1942
when I left to join my regiment in Northumberland en route to
India.

The outer world had changed. But in Westmorland little
had changed. The Tufton Arms had grown smarter and more
comfortable, the daguerreotypes of the Crimean War on the
walls of the dining-room, about which Constantine and I had

39

fantasised, replaced by china plates with pictures of wild flowers; there were tractors in the fields and many more cars on the roads; and the house where I had lived and enjoyed my colloquies with the rats had been equipped with electricity and sanitation and turned into a comfortable 'holiday cottage'. The old outdoor privy, in which I used to sit and look through the open door across the orchard and the fields to the distant Pennines beyond the River Eden, still stood, unused. There was nobody about. Half ashamed of my sentimentality, I passed water in this hallowed place.

Kate seemed to take this rather morbid revisiting of the past without demur; she had the present. But looking at these once familiar scenes again I had an uneasy feeling that the past was still there and still sounding through the years between and interpenetrating the present: the voice of Hitler seemed to rant through our ancient wireless set in the stone-flagged kitchen; a bicycle wheel whirred; a spade stood upright in the garden plot; young Constantine, impulsively self-exiled from Oxford, came loping up the lane to meet the girl friend I so greatly coveted for myself; in the nearby beech wood ancient boughs scraped and squeaked an ungainly half-forgotten tune; and then a high-flying German reconnaissance plane, prime symbol of everything that had vanished beyond any possible recall, droned overhead and for a moment imposed its now harmless ghost of fear. The sense of the numinous I had felt in those days had almost completely disappeared. But even being there induced an hallucinatory state. 'I think I've got a poem on,' I said to Kate. It was a phrase we had taken from a young would-be poet, in fact a public relations man, whom we had met in London, and we now used it as a familiar in-joke. 'I think I've got a poem on,' I said, 'but you can have it if you like.'

*

Sometimes we would go on the bus to Skipton, the nearest market town, still a simple place unexploited by tourism and not yet described in a thousand coloured brochures as 'the Gateway to the Yorkshire Dales National Park'. But it did have a gateway, the entrance to its ancient castle, where a stern, sergeant-major type of guide kept parties of visitors in strict order, thunderously rebuking Kate, who had strayed off by herself to peer up a forbidden stairway. We used to go to a somewhat forlorn little pub by the canal, now demolished, to play darts in a little square room with an old framed photograph on the wall. It was turning brown and showed a group of elderly men, mostly bearded, standing outside the pub with pints of beer in their hands; it was dated July 1911. The photograph took my fancy as a representation of human felicity. I asked the landlord if he would sell it; I was a collector of old photographs, I explained unconvincingly. He shook his head, his face instantly clouded with suspicion. 'Nay, it were me father's,' he said after a long pause for thought. But he obviously suspected that I 'knew something' about this photograph: either it was of great value in itself or it concealed in its mounting some document – a missing will, perhaps – which would make its owner a millionaire several times over. Next time we visited the pub, the photograph had gone.

This life, almost totally separated from others, a mild case of *folie à deux*, could not go on for ever. One day in late summer, when I was having a long recess from Manchester, we made an excursion by bus and on foot to what I called the 'Great Wilderness', the wild country at the head of Wharfedale – now invaded by visitors in hordes and disfigured by pseudo-forests of conifers – then a lonely region inhabited mainly by sheep and curlews. There, in an isolated farmhouse, clinging to the side of the fell and approached only by a rough track, lived a family Kate thought might make an interesting item for the radio about life in lonely places. She was anxious to help earn our living; and like all young women in what would now be called 'the media' she had an absurd and touchingly serious attitude to journalism.

We lost our way and struggling through bog and rough pasture to the farmhouse, got only a doubtful welcome in this tumbledown place where only the poorest and most desperate of Dales farmers would even then have thought of living. But Kate, unlike myself, was very good at getting on with almost any kind of people. She praised the sullen children playing among the sheepdogs and chickens on the stone-flagged floor; asked the farmer and his wife some lively questions, and took some flattering notes while I stared out of the doorway at the grey-green fell across the valley and the great slowly-moving clouds in the August sky.

We took our leave and, setting out on the right path, walked slowly down the hill to a place I had known since childhood, where the infant River Wharfe slid over limestone floors or fell with a delicious murmuring sound, over strangely hollowed rocks into deep pools. We sat together on the warm grassy bank beside one of these pools and I gave myself up to one of my favourite occupations: contemplating the sun-flecked water through half-closed eyes and listening to its eternal quiet laughter until I passed into a trance-like state which, once achieved, I would have liked to prolong for ever.

The minutes passed. 'It's time to go,' Kate said. It was not that she was unaware of the delight of being in such a place and of feeling lost in it. She was simply the more active one. I stopped plucking blades of grass in a self-hypnotising manner and got to my feet. 'I suppose it is.' Unwillingly, in what must have been a maddening way, I followed her and we walked off down the winding road to where human habitation began. In the first village we came to we drank some beer in the pub while we waited for the bus to take us to the end of the road which led to Amswick. But as soon as we had caught the bus we realised it would take us further down the valley to Haltonbridge, the place where on that very day, I remembered, they were holding the local agricultural show, the greatest day of the year in those parts.

It was early evening when we got there and the show was almost over. The sheep and cattle pens were already being dismantled, the winning animals, adorned with red, blue and yellow rosettes were already being hustled along with the losers into their trucks with much shouting and barking of dogs. The stalls were taken down, the hurdles stacked; the bookmakers who had taken bets on the fell-race up the crag and the trotting-races on the level showground between the hills and the river were packing up their stands and patting their bulging satchels; what remained of the cheap crockery, brassware and toys, prizes for the shooting gallery, coconut shy and boot-throwing competitions, were packed away; cars and coaches, with frenzied hooting, were already making for the narrow exits between the drystone walls, directed by policemen and helpers with ritual gestures. The declining sun shone on red, sweaty faces, on old and young; and from the departing crowd rose a collective noise of Yorkshire voices which I, never at a loss for the apt quotation, called 'the still, sad music of humanity,' scarcely acknowledging that my own more subdued voice was part of it.

It was a scene very familiar to me. My father, in his 'sheep-farming' days, would have enjoyed it, not only because he was at heart gregarious, but because it would have given him a chance to indulge, even in a small way, his passion for gambling. My mother never went near such places. She disdained the

43

crowd and maintained of its individual members that 'you never know where they've been'. My elder brother Geoffrey, who had died in the polio epidemic six years before, would have shunned it on principle, guarding his chosen solitude, though he might have been ready to show selected sheep there for the credit of his flock. I enjoyed such a scene as this all the more because of my family's disapproval. As for Kate, she enjoyed it because of its novelty for her; and because of her innate capacity for enjoyment. There could have been no greater contrast to the quiet solitude where we had spent the day.

There was a strong movement towards the open door of the King's Head, a long whitewashed building conspicuous in this very small hamlet built in the shadow of a huge limestone crag. We were both very fond of drinking. Constantine had said once, in his observant way, that Kate regarded pubs – which I imagine her devout Catholic family, however eccentric in some ways, seldom entered – as almost mystical symbols of liberty. We had met in a pub, the Stag's Head in Hallam Street, one of the statutory BBC pubs; it was on Kate's first visit to Amswick, in this very pub, that we had formally decided to get married, and had drunk in it several times since. It was very typical of the region in those days, before pubs all over England became uniformly gentrified and began to sell 'bar snacks' or, as vulgar signs announced, 'pub grub', or as even more vulgar signs later invited in the days of 'yobbos' and 'lager louts', 'Come in and Get Stuffed'.

It had a plain exterior and inside, flagged floors, simple furniture, two bars – one large and open, one smaller and cosier (this was the bar where we plighted our much-delayed troth) – and a few pictures on the distempered walls, caricatures of long-dead jockeys or local notabilities, and a big coloured lithograph, 'Friday', one of my favourites, in which a plump monastery cook displays a huge carp on a noble dish and the assembled *monsignori* raise their glasses in fine-ringed hands.

Yet it was no ordinary pub. It had a reputation for hard drinking and was notable for rapid changes of landlord. A previous incumbent, infamous in the neighbourhood, was said to have been almost continuously drunk. On Saturday nights, it was said, he was so drunk by closing-time that he was incapable of serving drinks or taking the money; so the regulars shut him in a cupboard and took over the bar themselves, drinking until the early hours of the morning and, being honest men, leaving a lump sum on the bar for him to count when he came round, provided he was capable of counting. The present landlord, an amiable man of about forty, was called Jacques Lebrun, but although his French name was often commented on in a wondering or jocular way, there seemed to be nothing French about him. Known as 'Jack', he spoke in a West Riding accent.

The only remotely French thing about him, and that only according to the popular myth of 'Frenchness', was his equally Yorkshire wife Cynthia, a small, well-made woman about ten years younger than himself, who exuded a powerful sexual attraction, all the more noticeable for her quiet demeanour. 'Hot stuff' was the general verdict on this slumbering volcano, and among her numerous admirers were some who either were, or earnestly hoped to be, something more than admirers. One of the farmers in the dale, Mr John Capstick, and a local garage man, Mr Tom Lambert, were deadly rivals for her favours; but unfortunately for them she was said to have a regular lover, a lorry-driver from Colne in Lancashire, whose vehicle was quite often observed standing for long periods outside the pub at times when it was closed to the public.

It may have been marital troubles which made the landlord

drink as much as almost any of his customers. Though he did not come anywhere near the level of his legendary predecessor he often complained of a morning hangover, jocularly saying, when offered a drink, that only a gin and Harpic or even a strychnine and soda would do him any good. In his later days, it was said, he drank more and more; tottering downstairs in the mornings, he could only bring himself to his senses by getting his wife, her sexual allure irrelevant in the circumstances, to fill up a glass with neat gin, place it on the bar and help him to lower his mouth upon it. Such alcoholic legends had a strong appeal for Kate and myself; Kate, for whom drinking, as Constantine had observed, had something of an ethical quality, was apt to judge people according to whether they drank or not and regarded those who did not as in some sense morally inferior.

On our previous visits to this place, usually in the early evening, we had found few customers and those quietly drinking and exchanging remarks on matters of local interest, with an occasional mention of politics, derived from the newspaper or the wireless. Because these people were not subject to saturation of information and entertainment by television, as their successors are, their opinions, though they may have been equally absurd or distorted, were at least their own. If it was nonsense, it was their own personal nonsense, not uniform nonsense pumped into their minds from a central source. Nor were they inhibited by fear and induced guilt about 'racism', 'sexism', or any of the other fraudulent bogeys which afflict us now. They would have laughed all such things to scorn, and they would have been right. It was a time when most of the international news was about troublesome denizens of the Middle East like Mossadeq, Neguib and Nasser. The only impression they had of Mossadeq may well have come from a newspaper photograph of him taken after his fall, showing him lying on a truckle bed, wearing striped pyjamas and crying bitterly. They could not understand how it had come about that our government, the government of a great nation which was supposed to have 'won the war' – and few at that time would have questioned that we had won it – was obliged to take such ludicrous and exotic foreigners seriously, or even take any notice of them at all.

On previous visits we had exchanged only a few polite words with the other customers. Some of them may have known that I had been at 'Oxford College' and an officer in the war and now worked with the BBC; they may have known that the young woman I was with was my second wife. They may have known the most amazing things about us, most of them partly or wholly untrue. We did not enquire, but sat in the small cosy bar by a tall window, with hens clucking outside and a view of old, stone-built barns across the yard, talking about whatever came into our heads, and were content. Had Constantine and Theodora suddenly appeared they would immediately have set about converting the pub into a distant fief of their dominions in Hertfordshire; but they would have found these stolid Yorkshire people, with their tradition of independence (an attitude summed up in the phrases 'I'll bow the knee to no man' and 'I'm as good as you are, whoever you are – and better') more difficult to convert to admiring subservience than the country people of the South, with their traditions of deference. Obstinacy, bloody-mindedness and even downright rudeness as well as the hatred of 'side', all well-established qualities of these West Riding people, elaborated in many a fearsome anecdote, are easily explained. There have never been great estates in the district – or very few – and those at the top have not been landed proprietors but industrial magnates who have risen from among people very like themselves.

47

The pub we entered that summer evening was very different from the place as we had known it. It was crowded with shouting drinkers from the show, some local but many from distant parts, sheep farmers from other dales, chance comers from Bradford, Keighley or Skipton, a few holidaymakers. Jack the landlord and the demure but dangerous Cynthia, with the help of a couple of young girls who had been taken on as temporary helpers, were frenziedly pulling pints, opening bottles and slamming glasses into optics as they tried to cope with the rush of orders. We entered unnoticed and made our way through the crowd with difficulty. Once served, we began to make for our customary corner by the window in the smaller bar. But in the press of people we collided with a merry-faced balding man a few years older than myself. Unlike most of the customers, he was drinking not beer but gin and tonic and had evidently had quite a few of them already. 'I know who you are,' he shouted in a friendly way. 'I've seen you walking by the river, aye, and playing catch, and I've seen you playing there with your baby. My name's Joe Tunnicliffe and I'm a terrible fellow!'

This was corroborated by several others who explained that he was 'noan so bad, really'. We soon found that this was so. Rapidly buying a round of drinks in which he included us, he confirmed what we had half-realised already from my mother's distinctly unfavourable remarks: that he lived in Keighley where he had a leather factory, and also owned the large white-painted wooden bungalow surrounded by shrubs and trees which lay on the other side of the river from the field where we played the Minoan Ball Game. He had a wife and three children, the eldest, a daughter, not that much older than Kate; but now he had been to the show and was on the loose.

Our new friend obviously had much more money than anyone else in the pub and was determined not only to enjoy himself but to ensure as far as possible that everybody else did so too. His sheer energy and *joie de vivre* were most attractive, and would have been so even if we and everybody else had not been getting rapidly into the kind of drunken state which inspires pure good-humour and pleasure. Yet we realised even then that Joe Tunnicliffe was more than a chance-met drinking acquaintance; that although we seemed to have nothing much in common (except, in Kate's case, difference of sex), he was going to be a friend. Later we found there were unexpected things about him, such as a love of music. Inheritor of a prosperous family firm, he had originally wanted to become a 'cellist, until the duties of business and an early marriage to the daughter of an even richer mill-owning family expelled such matters from his mind, though not entirely. All human faces in repose fall into lines of sadness; his, for all his habitual laughter and good humour, more strikingly so than most.

His father had sent him to a minor public school in the South of England. It was somehow typical that through a misunderstanding he had arrived at the wrong school and spent a whole term there before the mistake was realised. Like many West Riding businessmen of the time he was bilingual: in the ordinary way he spoke what is technically called 'improved West Riding', though without the sickeningly over-refined diphthongs and other phonetic prodigies of the womenfolk; but when he was in his factory with his workers he spoke with the broad accent without which they would not have respected him; and that was how he was speaking now with the even broader-spoken drinkers in the King's Head.

'Nah then, Mr Tunnicliffe, ista making a night of it?' one of these asked him in an accent which showed him to be native to the Dales, speaking a true North-Western dialect rather than the dialect of the West Riding which, though it would have

been tactless to tell that to its speakers, is more exactly called
North Midland. Not that anybody but myself was particularly
interested in the matter. What did George Borrow do when
people in pubs objected, as they must sometimes have done, to
his interrogating them about the way they spoke? It does not
bear thinking about.

'Aye,' replied Mr Tunnicliffe, 'we don't get a show every day
of the year, or such a fine day for it, or such good company.'
And he ordered drinks all round again. We were moving from
one bar to the other and back again by this time and so observed
that Mrs Lebrun had moved to the customers' side of the bigger
bar and was receiving burning glances both from Mr Lambert
and from Mr Capstick, one on each side of her, while she
herself looked remarkably cool and composed. The Siren of
Haltonbridge, as we came to call her, was quite used to such
situations and knew exactly how to deal with them.

'Where have you been all my life?' said Mr Tunnicliffe to
Kate, the first of a whole series of such stock gallantries, but
delivered in a highly individual way which made them seem
amusing even though I was now beginning to feel a twinge of
jealousy. It was therefore something of a relief when Kate
acquired another admirer, a rough-looking but amiable man
who turned out to be a sheep-farmer from Swaledale, one of
whose ewes had won first prize in its own class. 'Tha looks just
like my best prize yow,' he said. 'Don't be offended,' said Mr
Tunnicliffe. 'It's the greatest compliment he could pay you,
isn't it, Dick?' 'It is that,' said the Swaledale man, 'and if
tha comes to Swardale, tha'll be queen o't' whole flock.' His
compliment, for it was certainly meant for one, was not so far-
fetched as it might have seemed. Our old friend René Cutforth,
a man with great associative powers, had compared Kate, with
her long neck and strangely oblique 'Hunnish' eyes like his

own, to a llama. Seeing Kate the centre of attention and Mrs Lebrun temporarily relieved of her admirers, I tried to engage her in conversation. But I had scarcely begun my halting approaches when, after a mock tattoo on the main door of the pub it opened, revealing to my surprise that night had fallen.

A large, shambling man stood on the threshold, pulling off motor-cycling gloves from huge red hands, while behind him, below a flight of shallow steps, a motor-cycle and sidecar stood in the road. A general shout of laughter went up. 'It's t' policeman from Amswick!' bawled Mr Metcalfe. 'Has't come to put us all under arrest and convey us to thy dungeons?' he asked sarcastically. PC Albert Marsden, whom I now recognised from having seen him riding his machine about the roads in a diffident way and once making a terrible hash of directing traffic in Cassington, advanced into the room with a rather foolish smile on his big, lugubrious face and said in a hesitant tone: 'I know you folks have an extension till eleven o'clock, seeing as it's Show Day, but it's a quarter to twelve now, and if the Sergeant gets to know about this . . . ' He looked positively terrified. But his feeble expostulations were lost in a general shout of laughter. 'Nay, Albert,' said Mr Metcalfe, 'tha's blotted thi copybook wi't Sergeant often enough by now. I reckon he'll let thi alone this time. Come on, have a drink thisen.' With a great show of reluctance the policeman accepted a pint of beer and having swallowed that with immense speed and expertise, accepted another offered by Mr Tunnicliffe. Within a short time he was merely one among the crowd of drinkers, babbling away like the rest, though I noticed that from time to time a shade of alarm passed over his face.

PC Marsden, Joe Tunnicliffe told me, was a sad case. He was the son of a police superintendent from a town on the Lancashire border, a man of iron determination and stern devotion to duty. Albert 'had never wanted to be a policeman'. But his father had settled it in his mind that his son should join the force and if possible rise to a rank as high as his own or even higher. He died a disappointed man. Albert's heart was not in the job and although he did his best, telling himself it was 'a sacred trust', his repeatedly proven incapacity had ensured that he never rose above the rank of constable, finding himself in his late forties responsible for law and order in a place where there was seldom any crime more serious than riding a bicycle without a rear reflector. He was known to live in continual terror of his immediate superior, Sergeant Hoskins at Cassington six miles away, who was always threatening to put in an appearance in his fief and was 'particularly hot on drinking after hours'. It was believed that Marsden had an arrangement with sympathisers in Cassington living near the police-station, who had undertaken to warn him by telephone or by passing the word along whenever the Sergeant seemed to be heading in his direction. This accounted for his underlying terror now, even though he had drunk several pints of beer and had moved on to whisky. He had had no warning yet, but knew it might come at any moment.

Meanwhile he settled down to enjoy himself as best he could. 'You're a bonny lass,' he told Kate gallantly, gaining confidence for a moment. Then his face fell; I almost thought I saw tears in his eyes as a thought struck him. 'Do you know,' he said very slowly, 'I've had two wives myself and neither of them has been bonny.' This sad admission only served to produce more heartless laughter at his expense. 'What's Mrs Marsden doing tonight then?' somebody asked. 'Is it washday again tomorrow?' I remembered seeing a grim-faced, middle-aged woman of homely appearance pegging out washing outside the police house at Amswick. I also remembered Berner telling us, to my mother's outward disgust but secret amusement, that the policeman was said to wet his bed regularly and that his sheets were often to be seen on the washing-line, an object of derision to the villagers and an occasion for smacking any children who commented on them. The moral of all this seemed to be: don't have an overbearing police superintendent for a father; or if you do, run away to sea or join a circus as soon as possible. But the spirit of young Albert Marsden had been broken too early for that.

The arrival of the policeman seemed to have moved these rustic revels on to a new level of intensity. Mr Metcalfe had crossed to the publican's side of the bar and was trying to embrace Cynthia, who, as a sort of insurance, had her free hand tightly gripped by another admirer, Mr Baxter, who remained on his own proper side of the bar and seemed reasonably satisfied with this lesser share of her favours. As he was showing a tendency to slide to the floor, he may not have realised the true state of affairs. Mr Tunnicliffe was growing more and more gallant in his attentions to Kate, alternating these with beating time on a table as he tried to lead the singing of 'Ilkla Moor Baht 'At', 'Down at the Hole in the Wall' and other patriotic airs. Indefatigable, he suddenly pointed to a row of bottles on a high, remote shelf. 'Let's try some of those!' he shouted to the landlord. 'Nay,' said Jack, 'we haven't had any of those down for a good ten years. No call for them, you see.' I now saw, by screwing up my eyes, for my vision was becoming blurred, that the bottles had a thick coating of dust; it was just possible to read some of the labels: Danziger Goldwasser, a kind of schnapps with gold flecks in it, Parfait d'Amour, a sickly pink liquid, baleful Blue Curaçao and many other exotics. Where on earth had they come from, and what were they doing here?

'Have you got any of Mr Weston's Good Wine?' I asked the landlord. But this feeble, painfully literary joke, which I instantly regretted though half hoping Kate had heard it, was lost in a concerted roar of 'Get 'em all down!' and 'Drinks on the house!'. The landlord was clearly unwilling to oblige: did he fear the breaking of some ancient taboo which could only lead to misfortune? The matter was soon out of his hands. Somebody, possibly Mr Baxter, fetched a pair of steps, positioned it against the wall behind the bar and requested the landlord to mount. While he hesitated, his wife, perhaps taking the opportunity of escaping from Mr Metcalfe's embrace, climbed up the steps, displaying her slim form to great advantage for all to observe, and began handing down the bottles with graceful gestures, releasing clouds of dust which made everybody splutter and adding to the general confusion. The landlord, evidently resigned to whatever appalling consequences might follow, began to pour out a selection of exotic drinks for anyone who wanted them. He evidently felt they could not be poured into ordinary everyday receptacles; instead he produced from a shelf below the bar various strangely-shaped glasses: flat ones for champagne; tall ones for white wine; small squat glasses of ruby colour; a big narrow purple glass marked 'A Present from Redcar'; a calibrated medical glass; and even a frosted glass marked in wedge-shaped patterns which resembled cuneiform writing.

Had this been presented to him or a previous landlord by some eccentric assyriologist who had stayed for a fishing holiday in the pub in what I vaguely thought of as 'the old days'? Anything seemed possible. And now, with this injection of fantasy into a scene which though ribald and uninhibited, still clove to the realities of life in the Yorkshire Dales, all was altered. The smoke-filled air hummed and twanged; faces like those which appear in hypnagogic dreams, bunched like fists or folded like old gloves, advanced and receded or vanished altogether into shelves, walls or tall curtains. I stepped forward, trying to feel my way towards Cynthia through a curtain or tapestry which seemed to be made of multi-coloured pliable stained glass, but found I had stumbled over the body of the landlord, who lay on his back with his legs half under a chair, still holding level a miraculously full glass of purple liquid. From behind the bar came sounds of animal pleasure, but even if I had had my ordinary wits about me I could not have told who was making them.

Suddenly I blundered into the policeman, who was peering this way and that with a look of panic on his large, foolish face. 'Quick, let me out!' he shouted through the din. 'Sergeant's on his way! I know he is!' He stumbled to the door and opened it, and I heard his heavy boots clumping down the steps, and shortly after that the sound of his motor-cycle starting up and receding into the distance. 'So he's got away,' I thought, expecting, with some alarm, the appearance of the sergeant, unknown to me but evidently an austere disciplinarian: would he, I wondered, call an abrupt halt to the revels and charge everybody with offences against the licensing laws? Or would he, for all his devotion to duty, find himself instantly absorbed into the crowd, singing, dancing and shouting quite as idiotically as the rest of us?

The door opened slowly. But it was the policeman's face which peered sheepishly round it. 'Me motor-bike combination's in the ditch,' he mumbled so indistinctly that it was hard to understand him. 'And' – he was nearly in tears again – 'I've lost me teeth.' A great shout of laughter went up at this new misfortune. But a couple of men, including, I think, the sheep-farmer from Swaledale, who was perhaps beginning to sober

55

up a bit, went out to help him get his machine out of the ditch and on the road. They came back grinning. 'He's on his way. Just. But we couldn't find his teeth.' This struck me as irresistibly funny. The feeling of unreality, apparently induced by the exotic drinks, slowly evaporated. Instead a feeling of almost unearthly happiness seemed to flood this very ordinary room.

I opened the door, and found to my surprise a bright summer early morning; the sun was already shining gloriously on the hay meadows, the woods, the limestone scars ascending to the distant moors. I took Kate by the hand as we trooped out into the open air. With the rest we spent some time looking for the policeman's teeth but could not find them. With a politeness which was almost distinguished, and perhaps found only in men who have been engaged in a night of serious drinking, Mr Tunnicliffe drove us in his car, a powerful Jaguar, to the end of our lane and we parted, undertaking to meet again soon.

Clutching each other, we took the familiar stony path through the high meadow which led over the bridge past the field of the Minoan Ball Game towards my mother's cottage. Half way along the path I thought I saw something gleaming in the grass. Could it be a bright button mushroom? Or one of the country's small, exquisite snail-shells, some pink, some palest blue, some white like the pearl the base Indian threw away? Or the policeman's teeth? I bent to look again but now I could see nothing; and as I straightened up, by mischance I brought my elbow into Kate's face with enough force to bruise her cheek-bone. She cried out as I put my lips against it, then moved away. As we walked on, our separated shadows were long in the summer grass.

3
Unsteady Progress

As time went on, the 'Peter Simple' column began to gain a certain reputation, even notoriety. Its reactionary, 'eccentric' and independent opinions – in which my own Luddite tendencies and fervent hatred of scientific progress became more and more prominent – appealed not only to readers of the *Daily Telegraph*, then strongly identified with the Tory party, but to a wider public. There were, of course, people I met at parties who, when I told them what I did, said witheringly, 'I'm afraid I don't read the *Daily Telegraph*,' which, of course, settled the matter. It did not help when I said that as far as I was concerned I was still working for the *Morning Post*, the real true-blue Conservative paper which had been absorbed by the *Telegraph* as long ago as 1936. Even in its later days, when the *Telegraph* was no longer a Conservative paper in the proper sense of the word, and in its supply of scientific nonsense, low-grade entertainment and news of the world of 'showbiz', particularly television, became scarcely distinguishable from any other paper, there were people who regarded it as reactionary and looked askance at anyone connected with it.

There were, of course, people who disliked the column for its anti-socialist opinions, including some of my late colleagues (or, in a sense, continuing colleagues) in the BBC. 'It is pouring poison into the ear of England,' said one of them. But when, at the end of 1957, a paperback anthology of the first two years of the column was published by the *Daily Telegraph*, it received some surprisingly good notices even in quarters which might

57

be expected to be hostile, such as *Tribune*, the old left-wing weekly full of the sort of stuff we were lampooning. Its critic wrote of our work: 'bigoted, violent, well-written ... shrewd digs at pompous personalities and choice parodies of our more inflated culture-hounds'. Looking back at our quiet-toned, civilised 'satire' of that time (I suppose we must use this word, so lamentably devalued) from our *fin-de-siècle*, when writers compete for attention by outpourings of the most desperate obscenity and demented scatology, I am most pleased by the word 'violent'. We could not have been really violent in the *Telegraph* even if we had wanted to be, which I dare say we did. The whole tone of the paper, as of any 'serious' paper of that time, forbade it. Sir Colin Coote would have sternly suppressed any such tendencies.

This was the time before the trial of *Lady Chatterley* released 'four letter words' into the press. The spread of these once forbidden words was a gradual process; in fact they are not to be found in the *Telegraph* to this day, and when, many years later, Peregrine Worsthorne used the word 'fuck' in a BBC television broadcast, Michael Berry (or Lord Hartwell as he had then become, after taking a life peerage) sent for him and rebuked him in the following terms: 'You have disgraced your profession, your newspaper and yourself,' and forebade him to broadcast for six months on pain of dismissal.

We may have been violent and outspoken by the standards of the time but how the times have changed! They were beginning to change then, with the advent of 'satirists' like Lenny Bruce and Mort Sahl in America, followed by their imitators here; all, though glorying in their supposed 'revolutionary' ardour and unconventional attitudes, were, in fact, devoted to the most banal and modish opinions of the 'left-wing package deal', often attacking harmless targets like the Royal Family or the jam-

making ladies of the WVS. Such fashionable money-making
'satirists' became suitable subjects for my own satire as they
would have been for Juvenal; but, unlike Juvenal, I was handicapped by not being able to match them in obscenity.

So when Kenneth Tynan, the drama critic and celebrity,
famous for having used the word 'fuck' on the wireless long
before Worsthorne's unfortunate experience, praised Mort Sahl
of New York for his 'nonconformist satire', and complained of
the lack of similar 'liberal nihilist' entertainment in London
night-clubs (this decadent drivel was then on its way, so he
need not have troubled), I could only write:

> To call night-club liberal nihilists 'nonconformist' is nothing
> but a perversion of language. Nobody could possibly be more
> conforming than they are. They conform exactly to the
> fashionable desperation of their audience, its smart hatred of
> civilisation . . . that is why, far from being mocked and driven
> into the wilderness, they have grown rich and popular and
> fat with long-playing records. The role of Mort Sahl at
> Belshazzar's Feast, in that most expensive of Babylonian
> night-clubs, would have been to make liberal nihilist jokes
> about the writing on the wall, to the huge delight of his
> sophisticated audience.

I could operate only within the constraints of my newspaper;
those who came later, such as the writers in *Private Eye*, were
able to attack such people in their own language, a freedom I
sometimes envied.

Naturally the column, with its then unfashionable opinions
(some of them are unfashionable still) came in for a certain
amount of abuse. For example when Colin, I think it was,
pointed out, reasonably enough, that the white South Africans

had a perfect right to call themselves Africans (or Afrikaner), he came in for sharp attack from the journalist Bernard Levin, in whatever column he was writing at the time: he referred to 'Peter Simple' as 'still hobbling after Beachcomber's rear light'. This was fairly wounding but on the wrong tack. I thought, and think, Beachcomber at his best funny (though not in some of his 'funny' names such as 'Cocklecarrot' which I find painfully unfunny). But if my early writing in the 'Peter Simple' column was influenced by any other column it was Myles na Gopaleen's column in the *Irish Times*, which is in an altogether higher category, the work of one of the greatest modern comic writers. Sadly, his column ceased around the time when 'Peter Simple' was coming into his own, and Myles na Gopaleen (alias Flann O'Brien, real name Brian O'Nolan) fell into decline, illness and, in 1966, death.

I had first come across Myles na Gopaleen when, demobilised in April 1946, I lived briefly with my first wife in Dublin. His column, by far the funniest newspaper column in history, was a great solace in what were difficult times. Because of my interest in Irish matters (part of my immersion in 'Celtic studies') and knowledge of them I was in a better position than most English people to enjoy his more recondite linguistic jokes and allusions. I never met him while I was in Dublin, though I might well have done since I met, if only briefly in various bars, associates and drinking companions of his such as Patrick Kavanagh and Anthony Cronin. But perhaps it is as well I never did meet my literary hero; he is said to have been 'difficult'. He had every reason to be. In his lifetime he was scarcely known outside Ireland and it was only after his death and the publication of his novel *The Third Policeman*, written twenty-five years before, immediately after his other masterpiece *At-*

Swim-Two-Birds, that he came into his own in England and the world.

As well as the new friends and acquaintances we were making in the world of Fleet Street – the Welches, the Worsthornes, Henry Fairlie, Paul Johnson and many others – we still had our other circles of friends from the BBC and in Hampstead, some separate, some intersecting. The FitzGibbons still held court at Sacomb's Ash, still gave their splendid weekend parties. But their marriage was beginning to show signs of breaking up. It was not that they threw more or heavier objects at each other; if anything, these performances seemed to become more rare, or it may have been that I was not so often around to observe them.

The countryside around their house was also changing. Considering how near it was to London, it had always seemed surprisingly rural, with real country people in it who still talked about their own country affairs as their forebears had done. It was not surprising to find, in a pub Constantine and I discovered just over the Essex border, a genuine example of folk art: a glass case containing four stuffed ferrets playing cards. The landlord, a deaf man with a beautiful white dog which he called, with great pride, 'my Pyrenean mountain dog', could not explain the provenance of this artefact; he had 'always had it', and when we offered to buy it he looked every bit as cunning and dubious as the landlord in Skipton with his photograph of Happiness.

Now all this was changing. Hedges and trees began to disappear from this corner of Hertfordshire, between the little rivers Stort and Ash which, as Mr Rix (the landlord of the FitzGibbons' local pub) often said, the Romans had left alone as they drove their roads north and west across Britain, so that its inhabitants to this day were a race apart. They weren't, of

61

course; they were quintessentially English; but the idea that they were different was part of the peculiar charm of the place.

Now this was rapidly vanishing. Big fields were opened up: between them the winding lanes where I had bicycled so intensively a few years before in search of a cottage for Kate and Jane were laid bare between hedge-banks brutally stripped of vegetation by the new machines, losing their beguiling secrecy. Soon the very pub where Constantine and Theodora had ruled, imposing their ideas, often strangely modified, of life on Mr Rix so strongly that at one time he was found in the bar studying the maxims of Rochefoucauld – this splendid pub, with its brown-painted, beer-stained walls and kitchen always full of washing or baking, began to change. Mr Rix himself – whose forward daughter had 'got into trouble', resolved by marriage, but to an unsuitable urban-minded youth who owned a washboard, a primitive 'rock' musical instrument of the period – began to work part-time at the malt-works at Sawbridgeworth, returning on alternate evenings to tell of the new world which was coming into existence.

Soon he left altogether to run a pub nearer London. A new breed of customer from the outer suburbs began to invade the pub, ill-mannered and vulgar, forcing the locals into corners; not easily impressed by exotic visitors or conversation about books or foreign places but self-assertive and even hostile. Very soon a juke-box was installed, impeding if not actually superseding our old in-jokes and the public reading of Constantine's short stories. Even croquet on the lawn at Sacomb's Ash – that leisurely, supremely civilised game where you could carry your drink round with you as you played – began to lose credibility.

In the spring of 1958 the three-year lease of our pleasant maisonette in Downshire Hill ran out, and when I consulted our landlady Mrs Uhlman – wife of Fred the painter and writer, herself a Croft of Croft Castle in Herefordshire, one of the oldest families in England – about this, she told me with perfect politeness that she was not going to renew it because she had promised to let the place to a friend of hers, a psychiatrist called Dr Marie Yehuda. This was not altogether surprising. Neither our political views nor our manner of life was acceptable to the Uhlmans. They might have put up with the views, as did many people – for example, Margaret Gardiner, a rich, left-wing lady who lived in Downshire Hill and who, hearing of Kate's troubles before we married from her protegé Harry Craig, a soft-spoken Irishman, BBC scriptwriter and alleged relation of Theodora FitzGibbon, had offered to adopt her. It was not clear whether she meant to adopt the coming baby as well. In any case nothing came of the project. But we became quite good friends with Margaret, one of those people who 'knew everybody', including David Thomson, now married to a beautiful though somewhat enigmatic girl, Martina Mayne, in whom I had once taken a feeble interest. She was one of the great number of girls – Riette, Ann, Muriel, Glenys, Frances (two), Denise, Vera, Jenny, Molly and so on – who make up a roll-call of lost apparitions extending over my whole lifetime, occasionally appearing in odd trains of thought, or even in dreams, to haunt me with regret. I suppose it is the same with most men, and all think themselves uniquely stupid for not having taken all these girls to bed.

The Uhlmans could have put up with our opinions, vile though they must have thought them. What they could not put up with was our fondness for drink, drunken companions and noisy parties, let alone our charades and dramatic performances, which included set-pieces like 'the French Revolution', 'the Russo-Japanese War' or 'the Battle of the Somme', which had more than once brought Fred Uhlman out in his pyjamas in the middle of the night to dance with rage on the pavement below our windows, and caused the lady novelist who lived opposite to threaten us with the police. The police station, as it happened, was only a few doors away at the junction of Downshire Hill and Haverstock Hill; an added irony was that when my son Nicholas, who was about to proceed on a scholarship from Skipton Grammar School to Christ's College, Cambridge, visited us, he worked part-time in the police station canteen, amusing us with his close observation of police behaviour within the station, including a 'love triangle' between two constables and the canteen manageress.

The loss of our home, for, however temporary, a home we must have thought it, was a severe blow. We had two months to find another place in which to live and no means of buying one at a time when rented accommodation was becoming scarce. It fell to Kate, being the more energetic of the two, to deal with this crisis (and, of course, I was fully occupied with my work on the *Telegraph* four days a week). First she found a rather derelict, ivy-grown house near Edwards Square in Kensington which, though it had evidently been badly shaken by bombing during the War, was still standing up with the aid of a few iron braces. I was not at all keen on this house, but Kate for a time set her heart on it and once, when I demurred in a nearby pub where we had gone to discuss the matter, kicked me hard and painfully on the ankle because of my negative attitude. Negative I habitually was, but in this case I was right; I luckily got the support of 'Tommie' Rowell, a middle-aged friend I had met when she was a director of Wingate the publishers; she was one of Jane's godmothers and had always been most generous to us, allowing us to stay in her house when she was away on our visits to London from Manchester and overlooking, like the

good Catholic she was, our destruction of beds and other articles of furniture. It was she who now saved us by pointing out
that the house Kate favoured was liable to collapse at any
moment.

The day of our departure from Downshire Hill arrived and
we had nowhere to go. So now began a curious period of
nomadism, made more curious by the fact that I had to go to
Fleet Street to work at my respectable job and produce daily
offerings of humorous fantasy which, though Sir Colin Coote
remained sceptical, found more and more favour with the
respectable readers of the *Telegraph*. There were people who
declared that the column was the first thing they turned to in
the paper, and even a few who said it was the only thing they
read in it.

Letters would arrive: 'Dear Peter Simple – you have the gift
of expressing what I think but have no words to express. You
are an oasis of sanity in a mad world; more power to your
elbow'. I would read these encouraging remarks in the intervals
of wondering where I was going to spend the night. Fortunately
it was summer and the weather mainly fine. The enterprising
Kate had also hit on a means of mobility and of conveying our
meagre belongings from one temporary home to the next. 'We
must buy a car,' she said. 'I can't drive it,' I said, recalling my
notorious inability when in the Army to bring any vehicle to a
standstill within several yards of the point desired and my
desperate escapes from death on the roads due to my not having
the knack of doing several things at the same time, such as
changing gear while operating the steering-wheel and looking
out for other traffic – a thing absolutely essential to any driver.

Kate assured me she could drive, as indeed she could, so
she persuaded me to see Mr H. J. C. Stevens, the secretary of
the *Telegraph*, the man who had charge of the money, and ask

65

for a loan of £500 to help us set up house. Stevens was a large, rubicund, sardonic man with the reputation of being a bully and a habit of laughing loudly and flinging himself back in his chair as though what was said to him was too killingly funny for words. This was what he did when I made my request. But after a statutory show of insulting scepticism and reluctance he granted it all the same.

I had never before had so much money in my possession at one time. Nor had it occurred to me that I was a person who would ever own a motor-car. However, Kate had set her heart on a small plum-coloured Singer convertible which she had found for sale at a garage in Hampstead just before our expulsion, price £300. It was on this that we spent the greater part of Mr Stevens's bounty. Kate collected it without delay and housed it in the convenient garage which was part of the modishly modern ('split level') house of the artist David Gentleman, a friend and neighbour of David Thomson who lived near Regent's Park Canal. I cannot remember whether Kate had made friends directly with David Gentleman and his kindly, jolly first wife or through David Thomson. It is immaterial. She never had the slightest difficulty in getting people to do things for her, which was just as well for me and Jane in our circumstances at the time.

David Gentleman's house was our first place of refuge during that summer of nomadism, and we lived in it for a whole week while the Gentlemans were away on holiday, making occasional forays in the new car to contact other people who might prove suitable hosts 'until we got settled'. There were so many of them that I cannot distinguish them all. For a time we moved between several addresses in Hampstead; one, Lion House, I remember because of the stone lion at the doorway, which made a strong impression on Jane.

But after a time this wandering life began to have a worrying effect on her. Now four years old and still of enchanting beauty and intelligence, she was attending the private Catholic school in Hampstead where she had started her schooling during the last year of our life in nearby Downshire Hill; now, of course, she had to be driven there in the mornings, from wherever we had taken up temporary abode, and collected in the afternoons. As is not uncommon among girls of her age, she had invented a phantom companion or *alter ego* called Janice (a name Kate particularly deplored, but her attempts to change it to 'Lucy' or 'Caroline' had no effect). Jane would often tell us that Janice had thought or said such and such; Janice often showed considerable shrewdness in assessing our curious way of life. Soon Janice went further, maintaining that Kate and I were not really Jane's parents at all; her real father, to my chagrin, was a full colonel in the American Air Force, over here on temporary duty while his squadron remained in America. This story, which became further elaborated, persisted throughout that summer, fading out of Jane's mind when things became more settled. If they had not become so, what might have been the effect on her?

This was a question we might have put to a new friend we had made a short time before, now one of those who gave us intermittent refuge. This was the psychiatrist Dr Desmond O'Neill. We had originally met him at the house of Denis Barnes – already a high-grade and rising Civil Servant, who eventually retired with a knighthood as Permanent Secretary to the Board of Trade – and his agreeable, amusing novelist wife, who wrote under her maiden name of P. B. Abercrombie and whose broadcast talks I had produced for the BBC.

Desmond O'Neill lived in a tall house with a long narrow back-garden in Cavendish Avenue in St John's Wood. He was a Protestant Ulsterman 'from the Black North', as he put it, and carried thereby a 'VHL' or 'very heavy load' of guilt – an expression he told me was used jokingly by his psychiatric colleagues, who were, of course, all to some extent afflicted in the same way. A tall, slender man of about my own age, Desmond revealed a good deal of inner tension by his slightly anguished expression and by the excessive smallness and tightness of the knot of his tie. He had one distinction unusual in psychiatrists – while serving in the RAMC in the War, he had won a Military Cross. He was noticeably disinclined to talk about it.

At that time he was winning a reputation for his researches into psychosomatic medicine, which was only then beginning to be taken seriously, as doctors started to realise the absurdity, which should have been long obvious, of making a distinction between body and mind. He was a consultant at the nearby Hospital of St Elizabeth and St John ('Betty and Jack's') and showed me several fascinating research papers he had written on subjects about which very little – that is to say, nothing – was then known, or probably still is: one was on Sneezing and the other on Itching, both recondite forms of pleasure. As for sneezing, who has not found himself, at moments of emotional failure, sneezing uncontrollably perhaps as many as twenty or thirty times? As for itching, why is the Devil sometimes called 'Old Scratch'? Such were the apparently commonplace but in fact mysterious questions with which this remarkable man was concerned when I first met him.

Although Desmond was always formally dressed, with a sober tie and well-polished shoes, and had a most respectable appearance, his medical colleagues thought him eccentric and even 'Bohemian' – a word still used even in those days when the onset of democracy was beginning to give everybody the 'human right', as it would come to be called later, to behave in a Bohemian way. This tendency, which reached its apogee in the next decade with the phenomena of mass 'hippiedom' and 'flower power', was annoying for those who had always conducted their lives on such principles, or lack of principles. Certainly Desmond had unconventional friends and gave excellent parties in the large basement room we called 'the ballroom' below his consulting-room. He even joined in the charades which Kate, when tipsy, would suddenly set in motion, pretending to take pot-shots at him with an imaginary gun from behind a sofa in the Wild West saloon which his house had suddenly become.

He was a widower whose wife had been killed in a motor accident some years before; he had two adolescent children. He also had in his household a young woman he introduced as his ward and also his patient. She was depressed, withdrawn, enigmatic and reputedly rich. She showed neither pleasure nor irritation at the appearance in the house of my nomadic family. The garden was a good place for Jane to play and the room we had at the top of the house was a good place to write. One of the articles I wrote there was on the building of the first motorway, the M1. The piece had been commissioned by the eccentric Donald McLachlan, who later became the first editor of the Berrys' new venture, *The Sunday Telegraph*. Driven by Michael ffolkes, who was to illustrate the article, in his big brown Bentley of which he was inordinately fond, to Newport Pagnell, the operational base of the motorway, we stayed in an hotel there and spent a day inspecting the work: the new road, cutting a great swathe through the woods and pastures of Northamptonshire for a mere twenty miles or so, was the first small precursor of the great network which now covers large parts of the country with concrete. But I found it sufficiently horrifying to write a

somewhat Luddite article about it. McLachlan, who thought I
was a 'funny man' in his serious world of journalism, did not
object to my questioning the necessity for progress; it was a
time when this kind of crankiness could still be taken as merely
amusing.

Our new car, now that Kate had triumphantly shown she
could drive it, was a great success. It was a small, old-fashioned
machine which later, when we visited France in it, drew loud
laughter from the mechanics of le Mans. In wet weather we
had to put up its hood, which was in several parts, assembling
them for maximum speed in a series of drill movements which
I devised on the analogy of the drill I had so much enjoyed in
the army. The car, I was aware, was useful for Kate when she
wanted to meet her lover; I did not greatly resent not being
able to use it for similar purposes myself. I thought of taking
driving lessons but when I remembered my former hopelessness
at a skill I believed I was incapable of acquiring, I did not
persevere. As Kate grew more confident we drove further and
further afield. There was still great enjoyment in motoring in
those days when there were comparatively few cars on the still
unstraightened roads and it took two days to reach my mother's
house in Yorkshire.

That summer we even reached Scotland, spending a week
with the Tunnicliffes, who had become great friends and drinking companions, at Gatehouse of Fleet, their favourite place in
Galloway, then beautiful, wild, open country, a paradise so
changed and ruined by intensive conifer-planting later on that
I cannot bear to go there any more. On another expedition we
stayed with René Cutforth and his wife Marguerite, who had a
cottage not far from Aberystwyth. On the way there we spent
a weekend at the hotel built into the ruins of the Priory at
Llanthony in the valley of the Honddu. I had last been there

twenty years before on my wanderings through Wales with Pepi, my first wife. The place was unchanged, except that the road through the valley had been metalled. We slept in a four-poster bed, perhaps the very same one I had slept in on my previous visit. We were the only guests and had breakfast at the very same polished table, brought by a uniformed maid who had to be summoned by a brightly-polished brass bell worked by a pulley.

Kate was as delighted as I was by this splendid archaism, as well as by the beauty of the country round about. We walked to Cwyoy, lower down the valley, and looked at the little church, all askew on the hillside and said to have been knocked sideways hundreds of years before, when the vicar, entering the church one summer afternoon, found the Devil sitting on the altar and managed to eject him only after a fierce struggle. According to an even better legend, the landslide of the hill on which the church stood had taken place at the moment of the Crucifixion. We looked round the little, grass-grown churchyard, full of leaning tombstones of slate with fine-lettered, eighteenth-century memorial verses. One of them described the soul of some Jones, Williams or Davies as a bride, asleep and waiting for the Day of Judgement:

> 'Until she hear the Bridegroom say:
> Awake, my dear, and come away.'

The discovery of such a place, at a time (one of many times) when Kate declared, of course untruly, that she had given up her lover for good, brought us closer together. Then it was solitary and unvisited; now the whole world has been there and the Tourist Board is extracting from it every penny of extractable revenue. There are notice-boards, signposts, 'interpretive information facilities'. Nobody is permitted to find out anything for himself any more. I am glad to have been there before this happened. It is a privilege which we will not have again for hundreds of years, if ever.

We drove up the valley from Llanthony by the road, then a stony track, which my first wife and I had covered on foot, and reached the summit of the Bwlch yr Efengyl, the Gospel Pass, where we stopped to gaze over the Wye Valley far into the recesses of mid-Wales, where the horrible plantations of conifers were beginning to cover the hills and drive the hill-farmers from their farms in exchange for money. As a known Welsh nationalist, I did not speak of 'English imperialism' and a deliberate policy of extirpating the Welsh language and culture as I might have done. Kate would have been decidedly unsympathetic.

As the Cutforth's cottage was not big enough to accommodate all of us, they had arranged for us to stay at the pub in the village, where René, with his great gifts for entertainment, was already well-known. We spent most of the weekend in serious drinking. René had elaborated a mythical saga of his strange upbringing in Swadlincote, in the Derbyshire coalfield, even maintaining that he had spent his earliest years entombed in a mound or slag-heap constructed by his mother. This man had great literary talent which he had not really exploited in book form (except for one excellent book about his experiences in the Korean War as a correspondent for the BBC and another book of eccentric sketches of his experiences in Nigeria, which involved a good deal of African magic); instead he had put his gifts into story-telling, mostly in pubs, so that his fame will perish with the last of those who knew him. Does this matter in the long run? Did he not do better than I, with my persistent dream of literary fame and corresponding inability to live? René, a larger-than-life character if ever there was one, lived his life to the full. He was himself.

With multiple diversions the weekend passed agreeably enough. As with many Welsh villages in those days, and for all I know even now, the inhabitants were divided into two opposing factions: those who never went to the pub and were often militant teetotalers; and those who spent all their free time in the pub on weekdays, and on Sundays (this was one of the 'six-days-only' parts of Wales) in the local Liberal Club, whose main purpose was to provide a place for drinking. The moral power of the teetotalers, mostly supported by the women, was enough to terrify the drinkers into a certain furtiveness. One man who habitually took home a basket of bottles from the pub took the precaution of covering them with a layer of cereal or soap powder packets when carrying it home through the village, for fear the garage-man, who belonged to the abstaining faction, might refuse to repair his car.

The police station was opposite the pub and so zealous was the policeman that he spent almost the whole of his Sundays standing in his porch watching the pub door to check whether anybody was going in or coming out. People like ourselves who were staying in the pub were allowed to buy drinks, so some of the more fanatical drinkers used to go into the pub on Sundays carrying small suitcases and posing as guests. The policeman regularly staged a one-man raid on the pub, insisting on the suitcases being opened and spluttering with rage when he found toothbrushes, sponges and pyjamas neatly packed inside. All this, though it was a great joke, did not make him exactly popular in the neighbourhood; some months later, René told me the policeman was walking on the seashore, perhaps hoping to intercept a cargo of contraband liquor, when he was mysteriously run over by a tractor and went to hospital with an injured

73

leg. When he came out he decided to give up the unequal struggle and got himself posted elsewhere. He would have made a nicely contrasting successor to the policeman at Amswick.

We resumed our nomadic life in London. We had already arranged to take over the agreeable house of William ('Bill') and Ruth Sansom in St John's Wood. This was a cut above our average bivouac. I am not sure how we (or more likely, Kate) had got to know the Sansoms; perhaps through the Worsthornes, who 'knew everybody' in well-to-do social and literary circles. Sansom was then quite well-known as a novelist and short story- and travel-writer, and it was while they were on a fortnight's trip somewhere abroad that their house was available.

As befitted a successful writer it was very civilised, with great numbers of books and *objets d'art*, including one of those pictures which when looked at from one angle showed a child playing with a puppy, and from another a skull. I spent a good deal of my leisure-time trying out these effects. One of the conditions of our stay was to look after the Sansoms' two cats, Edward and Arthur, who occupied a capacious cubicle of their own next to the kitchen, with a separate entrance by cat-door to the garden. These cats were of opposed temperament, Edward being arrogant and bullying, Arthur meek and subservient. Kate, who had some fascist instincts, favoured Edward's right to dominate. I, who had the same instincts, only more so, felt I had to compensate for Kate's preference, at any rate where animals were concerned, by favouring the weaker Arthur and seeing that he got his fair share of food and milk. Later on, when some critic accused 'Peter Simple' of being a 'well-known protector of the powerful', referring no doubt to white South Africa, I remembered Edward and Arthur. Was it so certain even then, that the white South Africans were really 'the powerful'? They were only standing up for themselves, after all, with the whole world ganged up against them.

We had several acquaintances in St John's Wood. In the next street, with a house and a garden much like the Sansoms', lived R. D. ('Reggie') Smith, the marxist *bonhomme* of the BBC who had first brought Kate into its ambit by way of the Stag's Head in Hallam Street, and his wife, the novelist Olivia Manning. Olivia, though perhaps more sincere, was less unfailingly agreeable than Reggie, whose character as 'friend of all the world' is precisely captured in her novels. She even wrote a book of stories in which he figured with no more disguise than a change of name. I sometimes wondered whether he objected to being thus displayed to the public; but if he did, he showed no sign of it, which itself was very much in character. Theirs seemed a remarkably ill-assorted marriage, with no perceptible sexual tie. This may have been one reason why Olivia was inclined to be acerbic, even waspish in manner.

My fellow Yorkshireman Rayner Heppenstall, author of *The Blaze of Noon* and other novels, and a critic and producer for the Third Programme, said of Olivia in his modified West Riding accent, 'Now there's my idea of a really plain woman'. It is true that Olivia was no beauty (her impersonation by an attractive young actress in a television version of her 'Balkan Trilogy' years later made me smile faintly); but Rayner's remark may have been due as much to literary rivalry as sexual conoisseurship. Most writers are jealous of other writers; but Rayner carried this to extremes. He was jealous of the alliterative Ulster poet 'Bertie' Rodgers, who also worked for the BBC and as well as being a writer was irresistible to women, which Rayner, much as he would have wished to be, was not. Once, when 'Bertie' was holding forth at a party to a rapt female audience,

Rayner suddenly snatched up a small bunch of grapes and threw it at him, but without noticeable effect.

Rayner seemed to resent even my own meagre literary efforts. Finding to his surprise in the course of some research that a short story of mine had been published in the first issue of Connolly's *Horizon* ten years before, he made a point of telling me: 'It won't do, you know'. I did not mind this; he was right; the story was a mere pastiche of T. F. Powys. Indeed I did not mind Rayner at all, but liked him both as a person and a writer. Has he, like so many writers of that time ('Bertie' Rodgers is an outstanding example) sunk without trace? I hope not; I think his autobiographical novel about his absurd experiences as a psychiatric case in the army, *The Lesser Infortune*, a better book than the equally autobiographical but more pretentious and showy war novels of Olivia Manning, with their stock fictional characters and situations.

At this time Reggie and Olivia were much plagued by the *enfant terrible* of the BBC Features Department, Peter Duval Smith, a man of reprehensible and irregular life who was even more irresistible to women than Rodgers or anyone else I have ever come across. Like us, though without a young child to restrict his movements, he had no fixed abode and would often park himself on friends or acquaintances for the night. Reggie must have brought him home drunk one night to St John's Wood (for all Olivia's habitual cry of remonstrance – 'Oh Reggie!'), and left him to sleep it off on the sofa in their drawing-room, relying on him to make a quiet getaway in the morning. But a couple of weeks later Olivia, while entertaining some respectable literary friends, was aware, as they also must have been, of a particularly unpleasant smell. Later, when they had gone, she traced it to a valuable teapot on a shelf, which

Peter, unable to find his way to the lavatory, had used as a night-vessel.

Another friend in St John's Wood, though we never stayed with him, was the composer Humphrey Searle, an abstracted though friendly man whose dodecaphonic music was utterly unintelligible to me. Meeting me in the local pub, he asked me back to his flat, then, thrusting a drink into one of my hands and a sheaf of music into the other, he began to play his one-act opera *Diary of a Madman*, after Gogol, on the piano, supplying the vocal parts himself. I cannot read music (it presents something of the same difficulty to me as driving a car), but as he rumbled and tinkled, droned and screamed away, apparently at random, I dutifully turned the pages, watching him furtively in the effort to judge how far he had got. He reached the final rumble and scream when I was still only three-quarters of the way through the score. 'What do you think of it?' he asked. 'Splendid,' I replied, as I hastily turned over the remaining pages and glared at the final bars (did the thing have bars anyhow?) in as appreciative a way as I could manage. Did he notice my intense embarrassment? If so, he gave no sign of it. Perhaps he thought, not without reason, that I was always like that.

With such diversions (and all this time, of course, I was putting in four days a week at the *Telegraph* and receiving frequent letters telling me how much readers depended on my courageous commonsense and rocklike sanity) the summer passed and we were still without a permanent home. We had now used some of our temporary bivouacs several times over and the supply of suitable or willing hosts was beginning to run out. One of the last of our camping-sites was an elegant flat in one of the Regent's Park terraces belonging to my old sweetheart Laura, who was now, not surprisingly, separated from her film-producer husband and awaiting divorce so that he could marry a younger woman, this time a genuine rather than a fun-Communist.

Laura, who was now forty-five, my own age, had lost some of that patrician prettiness I had once found so irresistible that even her careless manner of dressing and her chain-smoking had been fascinatingly attractive to me. But although I no longer had any wish to go to bed with her, once the summit of my felicity, I was still fond of her – the feeling which never leaves such relationships. She had always got on well with Kate; if they had nothing else in common they had irrationality and a fondness of drink. She must have been lonely anyhow, and so quite glad to offer us temporary refuge. However, she was in a sad state altogether; indeed she was suffering a kind of nervous breakdown, which meant that she spent much of her time in bed and soon began to find our comings and goings irritating. Before long she and Kate had a blazing row, probably arising from some domestic detail of washing or cooking, and we were homeless again.

We had now quite run out of hosts and were reduced to putting up at a small private hotel in St John's Avenue on the slopes of Hampstead Hill. This was the last of our camp-sites. We contrived at this time to find a suitable unfurnished flat in Putney, a part of London quite strange to us and, though less agreeable than Hampstead, not completely unacceptable. We went on staying at the private hotel while waiting to move into the flat and it was in some ways the most bizarre of all our temporary homes during this summer of nomadism.

It was bizarre because of its intense banality. There was a resident population of commercial travellers (or sales representatives as they would now be called) who spent most of their spare time watching the primitive black-and-white television of this early period when the advance of the world's scourge was only starting and conversations overheard on buses on my journeys to Fleet Street were only just beginning to be dominated by discussions of the previous evening's programmes. The banality of the hotel soon became frightening. It has occasionally supplied material for some of my most highly specialised nightmares, in which boredom is a major element and even dominates the 'feeling tone'. I believe such dreams are very rare; and I am glad of it.

Our new flat, which we moved into as autumn was coming on, occupied the first floor of a large pre-1914 villa in Chartfield Avenue, one of a number of middle-class streets in the district west of Putney Hill, between Upper Richmond Road and a council estate which had been built on the site of one of the big houses on the edge of Putney Common. Some of its attractions – cedar trees and even a small lake – had been spared, so that this council estate had quite a pleasant air about it, and although its working-class inhabitants had nothing in common with the inhabitants of our bourgeois streets they seemed to be 'respectable' people who showed no tendency to stray outside their own limits.

Our house, which had a long communal garden at the back, was divided into three flats. The ground floor was occupied, when we first moved in, by a pleasant couple, the Prings. Mr Pring was a Clerk in the House of Commons; a subordinate of Kenneth Bradshaw, a friend of the Worsthornes who eventually became Chief Clerk and retired with the statutory knighthood. The flat above ours was occupied by the Smarts, who had a baby and several large dogs. We did not have a great deal to do with the families in the other flats; I do not think, however, that they were greatly bothered by our own noisy and tempestuous life; our frequent quarrels and drinking sessions. The

79

house, which was not unlike a small version of Duchy Grange, my mother's long-lost paradise in Harrogate, was solidly built and our flat quite roomy and comfortable in a disorganised way, especially after we had furnished it with some of the furniture from Downshire Hill which Mrs Uhlman, who had a certain inherited sense of *noblesse oblige*, had let us have for a nominal sum.

We borrowed some additional furniture from my old friends Ernst and Eithne Kaiser (née Wilkins, ingeniously gaelicised by her as Nic Liamóg) who had become, since I had last seen them just after the war, the world's greatest authorities on the Austrian novelist Robert Musil, whose works they translated and commented on for the rest of their lives. They had furniture to lend because they were leaving England to take up an appointment connected with Musil Studies in Rome. In spite of my esteem for Eithne, and, when I got to know him, Ernst, I could never manage to read the works of Musil; still less the works of Heimito von Doderer (in spite of his wonderful name), another monumental Austrian novelist on whom the Kaisers were authorities, though not the world's greatest. Kate did not care for Eithne, whom she thought somewhat affected and even 'twee', but she was glad of the furniture. However, she resented it in her robust way when the Kaisers made a detailed inventory of their possessions with a view to reclaiming them if they ever returned to England. She thought this showed a mean-spirited attitude.

The Kaisers, who lived in Belsize Park, not far from the house where 'Zed' gave his dreaded wine-and-cheese parties, had a number of high-powered intellectual friends. Among them was Elias Canetti, the renowned author of *Auto da Fé* and *Crowds and Power*, both of which I had read with a certain jealous admiration, the second with some difficulty, since I find it difficult to think in a systematic or even rational way at all. After a party at the Kaisers' one evening, I found myself having a drink with Canetti at the huge, cavernous pub in Swiss Cottage. I can't remember what we talked about, if anything. He may well have dismissed me as irredeemably stupid and frivolous; for my part, though probably drunk, I was alarmed by the powerful aura of cerebration which seemed to surround this short, square, dark, Sephardic person. We parted after a short while; such a meeting was typical of my fugitive and trivial experiences of the great and famous, people I feared all the more because of my never entirely suppressed aspiration to join them in their fame and greatness.

When we were both undergraduates at Oxford in 1936, Eithne, who was then a promising poet, had been very encouraging about my novel *Sheldrake*, which I had been writing with immense, not to say unheard of application in the vacation before my last term, when I should have been working for my final examinations. This preoccupation had been one of the reasons (the others being conceit and boredom) for my failure to get even the humblest pass and for my leaving Oxford without a degree. I did not care about this at the time, believing that I would immediately get *Sheldrake* published and become rich and famous, or at any rate famous. This did not happen and the book remained unpublished.

I had been desperately carrying the typescript about with me ever since, even taking a copy of it to India during the War. But I had virtually ceased to hope it would ever be published, especially since Anthony Gibbs and Charles Fry of Allan Wingate, the publishers for whom I had done ghost work, had, after some hesitation, turned it down.

So it was about this time that I was able to present Eithne with a nominal triumph which pleased her almost as much as it did me. The firm of Wingate had got into some sort of difficulties and had been taken over by one of the partners, Anthony Blond, a rich Jew of exotic personality and literary tastes more sophisticated than those of Gibbs and Fry, the latter a debauched and unhappy homosexual whom I discovered later on, after his suicide, in the pages of James Lees-Milne's enjoyable books on his work for the National Trust. The author describes him as 'the worst man in the world' and 'a positive Satan'; it was humiliating to find that of all the hundreds of variegated and often very distinguished people Lees-Milne mentions, Fry was the only one I had ever met myself.

After taking over, Blond set up his own firm, at first called Blond-Wingate and afterwards simply Blond, and the first book he ever published was my long-despaired-of novel, though in a somewhat shortened form. He was, I thought, rather mean in giving me an advance of only £75 ('might have run to a hundred') but I was so pleased to get the book published at all that I did not really mind. When it came out it got rather dismissive reviews, with one exception – Kenneth Young, a colleague on the *Telegraph* (he was assistant literary editor under 'Zed'), wrote fiction reviews on the side for the *Yorkshire Post*.

I was gratified to find that this true friend and fellow-Yorkshireman had given my book a 'rave review' in his weekly selection, singling it out as a work of genius and one of the most remarkable first novels published since the war. This was more than friendship and our common Yorkshire origin called for. The book, a fantasy about Bradford, hardly more fantastic than a what has subsequently happened to the place, has some originality but is, as I now see, over-influenced both by Kafka and by what might be called the conventional surrealism of the Thirties. But I was grateful to Kenneth Young, a bearded man with a mysterious background who had certainly been in war-time intelligence and may have retained some connections with it afterwards. 'Scratch me and I'll scratch you,' as the great Colonel Sibthorp used to say. But alas, I never had a chance to repay Kenneth's kindness. Not long afterwards, to everyone's surprise and to Sir Colin's open disapproval, he became editor of the *Yorkshire Post*. He kept the chair only a short time, vacating it in circumstances which I never understood and which, perhaps, nobody was meant to understand.

He took up a mysterious job as 'political adviser to the Beaverbrook Press', whose nature and purpose it was difficult to fathom, like much in this puzzling man's career. Twice he asked me, for no discernible reason, to dinner at the Beefsteak Club. On the first occasion he was called away for half an hour during dinner, leaving me staring, with a wild surmise, at the only other person present at the single large dining-table, Sir Henry d'Avigdor-Goldsmid, a prominent member of the English–Jewish establishment. On the other occasion I was just about to leave for the Beefsteak Club when I got a message saying that Kenneth had had a severe stroke. He never regained his faculties, but lingered, speechless, for several years until he died.

While he was editor of the *Yorkshire Post* he had done Kate and myself another service by arranging a meeting with his friend and fellow-Yorkshireman John Braine, who had just become famous with his novel *Room at the Top*. By a coincidence I had read the book in typescript but pronounced it 'promising but unpublishable as it stands' – perhaps my outstanding achievement as a publisher's reader, but one I did not mention to Kenneth or the author. At the time Braine was living with his wife and family at Bingley, a small town in Airedale between Shipley, my own birthplace, and Keighley, home of the Tunnicliffes. We were staying with my mother at Amswick, so we arranged to drive to Skipton and meet Braine at the Hole in the Wall in the market-place.

He arrived there after driving the short distance from Bingley in his brand-new 'mini'. As he had only just learned to drive (part of the price of his new fame and success) he regarded this as quite an achievement, which it undoubtedly was. We took to him at once, helped by a mutual fondness, which soon became obvious, for serious drinking. There was something both impressive and endearing about his unaffected delight in his success. He patted a magnificent new pigskin briefcase as he took off a new ginger-coloured tweed overcoat as fine as my own black Crombie, which I had bought after leaving the BBC as a pledge of my new life. 'Do you know what I've got in this briefcase?' he asked in his unimpaired West Riding accent. 'I'll tell you. My library books!'

There was a poignant symbolism here. Before his sudden elevation to best-selling novelist he had for many years been a humble librarian. It was not long before a man in the bar, who had been watching us intently in a judicial, Yorkshire way for some time, got to his feet and came over. 'I know you,' he said. 'I've seen you on television. Aren't you John Braine?' It was beautiful to see the author's innocent pleasure in this public recognition of his fame, so beautiful and even moving that it never occurred to me to feel the slightest jealousy. Soon we were beginning to find a pleasurable warmth stealing over us, and it went on stealing over us so insidiously that we suddenly realised with surprise that it was half-past two and closing-time.

This did not worry Braine unduly. 'We'll go to the Black Horse,' he said. 'I know the landlord – and he knows me.' The Black Horse was just closing when we arrived. 'Good afternoon, Mr Braine,' said the landlord, with a surprised glance at us and

an enhanced respect for people he had thought from our previous visits as of no particular account. 'Go up with your friends
to the upstairs room. There's nobody'll disturb you there and
you can drink as long as you like.' We stood drinking round
the billiard table, talking animatedly of this and that. We were
still drinking and talking when the pub re-opened at half-past
five. Braine, still clutching his briefcase, began to show signs
of uneasiness. We staggered through the market-place and
down to the railway station, where he had left his car.

He looked at it with alarm. 'Let's have one more drink,' he
said. 'All right, just one.' We shambled into the bar of the
Station Hotel, a gloomy establishment with horsehair-stuffed
seats and photographs of railway engines on the wall. A couple
of commercial travellers were drinking Scotch and chatting to
a hawk-nosed barmaid. Less interested in literature than the
habitués of the Hole in the Wall and the Black Horse, they
gave no sign of recognition. But Braine had had enough for
one day. The problem was: how was he to get home? None too
sure of driving at the best of times, as he admitted, he was
obviously incapable of driving now. In the end we put him in
a taxi and, extracting his address with difficulty, despatched him
back to Bingley. It was a good thing Kate had a strong head,
or she would not have got us home ourselves. We found my
mother in an agitated state. 'There's been a Mrs Braine on the
telephone, asking what you've done with her husband. Ee, I
don't know what you'll get up to next.'

We became good friends with John who, though he could
sometimes be boring in a ponderous Yorkshire way, was always
endearing. I ran into him from time to time at literary parties
after he moved with his family from Bingley into a mock-
Georgian house at Woking, a daft southern place if ever there
was one; moving away from the leftist orthodoxy which had

85

caused him to join CND at their 'sit-ins' in Trafalgar Square, he became a man of ultra-right views and therefore a great supporter of 'Peter Simple', sometimes sending me encouraging fan letters if I had written something which particularly pleased him. He varied between bouts of heavy drinking and total abstinence when, glass of orange juice in hand, he would lecture me half humourously on the evils of drink.

Sadly, he never repeated the success of *Room at the Top* and the film of it which was made soon afterwards, but declined gradually through less successful books and television films about his repulsive hero, Joe Lampton, until in the end he left his home and family in Woking to live with a late-found love in one room in Hampstead, where he died untimely and almost forgotten. Much earlier, after he had been to America, he found himself in conversation with a progressive bishop and praised that country highly. 'Well,' said the bishop, 'I suppose it's all right if you're not black.' 'I'm not black, you silly bugger,' Braine replied. I have always thought this the perfect 'existential' answer to all such remarks. Ever a hater of cant and conformity and a champion of freedom, Braine, when the campaign of terror against smoking was at its height, put special stickers on his envelopes: 'Smoking is Good for You; Smoke More.' He was a man of exceptionally sound instincts, convinced that if the Government told you not to do something you should make a point of doing it.

Kate, quite sensibly, had not been impressed either by the publication of *Sheldrake* or by Kenneth Young's review of it. But a second anthology of the column appeared at the end of 1958, further enhancing its reputation. Colin began to think of spreading its wings and with the approval of the editor, who was coming to accept it as a permanent feature of the paper with a certain regular following (though it is possible that even after it had become really famous many readers of the *Telegraph* were unaware of its existence, tucked away as it was at the bottom of an inner page), arranged several expeditions out of London. First we two, along with Michael ffolkes, went to Geneva for a week, nominally because some international conference or other, possibly about disarmament, was being held there. I wondered whether it had anything to do with the ghost of the League of Nations, which was certainly still hanging about. Michael ffolkes, who was fond of good living, had been looking forward to staying at a first-class hotel like the Beau Rivage (which, I remembered, had been one of my father's favourites in the Twenties, when my elder brother and sister had been at 'finishing school' in Switzerland, one of the absurd anomalies which were to distort and haunt their lives). But, just as if we had been in the army, a 'shambles' had been made of arrangements for our accommodation and we ended up in a 'self-catering flat'. There, in the mornings, we wrote our respective items and Michael drew his drawings, and in the afternoons we either saw the sights of the place or got drunk after a late, prolonged lunch.

Colin, always fond of argumentation, felt himself at a loss among companions less accustomed or inclined to it. Rather than not have an argument at all, he would provoke me by making some obviously absurd statement such as: 'Switzerland, per capita, is the poorest country in Europe'. We spent one whole afternoon arguing about this, then went out to drink at a bar. Colin, still arguing, became so drunk that he suddenly rolled off his chair onto the floor, his possessions, notecase, money, keys, passport, spilling all round him in the manner of a drunken sailor on shore leave. We had to take him back to our flat, undress him and put him to bed, still feebly maintaining the dire poverty of the Swiss.

Our next expedition was to a more mundane destination: Manchester. Here Michael ffolkes's predilections were better catered for; we stayed in the Midland Hotel, then the most expensive in the city, and made visits to the stupendous Gothic Town Hall with its wonderful frescoes (like 'the Danish Invasion of Manchester' and 'Dalton Discovering Marsh Gas') or the Free Trade Hall or Didsbury and Withington, calling up memories of my BBC days: the mild rule of Brian Cave-Brown-Cave, the sensitive Controller of the North Region and a member of one of the oldest families in England; the formation of a Marxist cell by the folk-singer Ewan MacColl; days among the derelict leadmines of Derbyshire with John Mort, the great barmaster of the Leadminer's Court; Professor Max Newman the mathematician, with his fondness for marmalade pudding and Enochian logic and his formidable wife who, as I learned long afterwards to my amazement, had not, at the time we lodged with them, been his wife at all. Why, being in Manchester again after only five years, did I not look up old friends and acquaintances? Had Kate, a friendly soul, been with us she would certainly have wanted to do so. But it never occurred to me. I had passed into another world which had no more connection with the BBC than either world had with the army or with my time at Oxford. All were separate spheres of my life and I must have felt instinctively that it would be inadvisable, even dangerous, to mingle them.

Our last expedition was to Dublin. We travelled by the night train to Holyhead, thence by boat to Dun Laoghaire (or Kingstown, as Colin, who did not share my 'Celtic' predilections, insisted on calling it). We had a nasty shock at the outset, for travel by air to Ireland had already superseded travel by train and boat for all except the poorer travellers. Though we travelled, of course, first-class as befitted substantial journalists, we found there was only one first-class compartment, indeed only a section of one, and that rather squalid and neglected, and part of the guard's van. When I had last travelled on this line, the year after the war, on my flight from my first wife in Dublin, there had been an excellent first-class service with meals adequate enough at a time of rationing. Now there was only a fry-up and an offer to make up a game of cards with the guard.

Michael was better pleased when we reached Dublin and put up at the Shelbourne Hotel, everything which an hotel should be. Here Colin was almost on home ground; we were met by his old friend from Peterhouse, Dr Desmond Williams, now Professor of Modern History at the National University of Ireland, a well-known character of mythological dimension, of whose charm, unreliability and wit a thousand anecdotes were told. Although lame from a bone disease and running to fat, Desmond was almost as irresistible to young women as his compatriot 'Bertie' Rodgers. He also had Rodgers's ability to be in two places at once; in fact he often improved on this by not being in any definite place at all, particularly if he had arranged to meet someone in a definite place or had invited someone to lunch there. Many of the most amusing stories about him were based on this peculiarity of his. He was also addicted to absurd flattery: I had hardly met him before he told me that some Cabinet Minister or famous writer had just told him how much he admired my work. I treated this, even before I had heard of his reputation, with a certain reserve.

Desmond had a German wife (he had been in the Control Commission in Germany and had married her, I believe, to give her British or Irish nationality) but had never lived with her. His present companion was a fierce South African woman doctor, Sheila Murphy, former wife of the Irish poet Richard Murphy and a woman of some means with a sad little eight-year-old daughter. She and Desmond lived in her expensive but squalid house in a superior part of Dublin. Their lives, which involved a good deal of drinking, were haphazard. She was good-looking but surprisingly dirty and ill-dressed and appealed to me more than she did to Michael ffolkes, whose taste in women was somewhat conventional.

Under Desmond's tutelage we met a great many people in Dublin, but for all I can remember I may have been drunk all the time – no uncommon thing on a visit to the Republic. I wrote a sketch about Conor Cruise O'Brien, who, himself decidedly drunk, walked out of a dinner party, offended by my reference to the *Táin Bó Cuailgne*, an epic poem he evidently thought no Englishman ought to have heard of. We met the solicitor and novelist Terence de Vere White in the Kildare Street Club, a man with an Irish voice of almost painfully exquisite refinement who asked us to his house, where his wife was quite amazingly rude, telling Michael ffolkes that he 'knew nothing' and asking her husband what he meant by bringing home low companions from the Dublin gutter.

One comparatively sober afternoon we saw a special performance of the film *Mise Eire* which George Morrison (or Seoirse Mac Giollamhaire) had made for Gael Linn, the Irish language publishing company. This presented the history of Ireland from pre-Norman times up to the 'War of Independence' by means of designs, and for the later period, photographs and clips from old films with a commentary in Irish. The music was by the composer Seán O Riada, a man of genius who might have been recognised as one of the greatest composers of this century if he had not lived in Ireland and died untimely of what is sometimes called the national malady, drink. For the film score he had used some of the finest Irish folk-songs (and there are no folk-songs finer) notably *Róisin Dubh* ('Little Dark Rose') in orchestral settings of great skill and beauty to produce an over-whelming effect.

By the end I was in floods of tears. It was enough to bring anybody to his feet, shouting support for the cause of Irish nationalism, that most tragic and hopelessly lost of all lost causes, lost when the Irish language was lost more than two hundred years ago. One generally overlooked reason why Ire-land, unified or not, can never be a nation is that when all the 'unhistorical nations' of Europe, the Czechs, Slovaks, Finns and so on, were asserting their nationality, only Ireland, though gaining nominal independence, lost her language beyond hope of revival. The latest heirs of that lost cause, the Provisional IRA, must know this in their hearts. Perhaps that is one neglected reason for their desperate savagery. When they are assembling their bombs or planning operations, do they use the Irish language? Are they not obliged, for their own sake, to use the language of the English enemy? It is the ultimate irony.

I came back to England with O Riada's music ringing in my head. That night Kate and I made love as we had not made love for a long time, and for the rest of that week spent success-ive nights of delicious love-making. It was an interlude I cannot explain. I don't think it ever happened again.

The FitzGibbons' ménage at Sacomb's Ash had for some time now shown unmistakable signs of breaking up. There seemed to be a correlation between this process and the change which was coming over the neighbourhood, a cloud of uneasiness and decline: its magic – at its best it had been that – was disappear-ing. Constantine's own behaviour was becoming more and more desperate. He had always been a heavy drinker; now he drank more and more, and his round face beneath a prematurely bald skull – Theodora said he 'looked like a mad Dutch baby' –

began to lose what had been its habitually amiable and friendly expression. He had a nervous trick of swinging his right arm in an arc of a circle; this gesture now began to express anger and aggression. On returning drunk from the pub at night he more than once took off his clothes outside the door, piled them into a heap and tried to set fire to them – a thing much easier in intention than execution.

I saw little of him at this time, but learned of the final collapse of his marriage from his neighbour Elizabeth Foster-Melliar. It seems he had arranged to abscond – where I cannot say – with the wife of another neighbour. Perhaps he only imagined, in his drunken confusion, that he had made this arrangement. But the woman changed her mind – supposing she had had a mind to abscond at all – at the last moment and failed to keep the assignation. Constantine therefore went home with his packed bag to face what may have been one of the most remarkable of all the FitzGibbons' scenes of controlled violence. Or it may be that with things getting really serious the throwing of food, drink, plates and bottles was inadequate to express their feelings. There had always been an element of fun and affection as well as theatrical contrivance in these displays.

It was not long before Theodora made a far more effective counter-move by herself absconding in fact. She went to Ireland, which she had always claimed was her native country (she had been, she used to say, the daughter of an Irish peer, guarded in her nursery by six gigantic Irish wolfhounds). An old admirer, George Morrison (who made the wonderful film *Mise Eire*), was waiting to give her refuge and after the divorce had gone through they married. For a time Constantine stayed on in his house, either alone or consoled by one woman or another. But he was a man of great resilience; it was not long before he found another wife, Marion, a dark, rather mysterious person who, though she lacked Theodora's gift for fantasy and amusing rudeness, and probably her outstanding gift for cookery, no doubt had other qualities I did not discover.

It was not long, either, before Constantine, whose ability to go on writing books even under the most adverse circumstances I admired and envied, wrote a novel about a coming Communist takeover of England, *When the Kissing Had to Stop*, which was serialised in a newspaper and even televised, making him well-known for the first time, and put him really in the money. His reaction was characteristic. He sold Sacomb's Ash and bought, with a typical illusion of grandeur, an immense, rambling, dilapidated house in Dorset called Thornhill. He and his new wife had not nearly enough furniture to furnish it, nor enough money to keep it up. This did not prevent him from giving a wedding party in the empty, echoing house, the last of his memorable parties I ever attended, full of improbable people from the top of his league tables, such as the novelist Sibylle Bedford, Noel Annan the thinker and Constantine's vast, rumbling uncle, Sir Philip Antrobus of Avebury Manor in Wiltshire, whose family had once owned Stonehenge and who, whatever else he was, seemed every inch a baronet to me – I had, at that time, met very few baronets.

Rapidly 'outsoaring the shadow of our night', as I told Kate in a self-pitying moment, though remaining just as friendly as before, he soon sold Thornhill and moved to a somewhat smaller but much more beautiful house not many miles away, Waterstone Manor near Puddletown, famous for appearing in Hardy's *Far from the Madding Crowd*. Here I stayed once or twice (Kate, I think, never, for she had by this time incurred Constantine's permanent displeasure, partly by her serious infidelity to me, and had dropped out of the league tables altogether). There was still not enough furniture to fill this large

93

house, but there were many of the right appurtenances, such as a sideboard in the breakfast-room with dishes on a hot plate – bacon, eggs, mushrooms, kidneys, kedgeree and so on – from which guests helped themselves in approved country-house fashion.

There was a terrace, there were fine lawns and stately trees, even a dower-house where Constantine's formidable American mother was, I think, meant to live in her old age, though I doubt she ever did. For me there was a particular bonus: a mysterious avenue leading from the garden to a prospect of distant blue downs; I had only to walk along it a short way to feel that clouding of the mind, that sense of the numinous I had known in childhood and youth but thought lost or only faintly recovered. Constantine showed me this avenue with great pride; he also knew what kind of feelings it was likely to arouse in me, even though he may not have shared them himself. It was as if he were giving me a special treat, as indeed he was.

Here in this beautiful place Constantine lived for several years, writing with his usual diligence though never repeating the success of *When the Kissing Had to Stop*, and entertaining in his usual generous, if unpredictable, way, until that marriage too broke down in acrimony after producing his first child, a son, Francis, and his dark lady departed, leaving him alone again.

It was not long, of course, before he found another wife. I am not sure whether this was his third marriage or his fourth. There had been rumours of a very brief marriage when he was at Oxford, to a beautiful Burmese girl, Margaret Ay Maung; but this, if it ever took place, was soon obscured. His latest wife seemed to me by far the best of them. Marjorie was a very attractive and amiable young American, formerly married to a millionaire and presumably well provided with alimony. With her he left Waterstone and England for good and settled in Ireland, at first in west Cork, where there was a considerable English colony attracted, as Constantine himself must have been to some extent, by the Republic's remission of income tax to all residents who could show themselves to be 'creative artists' by having published a book or musical work or held an exhibition. He soon tired of these people and moved to Dublin where he had a house in the superior suburb of Killiney, an establishment of some splendour, I was told; mainly through apathy, I never visited him there.

Very soon, he took Irish nationality (his father had been Irish-American) and with it Irish nationalist opinions which gave rise to several books on Irish history such as *Out of the Lion's Paw*, an account of the last Irish struggle for independence. Apart from his writing and his family (Marjorie produced a daughter, Oonagh) he devoted himself to two ambitions: to become a Senator of Ireland and to establish his claim to the Earldom of Clare, extinct since 1864. Considering that the first and best-known Earl of Clare, John FitzGibbon, had been the most prominent Irish supporter of the Union of 1801 and was accordingly one of the greatest of all Irish historical villains in nationalist eyes, this seemed an odd ambition indeed.

He succeeded in neither ambition. But he was, I think and hope, reasonably happy with this best and comeliest of his wives. He certainly ought to have been. But he was a conspicuously 'difficult' man to live with. He told me, on one of his visits to London, that he had been doing his best to wreck his marriage to Marjorie, 'just as I always do'. If so, he did not succeed. But I have no doubt he was angered and frustrated by the decline of his reputation as a writer and, it may be, by his unacceptability in Dublin literary circles as well as English ones. In his later years, heavy drinking passed into dipsomania. He wrote a book about this, confident, he told me, that it would re-establish his literary reputation and be a bestseller. This did not happen.

Toward the end of his life his misfortunes multiplied. He had an operation for double cataract, which left him with 'tunnel vision' – he could see only straight ahead with the aid of immensely powerful spectacles. Claudie, whose mind was inclined to dwell on such things and who disliked him anyhow, told me she believed he had had a colostomy, one of the ultimate medical horrors. However that may be, it is certainly a fact that on my very last meeting with my old friend, only a few months before his death in February 1983, he seemed to be partly paralysed. Yet he faced all this 'with immense courage and cheerfulness', a cliché which in his case was no more than the truth. In the pub where we met he drank several pints of beer and talked excitedly of a book he was writing about Charlemagne. As I put him in the taxi which was to take him to the airport for the plane to Dublin, he smiled just as he had smiled in the Fitzroy Tavern where I first met him in 1937, a precocious young man of seventeen just back from a sort of Grand Tour of Europe and full of ideas for writing.

It was curious and also sad that I, whose unwritten books he had offered to write for me in Sacomb's Ash days since I seemed utterly incapable of writing any for myself, slowly attained, even though pseudonymously, a greater literary reputation (of a sort) than he, whose writing career had started off with such a bang. But for him I might possibly never have written anything at all, but have remained, a fading hanger-on, on the margins of the BBC, gradually declining into alcoholic hopelessness – if, that is, I could have found enough money for the alcohol. It was he who, in my wandering life after Oxford, showed me the possibility of better things by encouraging what some people might have called snobbery but others discrimination.

96

It was he who had brought me into the circle of Much Hadham, the Welches, Worsthornes, Moores and Foster-Melliars by which I eventually secured, on the *Telegraph*, the first regular job I ever had in my life. And he had been, in spite of all the nonsense of social league tables, a warm friend. We shared, up to the end, a whole domain of jokes and associations which were renewable whenever we met: the days before the war which my first wife and I had spent in Chelsea, rapidly moving from one bed-sitter or half-furnished flat to another, one rented from the 'married' homosexual pair, Potter and Baxter, whose screaming rows with each other and with Quentin Crisp, a flamboyant homosexual who later became famous, were promising material for fiction; summer days in Westmorland at the beginning of the war; the statutory pub crawl of the nine pubs in Appleby, in one of which, the Golden Ball, Constantine had only just escaped being arrested as a spy because, though dressed in the uniform of a bandsman in the Irish Guards, he had been heard speaking German; odd meetings during the earlier part of the war, when I had spent a weekend at Grosvenor House with my rich Yorkshire girlfriend and we had got drunk with him at a night club, the long-lost Coconut Grove; parties at Sacomb's Ash when we 'went on' to a curious, dilapidated country club called Gilston Hall and sometimes stayed the night to resume drinking at dawn: alcohol, though not the only bond between us, certainly suffused our relationship with its kindly influence, making possible a friendship between two people as disparate as could well be.

A weekend I spent at Waterstone in the Sixties before his final departure for Ireland – the last occasion I saw him for more than a few hours at a time – was typically bizarre. I knew his second wife had left him, and as far as I knew he was not yet in the way of acquiring a third. What I was not prepared

97

for was to find George and Theodora, by this time Mr and Mrs Morrison, installed as a sort of butler and housekeeper and running his house with commendable efficiency. He had sent for them from Ireland in his imperious way and there they were just as if nothing had ever happened between them. Theodora had always been a magnificent cook (she was now making a name for herself as a cookery writer, author of a series of books illustrated by George's fine old photographs of peasants and fisherman – *A Taste of Ireland, A Taste of Scotland, A Taste of Yorkshire* and, for all I knew, *A Taste of the Back of Me Hand* – and was in her element in the Waterstone kitchen, turning out splendid feasts as in the old days.

I was glad to find she was still as free as ever with her insulting witticisms ('I've taken an instant dislike to you,' she would say to someone like myself whom she had known for years, or 'Look, his little face is all puckered up with disappointment'). George, a large, quietly-spoken leprechaun, asserted his place in the world in a whisper which contrasted with Theodora's shout. But there was no mistaking their good opinion of themselves, which went with a certain puzzlement at my own self-depreciating attitude ('But then,' Theodora said, 'you always were peculiar'). And so, after a pleasant weekend of serious drinking in the old style, I left them to play their peculiar charade.

As positive and eager to extend the bounds of our lives as I was negative and inclined to shrink from new enterprises, Kate decided to make new, sensational use of our curious little car. We would go to the South of France in it. So, in the autumn of 1959, through one of her innumerable friends and contacts (she was now quite successful with her journalist's work, and for a time had a well-paid job writing for a mysterious body called the Wool Secretariat, pattern of all the proliferating organisations set up to publicise and promote anything you can think of) Kate arranged to rent for a whole month a small house in the forest near Vence, only a few miles from the Riviera. With misgivings on my part we set off from Putney in the little car, the back part of which was so crammed with luggage that Jane, then nearing her seventh birthday, had to fit into a little nest in one corner.

As often with Kate's enterprises, my misgivings soon vanished and gave way to what most people would have described as pleasure when we boarded the car ferry at Dover and savoured the delights of 'going abroad', not yet a thing which almost everybody in England did. The democratic horrors of mass tourism were still ahead. It was ten years since I had last been to France. Then it had been my BBC girl friend Anne who had organised our holiday in a château on the Tarn. Now, under a different tutelage and with a beloved young daughter to enjoy unfamiliar sights, sounds and smells and wonder at the foreign people, thus providing vicarious wonder for myself, all was changed. In 1948, what was more, Anne and I had had to subsist for a whole fortnight in France on the travel allowance the Labour government allowed us, £25 each; now, with the Conservative dispensation, the travel allowance, if it existed at all in practice, was much more generous; besides, I was now rich, or if not rich, had a great deal more money than I could ever have expected.

We loaded our car onto the train at Calais and reaching Lyon in the early morning, drove steadily south and down the Rhône, through the brightly-coloured country by way of nougat-infested Montelimar (fascinating only for Jane; I suggested buying a twenty-ton block of the stuff but was persuaded to reduce it to reasonable proportions). We spent the night at Les Baux in a pleasant enough inn, excited by all the signs that we had reached the true South – the sound of massed cicadas, the smell of pine resin and lavender. Next morning I was astounded by the strange mirage-like Alpilles, which I had never heard of before and had not even noticed on the map. Entrusted with the map-reading, one of my few practical skills, I deceived Kate by choosing, instead of the obvious main road, a lesser one which took us through the inland hills, with their beautiful forests, ruined villages on hill-tops and small towns where nothing much had changed for centuries. So by the time we had taken on necessary supplies, further restricting Jane's nest-space and overloading the car, and were nearing our destination, it was late evening. We lost our way, descending a steep, rugged track in the gathering darkness, then, saved by a skilled piece of reversing by Kate, who was getting more confident in her driving every minute, came upon our little house, buried in trees and in a labyrinth of tracks, almost by accident.

The house, amid olive trees and pines, was in a place near enough to the coast to be occupied by many similar though widely separated houses belonging to French or Belgian bourgeois, largely retired, and a few foreigners, none English. The cleaning woman, supplied by the owner, was a monopod. This fascinated Jane, who may have acquired from this experience her later fascination with cripples, physical cripples at first, later mental. There was also a beautiful tabby cat named Baudouin after the King of the Belgians, whom Jane grew fond of, inventing a chant she sang when Kate crossed her: 'Beautiful Baudouin, Horrid Mummy'. I seldom crossed her myself ('you spoil that child,' Kate would have said if she had been addicted to talking in such familiar clichés).

The holiday started badly on the first morning when we went to Cagnes by the sea, the scene of Cyril Connolly's book *The*

Rock Pool, whose hero, Naylor, has such a disquieting resemblance to myself that I have always wondered on whom, apart from the author, he could have been based. This must have been the time when the Riviera was beginning to turn into a squalid inferno (the strange villas of the rich still remaining here and there, with rocky steps leading down to private beaches, gallantly defended against the hordes of the too-many, to serve as a reminder of the paradise it must have been). The beach of Cagnes was not only smelly and bleak under a grey autumnal sky but almost deserted. It was a horrible let-down. Careless of Jane, for whom it was perhaps enough to be by the sea and in a foreign land, we quarrelled fiercely.

The holiday was not like that all the time. There were more agreeable beaches; there were cafés where we sat drinking and watching passers-by; there were expeditions to Vence (already famous for terrible amateur and professional painters, tourists' knick-knack shops and false potteries), Grasse, Miramar and Vallauris (famous for Picasso); and one day we even set out for Italy, a country where neither Kate nor myself had ever been. I had absurd plans to reach Liguria and even Tuscany, unwilling to accept that the distances were too great for such megalomaniac ideas; in the end we got no further than the unpleasing coastal resort of Diano Marina, spending the night in an inferior hotel where we were kept sleepless by our first experience of the amiable noisiness of Italians. Next morning, on a beach occupied almost entirely by fat Germans, there was another treat for Jane: an artificial leg lying ownerless on the sand, a striking symbol, but of what? ('I've got a poem on,' we both said simultaneously, united for a moment.)

We turned back towards France under grey, thunderous, menacing skies; through San Remo where, hot and fly-tormented, we ate a disgusting lunch, looking disgustedly at the dull Alpine foothills, bristly with scrub and disfigured by dried-up ravines. But next day, the 16th of September, was Jane's seventh birthday; asked what she wanted for a treat, she chose the beach of Juan-les-Pins, with its expensive beach-huts and umbrellas, delicious iced drinks and the occasional bit of swimming, of which she was already inordinately fond.

Now we had only two days left. Next day the postman brought a shock for Kate from England: a letter from her Kenneth, telling her that his wife had discovered their affair (it was amazing that she had not discovered it long before; there is a proverbial but true saying: 'the wife is always the last to know') and consequently it was all over. Kate set her considerable jaw: 'Oh no, it isn't,' I could almost hear her saying (and there, of course, she was right). As was her habit, she made no secret of her private life to people in general, least of all to me, and was soon telling me all her troubles. Was this openness, even boastfulness a part of her persistent wish to flout her family's Catholic conformity; or was it part of her persistent need to reassure herself that she was lovable and loved?

We set off on the long journey to Lyons and home in a mood on her part, half despairing, half determined; on mine, passive, no longer caring greatly one way or the other. We simply gave ourselves up to the pleasure of the journey. We spent the night at an hotel in Avignon after duly inspecting the papal palace. Its restaurant was fascinating to all of us in different ways. At the next table was an elderly French couple who gave an amazing exhibition of greed, putting on protective clothing when they ate shellfish, then laying it aside as they got down to business with enormous helpings of *coq au vin*. I had always annoyed Kate with my seemingly perverse but in fact genuine dislike of French cooking ('perfectly good food ruined with ridiculous sauces') but here was an exhibition of gourmandism which even she, with her claim to sophisticated taste, could laugh at with me.

These people even talked about food as they ate it. 'What do you do,' said the man, 'if you wake up hungry in the night?' 'I always keep a chocolate cake under the bed.' The man considered this. 'Moi,' he said at last, 'je prefère un Port Salut.' We could hardly contain ourselves, and failed to notice that Jane was amusing herself and propagating anglophobia by blowing into the long narrow paper containers of bread fingers and propelling them to great distances across the room. Next day we caught the car-conveying train at Lyons and reached Calais in the early morning. It was a beautiful, golden autumnal day, the sea like glass, and glass of a very high quality, as we crossed the Channel back to England and our various troubles; we reached Putney on an afternoon so calm and warm in golden light that I imagined I could hear cicadas in the gardens beside the leafy suburban roads.

4
Evenings in Fleet Street

With the success of the column and our growing prospects we began to acquire, in our Putney villa, some of the appurtenances of middle-class life. We bought a new, or rather second-hand, car to replace the comical little machine which had given such good service, a smart-looking green Hillman Minx convertible, a popular model at the time. We also began to have *au pair* girls to look after Jane when either or both of us were away and to take her to and from her new school, the Virgo Fidelis Convent School in Kensington (Kate, a lapsed Catholic, was anxious that Jane should have a Catholic education, though this, whatever it may have done for her moral welfare, and it probably did a lot, meant that she suffered disadvantages in an academic sense). The first *au pair* girl we had was a large, dark, fierce and overpowering German with lesbian tendencies. She did not stay long and was replaced by Gabriela, a plump Italian girl of amazing amiability and simplicity who was quite happy to put up with unlimited teasing and practical jokes.

In the summer of 1960 we took Jane to Ireland. We stayed at the Glenbeigh Hotel on the Ring of Kerry, recommended by some friend of Kate's, an extremely jolly establishment and a credit to the efforts of Terence Sheehy of Bórd Fáilte Eireann, then beginning to attract tourists, both English and foreign, to a country which, outside Dublin, had had few good hotels. The more convivial guests, that is to say most of them, gathered in the bar every night for drinking, singing and other entertainments. A Dublin barrister, Dermot Kinlan, was famous for a

recitation in which he reproduced in succession the accents of
the four provinces of Ireland, ending with that of Ulster, whose
harsh back-vowels and grimly menacing tones caused much
amusement. Who would have thought, at a time when peace
seemed to have settled on Ireland for good and nobody seemed
to take old hatreds seriously any more, that twenty years later
those tones would be no matter for merriment?

One evening we went to the celebrated Puck Fair at Killorglin, where a goat is hoisted to a high platform but no longer
sacrificed as it must once have been. Satisfactorily, the electric
lighting in the town failed that night; we peered into a rough
and primitive bar and saw by flickering candlelight a crowd of
dark wild faces which had not changed in essence from those
a traveller might have seen a hundred, even two hundred years
before. All this delighted me; the Tourist Board was probably
beginning to think about the touristic possibilities of this pictur-
esque Fair of Killorglin, but then it still belonged, without selfconsciousness or artiness, to the Irish farmers and tinkers as it
had for untold centuries. We must have seen it in its last
days before it was swallowed up by the 'modern world' and
transformed into a show, an entertainment for everybody to
gaze at on the television screen, with a neat commentary, perhaps, and a discussion by 'experts' in which its ancient symbolism would be analysed at a simple-minded, even moronic level,
enough to justify its being described by people who should
know better as a 'serious programme'.

In old age I have 'gone off' the Irish, and even begun to
doubt whether there are any people, apart from the aboriginal
Gaelic-speakers of the west, who can really be called Irish at
all. In my youth, and even up to the time of this holiday in
Ireland, I was as fervent a believer in the myth of Irish nationalism as any of those English people, such as Arnold Bax the

composer or Cecil Day Lewis the writer, who upheld the romantic cause of what might have been called 'England's little playground in the west'. I even tried to learn the Irish language, which is far more difficult than Welsh, but although I occasionally pretended to understand it, I retained little from my studies. Rolleston's *Myths and Legends of the Celtic Race*, particularly the Irish part of it, was a powerful influence on my childhood, and to this day I can reasonably claim to know much more about the background, mythical and historical, of Ireland's troubles than the majority of English or for that matter 'Irish' people – which is not saying much.

It was the blatant failure of the Irish nationalists to create a nation; the fiasco of the language movement (de Valera was right when he said 'without our language we are only half a nation'); the headlong surrender of the Irish in the Republic to the 'modern world' I abhorred so much, typified by their setting up a television service (I had advised them in the column to set up a jamming station instead, preferably one powerful enough to do England a good turn by making it impossible to receive television programmes there either): these were the things, fatal to my reactionary hopes, that cured me of any Irish addiction and left me weary and cynical about that country which seems, in spite of the outburst of violence in the North, to be growing more like England (and the worst things in England) every day. As Hitler in a more serious context said of the Germans, I have felt like saying, 'My Irish have failed me'.

We had only just got back to England when Colin (who for some time had seemed to have something on his mind) announced that he was leaving the column and that if I wanted to take it over it was mine. He was ten years younger than I and took his career as a journalist more seriously. He felt, rightly, that the column was a dead end. It could not help him to achieve what he wanted, which was, of course, to be an editor, preferably, I suppose of, the *Daily* or, failing that, the *Sunday Telegraph*. Meanwhile, he proposed to revert to what he had been before the column started, a leader writer.

I felt a certain amount of panic, for although I had got used to writing the fantastic, whimsical or 'satirical' parts of the column, I doubted whether I could manage the political side. However, it would mean more money; and I would become the 'head of a department', responsible only to the editor. Of course I agreed, after an uneasy interview with Sir Colin Coote. He was anxious that I should have an assistant. This I did not want, mainly because I preferred to be in charge of something which was entirely my own. So without actually refusing to have an assistant I left the matter in abeyance, and in fact never had one. Not long after I took over, a candidate presented himself. He was young Auberon Waugh, then working on the *Telegraph*'s Peterborough column but maintaining that nothing he had ever written had ever appeared in it. He would probably have done very well – perhaps too well; my unconscious reason for refusing his offer, which he made with great charm and politeness, may well have been a fear, typical of me, that with his superior social connections and greater confidence in himself he might soon have taken over the column altogether.

I did have a regular contributor who could write the column when I was on holiday. This was Colm Brogan, a famous journalist in his day, who had written eloquent pamphlets against the post-war Labour government but had since fallen into comparative obscurity. He was a Glaswegian, a Catholic and a vehement 'reactionary', a man to love and admire but one who was often described as 'his own worst enemy'. He was handicapped both by his bibulous appearance – a fiery red face on a small but wiry and energetic body – and by his Glasgow accent, which made him difficult to understand in person until you got on to the right wavelength, and on the telephone completely unintelligible. But he was a witty and forceful writer who in those early days was a great help to me.

The column had, of course, started as the work of several hands, including my own, and this it continued to be, though less and less so (I never wrote less than four-fifths of it myself from 1960 up to the mid-Seventies, and after that I wrote all of it). One fairly constant early contributor was Charles Herring, a big, lumbering, very shy man who lived in Birmingham and sent in a weekly supply of material in which amusing ideas were apt to be embedded in overmuch verbiage but, when edited, were often useful. Later on, an established humorist, Michael Green, author of popular books about sport (*The Art of Coarse Rugby* and so on), wrote occasional items. It was he who invented 'Squire Haggard', the wicked landlord of eighteenth-century Stretchford, extracts from whose journal, said to be edited by my fictitious all-purpose literary hack, Julian Birdbath, appeared regularly in the column over a period of ten years and were sometimes singled out for particular praise by readers, causing me some slight mortification.

They were, in fact, very clever and funny pastiche, different in their broader, coarser humour from the rest of the column. Green, a sardonic man whose character I found difficult to fathom, was, unlike Herring, a professional writer and after a while secured legal copyright in the character of the wicked squire. It was when he began to claim rights in other columnar characters I had already invented, on the grounds that he had written items about them, and to intimate that I was getting the credit for his work, that we fell out. I pointed out, reasonably enough, that the column was pseudonymous, that I had never claimed copyright in my own inventions and often got no credit for them myself – many people, never having heard of me, believed the column was written by A. P. Herbert, Lady Pamela Berry, Randolph Churchill or all of them at once. But, muttering that it was 'all very well for people who got a regular salary of seven thousand a year', he seemed unconvinced, went his own way and I saw him no more.

Soon after I took over the column, Claudie Worsthorne gave up her job as columnar secretary, not because she was unwilling to work for me (in fact she returned in 1969 and was secretary from then onwards) but because of her domestic and social duties. As her successor she introduced Annabel Dilke, a granddaughter of the notorious Sir Charles Dilke, a stunningly beautiful girl about twenty years old, amiable and intelligent (she later wrote novels and married Georgi Markov, the Bulgarian exile who was murdered by a poisoned umbrella). I was somewhat taken aback by this apparition. But she seemed quiet and anxious to please, and though we never became really great friends we got on together well enough. It might be thought that I would find it distracting to sit at my desk every day opposite a strikingly attractive girl of upper-class background. But very beautiful upper-class girls never appealed to me, perhaps from a deep-seated feeling that I was not good enough for them. If Annabel had had some defect in her beauty, such as my favourite 'goofy teeth' or had been of an inferior class or no class, like myself, things might have been much more awkward, not to say impossible. But as it was she never gave me a single moment's uneasiness. People like Michael ffolkes, who was habitually gallant to all attractive girls, sometimes commented on this, but I noticed that they never 'got to first base' with Annabel either.

Thus I toiled on, with a narrow scrape very soon after I took over the column, when the deputy editor, John Applebey, suggested a radical change in its function: I was to travel about England, writing it from various different places. Applebey, who had taken over from the eccentric Donald McLachlan, was a serious-minded man, unmarried, a teetotaller, non-smoker and devout Anglican. There was no nonsense about him, which made his suggestion – presented almost in the form of an order – even more alarming to me: I instinctively objected to change of any kind and thought that on the whole things were very well as they were. Perry Worsthorne, whose mother, Lady Norman, was associated with Applebey's sister in some charitable work, had once called at the Applebeys' semi-detached house in Wimbledon. Accustomed to the halls of the mighty, he reeled away incredulous. 'Do you know, they live – I can hardly believe it – they live in – in' – he was at a loss for a comparison ' – a postman's house!'

This suggestion by Applebey threw me into dread and confusion, with nightmares that lasted a whole weekend. I was delivered by astounding news. Applebey, who was about forty and looked extremely healthy, had suddenly died of a heart attack. Was I responsible? Was I the possessor of supernatural powers, evil powers at that? It was not the first time something of this kind had happened, I remembered. At my Harrogate prep school a games-crazed tyrant among the masters who, I believed, would make my life a misery, had suddenly died of a heart attack soon after my arrival. But I cannot say that either coincidence – what else could it have been? – worried me for long.

A minor event was my dispossession from the office which Colin and I had jointly occupied; the authorities now thought this was unduly large for me alone. It was proposed that Reg Steed, a leader-writer, should share it. In vain I made representations to the editor: my work, I said, was not routine but had a 'creative' element. I therefore needed solitude and quiet. I can imagine what he thought of this; but he rejected my plea politely and Reg Steed was installed. I had no objection to Steed, indeed liked him very much. But I looked for another home and soon found one in an obscure corner at the back of the third floor.

It was a small room, formerly occupied by three music critics, and had a door at the back of it marked 'Fire Escape', for the very good reason that it led to one. So it was with this notice at my back in this uncarpeted room with a restricted view of a courtyard that I sat at my desk, weaving my curious fancies, for the next fifteen years, until moved, greatly against my will, to superior, standardised, carpeted accommodation on the fifth floor under a scheme of reorganisation. There was something about my tiny room, which had just enough space for my desk, Annabel's desk, a table, a cupboard, a bookcase and a large old-fashioned hatstand, which appealed to me strongly. What did not appeal to me was a disaster which occurred when Annabel innocently put the greater part of my books in an outsize waste-paper basket, ready for removal. The night-time cleaners, taking it for rubbish, sent the whole lot for burning. So perished, among other treasures, my rare copy of Marsden's translation (with notes) of *The Protocols of the Elders of Zion*. Did it cry out, I wondered, after the manner of the Old Orange Flute burned by the Papists, 'Perish Judah!'? I did not reproach Annabel. Perhaps she had done me a good turn.

There was certainly no lack of material in the world for me to write about. This was the time when all the main themes which were to occupy the column for the rest of its existence first appeared; the time when the quagmire foundations were laid of the tottering England we now inhabit.

The column as I began to develop it became more and more

'controversial' and a byword for 'right-wing' opinions, that is, the opinions which most people in England held before the 'great semantic shift' by which the Left gradually took over the Centre and what had been the Centre became known first as the Right, then as the Extreme Right and finally the 'backwoodsmen' and even the Fascists. This meant that I got a good deal of correspondence, both for and against, both congratulatory and abusive, both, since on the whole intelligent people do not write to the papers, largely based on false premises.

The only threat of actual physical violence I ever had was from a member of the National Front. I had written, apropos of the arrival of Ugandan Indians fleeing from Idi Amin, that there must be plenty of these Indians I would rather have in England than some of the people who were here already. 'Traitor!' wrote this patriot. 'We counted you on our side and you have let us down. If I wasn't too busy I would come round and punch you on the nose.' Another time a sausage-shaped, flexible parcel arrived. 'Don't open it,' said Claudie. 'I know it 'ees sheet.'

Another time a small irregularly-shaped parcel arrived; it proved to contain two crossed straws, a pebble and a small empty bottle smelling faintly of urine, probably horse's. It was a genuine African 'bad juju'. But the parcel was marked 'Insufficiently secured and repackaged in the Post Office'. In some London post office, I suppose, an innocent clerk had opened it, received the full blast of the magic spell and dropped dead on the spot.

To balance these hostile manifestations there was an equal or greater number of favourable ones, equally mistaken. Many *Telegraph* readers became tremendous fans of the column mainly because, particularly in the 'lead' or 'serious' first item, it could be taken to support their most dearly-held prejudices. I had one letter from a reader who applauded my views about Ireland and 'the blacks'; as far as he was concerned, he wrote, they were all the same and he could not distinguish between them. This was an interesting survival of an English prejudice which must have been quite common among uneducated people in the first half of the last century. I got plenty of letters commending my support for hanging and flogging, neither of which I had ever written about, let alone recommended. Such people held a complete set of opinions corresponding to the 'left-wing package deal' and equally immovable by any argument. I preferred them to the Left, however, because, being simple-minded English people, they were at least instinctively on their own side, unlike the bigots of the Left, with their imbecile assumption that their own country must always be in the wrong.

I came across another kind of misconception among some of my middle- and upper-class readers. They thought I must personally resemble the aristocratic, Blimp-moustached figure, with his deerstalker, gold hunter and glass of port which Michael ffolkes had drawn as the writer of the column and which, of course, I had self-mockingly fostered myself. These people, who sometimes invited me to luncheon or even dinner parties, were taken aback to find that I was not like this at all, and far from being a brilliant conversationalist I was usually tongue-tied, or, if my tongue was loosened by drink, tended to rant away about subjects they knew and cared nothing about, such as the Welsh mutation system or the methods by which a new incarnation of the Dalai Lama was identified. Besides, I knew none of the rich, famous or well-connected people they talked about, so that embarrassment made me more uncommunicative than ever and ensured that I was never asked again.

Such people might just as well have lived on another planet; afterwards I thought of these occasions as affording a glimpse of some unattainable paradise. A rich and cultivated Jewish property developer, who had given up property developing, I think, because he had been among the first to make a great deal of money in this way and was not interested in making any more, took it into his head to ask me to lunch at his house in Hill Street, in Mayfair. The marble-floored entrance-hall, the Portuguese manservant who took my coat, the drawing-room with its original Zoffanys – boring paintings in my opinion but very valuable, I suppose – on the walls, the bibelots of jade or Roman gold on ormolu tables, the magnate's tall, blonde and beautiful young Italian wife with her stunningly elegant clothes and stunningly elegant jewellery: all these things made my head swim, the more so from the fortifying drinks I had taken before-hand and the powerful additives this excellent host was now supplying.

The company at the table in the elegant dining-room reinforced this dreamlike impression: a young English Marquis and an older Earl with perfect, easy manners; a woman older and less beautiful than my hostess, but equally elegant; a famous journalist whom, to my host's surprise, I had never met before; a retired soldier famous for his wartime exploits and for peacetime activities which made him a prime object of suspicion to the Left . . . what was I to say to these people or they to me?

They could not understand that everybody was not as rich as themselves. 'When you fly to Australia,' said my neighbour the war hero, 'have you ever thought of travelling via Samarkand? It makes a change. I found it most interesting to stop overnight and have a look at the place.' 'I don't suppose it's very romantic any more,' I said, evading the original question. 'Well, no, it isn't,' he said, looking at me suspiciously.

I did not even know how to take my leave. At last, stammering and bemused by this glimpse of fairyland, I staggered out into .

the grey world and back to my desk as though waking from a dream. It took me hours, even days, to recover; for quite a long time I had a fading sense of lost opportunity. But what in fact, hopelessly unequipped as I was by nature, by training or by experience, could I have done to secure even a foothold in such circles? I have never ceased to marvel at people, obviously no better equipped than I, who have contrived to do so. What is their secret? A firm self-confidence? An ability to overcome the shyness which springs from acute selfconsciousness? I gradually learned, after a few experiences of this sort – and I always accepted these invitations in the never quite extinguished hope of doing better – to resign myself to personal obscurity. It was galling to be at the same time pseudonymously famous.

Another class of readers, and among the most numerous and tireless correspondents, were the cranks and adherents of 'conspiracy theories', who as time went on found plenty of material in my column to encourage them to think I would be sympathetic. To some extent I was. It is not difficult to believe that the world is shaped by secret influences which move it ineluctably in a certain direction; how else to account for what has happened in two world wars and all that has flowed from them: the destruction of Europe, the end of the British Empire, the predominance of the United States, the establishment of the State of Israel and its key role in the world; the power of credit or imaginary money especially condemned by some of my conspiracy-theorists, who owed a lot to the Social Credit theories of Major Douglas which, though unintelligible, had attracted me so much before the war?

Some of my correspondents were straightforward believers in the Jewish World Conspiracy. An obvious objection was that, if this conspiracy was, as they maintained, all-powerful (it secretly controlled both the United States and the Soviet Union and even Hitler had been in its service) as well as being hidden not merely from the masses but from most of the world's statesmen, what hope was there of resisting it? They did not seem at all clear on this point themselves. Other correspondents at least had an answer: to them the world was in Satan's hands and awaiting the Apocalypse, when Satan would be cast down and God would triumph in the Second Coming, and all would be transformed in a new Heaven and a new Earth. But this scheme of things was also pre-ordained; and if the principle of Good was going to triumph in the end over the principle of Evil whatever anyone did, why should anyone do anything?

In the course of time I amassed a vast collection of 'conspiracy literature' sent in by readers, much of it of American origin (there is even a 'Conspiracist Publishing Company' somewhere in the States, with a copious catalogue). But I contrived to avoid meeting the conspiracy-theorists; one of Annabel's main duties was to ensure that they got no nearer than the other end of the telephone. Only once, and much later in my time at the *Telegraph*, did I actually meet one of these people, and he was obviously untypical. He rang up one day when I was without Annabel to discourage telephone-callers, and in a pleasant public school voice explained that he was obliged for certain reasons to use an assumed name; but would I do him the great favour of lunching with him at a certain restaurant in London where we could be sure of having a quiet conversation?

It was a restaurant I had heard of, an unfashionable but expensive one; I accepted. My host turned out to be a youngish man, well-dressed and with excellent manners. His opening remark was, 'Before we go any further, I must tell you that I think your column is a work of genius'. I could hardly fail to be predisposed in this man's favour; and we did in fact have a most enjoyable luncheon, helped by two bottles of delicious

Sancerre, almost all drunk by me. As I got more and more pleasantly drunk, he gave me his views of the world. Some of them were already familiar from correspondents who certainly did not patronise this kind of restaurant, or wear gold cufflinks or bear, as it turned out this friendly and agreeable man did, an aristocratic name. But now I heard them laid before me with quiet certitude; and the more outrageous they were to generally accepted opinion the more quietly certain he seemed to be of their unarguable truth. Of course the American astronauts had never reached the moon; it was a transparent confidence trick intended to deceive the people and divert their attention from what was really happening in the world. Hadn't I noticed in the television film that the simulation of the supposed moon-landing was far more convincing than the 'real thing'? If I had looked carefully in one corner of the screen I would have noticed that the identical boulder shown as being on the moon could also be seen in the Arizona Desert. All this seemed extremely per-suasive.

My host asked me, when the conversation (or monologue) turned from the supposed moon-landing to other things, what I thought of Pope John Paul II. I said, as most people would have said, that I thought him a remarkable man who promised to have great influence for good and might even reverse the destruction of the Roman Catholic Church. He laughed, though without patronage or unkindness: 'My dear fellow, my dear Michael' – we had got on first name terms by then – 'how can you be so easily deceived? We live in a world in which everything is turned upside down. What is generally thought good is bound to be evil, however cleverly it is disguised. No, the mere fact that the Pope is universally praised proves that he is an agent of the Devil.'

I did not try to argue. What would have been the use? And

the easy hospitality, as well as the charm of this strange person-
age made him most persuasive. What was I to make of him?
Was he himself an agent of the Devil? He ended by telling me
that I must enter the Catholic Church without delay. I explained
that I had no faith. 'Go and see Father So-and-So' – he named
a priest in South London – 'and mention my name'. I said I
would think it over. I did nothing about this. Some weeks later
I had a letter from my strange host. It ended: 'I fear you are
determined to fry in Hell ever more. Yours, with very best
wishes . . . '

Another kind of misconception may have arisen from what
hostile critics might have called an occasional 'high camp'
element in the column. A high-ranking naval officer professed
to be a great fan and even sent in some suggestions and ideas,
some of them quite good ones. Meeting him for a drink I found
a gentlemanly person of unmistakably homosexual temperament, discreetly and skilfully made up, who after some amusing
conversation invited me to spend a weekend at Plymouth on
the ship he commanded. I was non-committal. Later he asked
me to a party in a flat in Battersea; it was in one of those
mansion flats along the south side of the Park where I was later
to live myself, though in a humbler block (this one had a lift
and central heating). It was a good party of decidedly upper-
class people; the waiters were young naval stewards, all noticeably good-looking and wearing white gloves. One of the guests
was the current Chief Scout. He told me of a disastrous jam-
boree held in incessant rain on a Scottish island; 'but the worst
thing was, do you see, they had sent the wrong kind of claret'.
But I had taken Kate along to this party and although she was
a great success I heard no more from my host the naval officer.

Another invitation came from a rich middle-aged Parsee (a
tautology; in my experience all Parsees are rich) who was living

at one of the big hotels in Park Lane. He asked me to come and sign a copy of my latest anthology. Flattered, I was even more flattered to find that he wanted me to sign copies of all the previous anthologies as well; he had had them beautifully bound in dark green leather by a bookbinder in Lisbon 'where I lived until this ghastly revolution . . . ' – it was 1974 – ' . . . made things so disagreeable that I simply had to leave. So now I'm camping out here with some of my furniture. I'll move on somewhere else in due course. I suppose I'll die alone in some hotel like this one.' he said, and I had a vision of the sad death of a rich, lonely homosexual. 'Where would you think of moving if you were me?'

Here again I had come across the inability of the rich to acknowledge that there are any other kinds of people, though my shabby mackintosh folded on a chair should have suggested there might be. I murmured non-committedly. 'I thought of Lausanne,' he said, 'dear, dear, little Lausanne. But no, it is not what it was. Istanbul, perhaps. I've always loved it. I once bought a kitten there from a brute who was going to throw it into the Bosphorus. And do you know, when I got home I found it was dumb! How I loved that kitten!' He looked at me with mournful eyes. 'Did you ever think of living in Persia?' I asked desperately. I had noticed that he used a Mongol–Persian version of what must originally have been a distastefully Indianised Parsee name. 'Oh, no, never!' he exclaimed in horror. 'You see, the Shah's courtiers are so terribly *common*.'

The conversation languished. 'What school did you go to?' he asked. I told him, but it was clear that the Bradford Grammar School meant nothing to him whatever. 'I was put down for Eton,' he told me. 'But I was too delicate.' He smiled delicately. 'So I had tutors. My mother was a Wardha.' I nodded acknowledgement of this fantastically rich Parsee ship-owning family.

'I always loved dear Queen Mary,' he said, the ghastly common-ness of the Shah's courtiers evidently still on his mind. 'Didn't you?' Later I wrote him a note of thanks, but got no reply.

There was yet another class of correspondent, probably representing a much larger number of *Telegraph* readers. These were the people who thought my column was simply part of the news, or at least was meant to be taken literally. I had only to mention a book by Henry Miller, *The Naked Afternoon Tea*, to get a letter from a reader complaining that she could not get it at any bookshop (it was said to be published by 'the Lavender Press', and I got another letter from a real Lavender Press, pointing out angrily that they had never published any such title). I had only to write about the sole Tibetan monastery still remaining in South London to get readers complaining that in spite of following my directions they had been unable to find it, and what did I mean by misleading people? I wrote a 'Lingu-aphone' advertisement, 'Learn Etruscan the Way He Did', offering gramophone records, with a drawing of an Etruscan warrior by ffolkes; I got so many requests for the records that I had to write another item saying the Etruscan records were sold out, but we still had stocks of Old Prussian, Aztec and Pictish. And sure enough, several requests for these came in.

Colin Welch, who in due course rose from chief leader-writer to deputy editor before leaving the *Telegraph*, had been right when he said the column was a dead end. But it was a dead end which suited me. I was not, except in a formal sense, a journalist and had no ambitions to rise in that profession. As I had never been a reporter, my knowledge of its technicalities was nil and I surprised the printers on the 'stone' by wondering at their skill in reading upside down and in reverse when we dealt with the beautiful lead galleys of my column in their wooden frames. Oddly enough, I got on quite well with these blue-dungaree'd printers, Jim or Fred or Frank, with their absolute self-confidence and assurance. No wonder they were like that; in those days the printers ruled the newspaper; they had only to stop work and bring the presses to a standstill to face their employers with enormous, daily mounting losses. No wonder the employers always gave in; they had no alternative, and it was quite forbearing of the Father of the Chapel, a suitably huge and complacent man who regarded journalists with kindly contempt, not to call a strike every other week. As it was, the printers must have been among the most highly paid of all English workers.

They were also the most truly conservative people in England, resistant to all change and operating a strictly hereditary, hier-archical system which made it impossible for anybody to enter their trade unless he had a father or other close relative who had already been in it. I used to maintain that all the printers were descended from Caxton's apprentices. Certainly the names on the duty rosters were splendidly and transcendentally Eng-lish: Bates, Charlton, Breakspear, Muggeridge, Mudd. It would have been no more impossible for a dog to become a printer on this or any other national newspaper than for an Indian or a Negro or indeed any foreigner. As for a woman printer, they would have thought you were daft if you had suggested it; and you would have been. All this delighted my reactionary soul.

I was not, of course, socially acceptable to the printers myself, though tolerated as a harmless freak. In my leisure hours in Fleet Street I did not drink with the printers in the Kings and Keys. They kept to themselves, and in the early days, before it was tarted up with flock wallpaper, electric mock candle-holders and an elaborate wooden ceiling with gilded emblems of crowns and keys, it had a separate bar, a small cubicle near the doorway which non-printers entered at their peril.

One of the few who occasionally tried to do so, with mildly violent results, was Philip Weston, a senior leader-writer with masochistic tendencies and remarkable drinking habits. He was to be found every evening in the Kings and Keys or in the alternative *Telegraph* pub, the Falstaff, on the opposite side of the street. So was a regular group of senior *Telegraph* journalists, including myself, though I was not as regular in my attendance as some, occasionally drinking in other places, such as the celebrated wine-bar El Vino, though this I found uncongenial because it was patronised by the famous – or sometimes not drinking at all, or even just going home.

It was a well-known fact in those days, though most of the *Telegraph* readers would have been shocked and incredulous if they had known it, that some of the hardest drinkers and most eccentric, even disreputable, characters in Fleet Street were members of the staff of what was to them one of the most respectable newspapers. Whereas many journalists on the low, tabloid papers, who daily dealt in smut and scandal (remarkably harmless and innocent though it was, compared with what was to come) regularly caught trains, after finishing their work, to places like Oxshott or Esher, where their wives met them at the station and drove them home, the *Telegraph* journalists remained in the pub for hours, some of them getting so drunk that by closing time they were in a state bordering on mania.

Of these Philip Weston was by far the most remarkable. A tall, distinguished-looking man of about the same age as myself, in his late forties when I first met him, well-dressed and always carrying a furled umbrella, he was, when sober, charming, intelligent, reasonable and amusing. It was impossible not to like him. But he had another quite different side. I used to maintain that if various data – quantity of whisky drunk, food (if any) taken, temperature, barometric pressure, wind force and direction and so on – were fed into a computer, it would be possible to forecast the exact moment when he would 'go critical'. He was one of those drinkers who become drunk, or at least change their mood, in the middle of a sentence, switching unnervingly and without warning from rational amiability to raging fury.

His speciality, for which he became notorious, even famous, was outrageously insulting rudeness. For this he was specially qualified by an instinct for spotting the weak point in the person he had chosen to insult and then concentrating on that, so that his remarks, however fantastic and exaggerated, always seemed to contain a proportion of truth, however minute, which could be worrying for the victim. He was a novelist, perhaps even a poet, *manqué*, and this, I think, may have been one source of his latent anger. His brother Robert was a painter, once quite well-known, of the *avant garde* variety and was even ruder than Philip, though without his artistry. Awarded a prize for painting in some provincial competition, he was photographed aiming a kick at his own winning 'abstract' picture, rightly observing, 'If they give good money for rubbish like that, they must be out of their bloody minds' and loudly demanding his cheque for £1,000 forthwith, so that he could get the first train back to London. He was also perhaps the only man who ever reduced Kate to speechlessness, instantly shouting when she tried to order drinks in a pub, 'Shut up you! Can't stand bossy women!'

But this was feeble stuff compared with his brother Philip's performances. He had developed a special voice, between a croak and a snarl, which made him sound like a demented bird of prey as, having 'gone critical', he selected a victim among the people in the bar and set about him.

He was particularly insistent on the niceties of behaviour in pubs, which may seem paradoxical but was not. He believed in a strict code which would have involved the exclusion of certain people from 'his' pub altogether. So when the editor – not Sir Colin, who had almost certainly never been in a pub in his life, but his successor Maurice Green, a more easy-going person – appeared in the pub one evening, perhaps to pursue some point in a leader, Weston, who had just 'gone critical', was extremely angry. 'Get out!' he croaked. 'This is no place for you! Get back to your gentleman's club where you belong!' This probably deserved the sack. But Green, who knew about Weston's act, wisely took no notice at all and Weston had to seek another victim.

One member of the staff whom Weston thought had no right to enter the pub was Perry Worsthorne, partly because of his upper-class status and partly because he had become deputy editor of the *Sunday Telegraph*. One evening he came in and, with an unconscious infringement of Weston's sense of what was fitting, said to the barmaid, 'Oh, get me a Scotch, would you?' Weston's furious croak was heard at once: 'Get me a Scotch, would you?' he mimicked hideously. 'If you don't know how to behave in pubs, don't go into them! Now get out and don't let me find you in here again!' A few weeks later Perry disobeyed this order and, as Claudie, who was with him, told me later: 'Weston was like a madman' – she pronounced the word with the accent on the second syllable. 'He came crouching forward and I 'ad to place myself between them!'

But this was not the last encounter. One evening, when Weston found Perry, who was for some reason in an over-wrought and nervous state, seated at the bar with Claudie, he at once began a high-flown tirade which ensured total silence. 'You're a phoney!' he croaked. 'You're a hollow man! You're a tinsel king, on a cardboard throne!' He went on like this for some time. Big tears had begun to roll down Perry's cheeks, but this phenomenon, watched in fascination by the whole company, did not deter Weston in the least. 'Look!' he cried in glee. 'Look, I've made him blub, I've made him blub!' Perry could take no more. But as he left, Weston looked round with glowing eyes. 'I made him blub! I made him blub! Now who shall I make blub next?'

He had a regular sparring partner, an assistant editor, Martin Jameson, a fierce-looking, red-haired man, professionally a strict disciplinarian and much feared by his subordinates. Jameson was able to give as good as he got, but of course he could not match Weston in style or imaginative power. One day I came into the pub to find a strange battle in progress. The two men were standing side by side at the bar, both obviously very angry. Weston had just poured salt in Jameson's gin and tonic. Jameson had countered by putting pepper in Weston's whisky. 'Pass the mustard!' shouted Weston. 'Bring me the biggest sausage in the place!' Such scenes as these, which seemed to take both these successful journalists and esteemed employees of Lord Hartwell back to their schooldays, were nothing out of the ordinary.

Weston's performances, of which I can give only a faint, inadequate impression, became quite famous. He would sit on a barstool convenient to the door, eyeing each new arrival as he or she came in and estimating his or her fitness to be insulted. He did not spare women; and the unmistakable element of masochism in his nature was shown when he insulted a hefty blonde reporter, who instantly fetched him such a clout with her handbag that he fell headlong to the ground. Next moment he was up again, laughing as though in triumph. He made a particular point of trying to get knocked down by printers, but only once succeeded even in getting one of them to trip him up. I have seldom seen him look so pleased with himself.

The Master Insulter, though obviously proud of his gifts, was overtly modest about them; when sober and in what might be called a normal state of mind he was capable of discussing his achievements as though they belonged to another person altogether; it was as though he wondered at an inspiration that might have come from another world. His consumption of whisky was stupendous. Once he told me that when he consulted a doctor about some ailment or other, the man asked whether he drank at all. 'Yes,' said Weston, 'a certain amount, I suppose.' The doctor hemmed for a bit, then said: 'Well, if I were you, I'd try cutting out that second glass of sherry before dinner.' Minutes after Weston had amiably shared this joke with me, he had 'gone critical' and was roaring abuse.

He became a legend. There was talk of sending him on a world tour, so that he could insult people of all nations in the interests of world peace. It was said that psychiatrists were sending some of their patients to the Kings and Keys to be insulted, believing it had therapeutic value. But he received a check to his all-conquering career one evening when he was performing at the Falstaff across the road. This he occasionally did, as it was said, 'by special request', though the landlord there, a stolid Englishman, eyed him less favourably than the Irish landlord of the King and Keys who appreciated the wild poetry and eloquent flights of fancy of the man. A party of elderly American women, Daughters of the Revolution with blue-rinsed hair and the earnest mien of cultural tourists, entered. 'Pardon me, sir,' said their leader, addressing Weston, who was waiting expectantly for a victim. 'Pardon me, is this your Doctor Johnson's house?' Weston, brandishing his umbrella, rose to his feet. 'I *am* Doctor Johnson,' he croaked maniacally. 'Now fuck off!' The ladies fell back in confusion, turned and fled.

'Right, Mr Weston,' said the landlord. 'That's enough. You have gone too far for once. Please take your custom elsewhere. You are barred.' Smiling in triumph, Weston crossed the road to the Kings and Keys, where he found me talking to Sheila Murphy, Desmond Williams's companion, over from Dublin on a visit. 'Who's this?' shouted Weston. 'I know all about you, whoever you are. You've got a purple bottom!' Whether Sheila actually had a purple bottom I have no idea; but such was the force of Weston's personality that it seemed perfectly possible, even likely, that she had.

The landlord of the Falstaff's ban on Weston did him no good. Next time the brewer's man called he noticed from the records that the consumption of whisky at the pub had sharply declined. 'We had to bar one of our best customers,' the landlord explained. 'Well, get him back at once!' ordered the brewer's man. But Weston, who claimed he had never been so insulted in his life, refused to patronise the pub any more. Soon afterwards it went out of business, but not before Jameson and myself, visiting the place for a quick drink, had had a curious experience. Instead of serving us, the landlord took a thick photograph album from a shelf and consulted it carefully. 'I thought so,' he said. 'I'm afraid I can't serve you gentlemen.' 'Why on earth not?' 'You've been seen in the company of that Mr Weston, and I've made a rule not to serve him or any friends of his.' Such was the terror of the man that he could even impose guilt by association.

As time went on, Weston passed his peak. His inventiveness declined. He began to content himself with shouting 'Poofter!' or 'Superficial!' or 'Homosexual South African policeman!' – this to my friend and columnar contributor Charles Herring who, needless to say, was none of these things, yet somehow *looked* as though he might be any or all of them. Weston still had one or two minor triumphs. One evening he accused a Salvation Army man who was selling the *War Cry* of being a rapist wanted by the police in three counties. But the strange thing was that this frenzied behaviour in drink, abhorrent though it seems, had nothing evil about it but was curiously innocent. Most people enjoyed it as pure entertainment, even when they were the victims. I certainly did myself, but I noticed that any attempt to encourage Weston to go into his act produced a perverse refusal to do so. He was an artist in insult and would perform only in his own good time. Nobody who heard him perform when he was at his best will ever forget it.

This sustained act of Weston's was not, of course, an isolated phenomenon; it was the centrepiece of a drunken 'Theatre of the Absurd' which was played out nightly over a considerable part of my time at the *Telegraph* and (not to be pompous) anticipated in some ways the 'alternative comedy' acts which became fashionable in the Eighties, though these made much more use of obscene language and sexual and scatological material. Weston had certainly missed his vocation, as he must have realised. But there were other actors besides him. Jameson, a stern disciplinarian in the office, was almost as heavy a drinker as Weston and occasionally contributed a solo comedy act. At one time he had a part share in a racehorse. This was the cause of a lot of derision and teasing, particularly when it was entered for the Derby. But in the event it ran surprisingly well, finishing fifth or sixth, and thereafter had several wins and places until it unfortunately broke a leg. This was a bitter blow to Jameson. That evening in the pub he became spectacularly drunk, for once upstaging Weston, and ended up lying on the floor with his arms round a big well-mannered woolly dog belonging to the landlord, crying 'this is my *Cavalry*,' as though the spirit of James Joyce had descended.

There were other stock characters too, such as Stephen Daneff, the witty, polyglot Communist Affairs Correspondent, since his boyhood an exile from Bulgaria, where his grandfather had been prime minister. He had a great deal of out-of-the-way knowledge which matched my own, and we would sometimes find ourselves, when agreeably drunk, discussing the Bulgarian Exarchate or the history of the Bukovina in the midst of a roar of raving voices, among which Weston could be heard shouting: 'Look at them! Poofters! I know what they do when the pub closes! They've got a room in Soho they go to! Haven't you? Haven't you?' In fact Stephen, who became a great friend, would sometimes take me back to his highly civilised house in Chelsea, where we sobered up at supper with his highly civilised, long-suffering, agreeably sphinx-like and very pretty wife, a dark-haired member of the Welsh squirearchy who owned a country house on the outskirts of Welshpool. After supper we would listen to Bruckner or Wagner on the record-player and in the small hours I walked out into the night and got a taxi back to Putney.

Other supporting players appeared from time to time: Ronnie Payne, a large, friendly, bearded Yorkshireman given to elaborate charades and rôle-playing and with something enigmatic about him which may have been due to his being an expert on espionage and Middle Eastern terrorism; Ron Hall, the archetypal journalist, another Yorkshireman, a man of great goodness and generosity of character, a militant atheist whom I offended by telling him he had a naturally Christian soul; and besides these there was a large supporting cast of journalists, any one of whom might suddenly acquire a non-speaking part and attain negative stardom by being singled out by Weston as the victim of the evening.

Although the Theatre of the Absurd dominated the pub in the evenings and also for occasional matinées, there was one group which was outside its domination, and because of its moral authority was largely immune from Weston's histrionic insults. I had the impression that the landlord would not have tolerated any attack on it, though he was generally indulgent to Weston's antics, perhaps because he knew they were good for business. But his forbearance was not entirely for this reason.

Mark O'Donnell was no ordinary landlord (we called him 'the greatest publican of the twentieth century'). A handsome and intelligent Irishman whose brother (he occasionally appeared at the pub with a good deal of ceremony) was a member of the Dáil, he had seen something of the world, spoke French fluently and obviously enjoyed Weston's performances as much as anybody, as he watched sardonically from his own side of the bar. An altogether more sophisticated man than the old landlord Seán Macnamara, he yet had certain gifts in common with him. It was noticeable that if by ill chance some stranger who did not know the conventions of the place was so grossly insulted by Weston that he put up his fists and threw a punch at him, it was not Weston but his victim whom the landlord asked to leave and, if he seemed unwilling, came round the bar and threw him out into the street in a practised manner one could not help admiring, however unjust his action may have seemed.

The group which O'Donnell quietly watched over and protected was that which gathered round one of the most distinguished journalists in Fleet Street, T. E. Utley, always known as 'Peter'. He had been totally blind since the age of eight, but had surmounted this and other difficulties – he was, I think, an orphan – in what can only be called a heroic manner. He was now a leader writer on the *Telegraph* and an authority on two subjects, the politics of Ulster and the Church of England, particularly in matters of 'faith and morals'. Should a leader be required on either of these subjects, it was Utley who wrote it, and as he was one of the few journalists on the *Telegraph*, or for that matter any other paper, who could write English in an elegant and lucid style, his leaders and other writings were always worth reading.

He was a slight man of middle height, carelessly dressed and usually with a good deal of dandruff on his shoulders, fallen from hair worn rather long and curling up over his collar from the pressure of the black ribbon which held in place the eye-shade over the crater of his damaged eye; his other eye, equally sightless, was of a disturbing milky blue. Perhaps to compensate for his blindness he had a very loud, vibrant voice which sounded overbearing and exaggeratedly 'upper-class', causing ffolkes, who was as conscious of class distinction as I was, but did not mind who knew it, to take an unjustified dislike to him. Utley described himself as idle, but was in fact a man of great energy both for work and social life. He was said to be one of the most rapid readers of braille in England, but needed an efficient secretary to read the morning papers aloud to him and do any research he required.

As for his secretaries, he seemed able to command the services of an unlimited supply of young girls. These were invariably personable and in some cases extremely attractive, so that jealous fellow-journalists sometimes wondered whether he could really be blind at all. But he always claimed, when asked for the secret, that he could tell by a woman's voice whether she was attractive or not; and he may have supplemented the clues he got by ear with easily-acquired tactile data. He could

often be seen sitting in a certain corner of the pub, especially
at lunchtime, in the middle of a circle of attractive girls, including his present secretary as well as some of his past or future
ones. If any other member of the *Telegraph* staff required a
temporary secretary he could usually offer a choice of two or
three. I came to think of him as the T. E. Utley Secretarial
Agency. There he sat with his circle in the Kings and Keys,
imperturbable, booming wisdom, with something legendary and
noble about him as he reached with a blind man's vagueness
for his glass of whisky and soda, or waveringly held out his
cigarette for a light, chain-smoking and dropping long tubes of
ash anywhere but in the ashtray.

The circle he presided over was not, of course, confined to
girls; other members of the staff such as Colin Welch, Nicholas
Bagnall, a learned, likeable, sometimes irascible man with a
game leg, later literary editor of the *Sunday Telegraph*, and many
others also joined it. And Utley could sometimes be seen in
earnest private conversation with people who could be recognised by some instinct as Ulster politicians or others concerned
with the affairs of the province. In spite of his blindness, Utley
was extraordinarily good at getting about by himself. He often
visited Ulster even at the height of the Troubles. He was, I
think, totally fearless, nor was his courage the less admirable
because, so it was said, the Provisional IRA themselves had
declared they would not assassinate a blind man, even though
he was, with Enoch Powell, by far the most intelligent and
persuasive of all exponents of the Unionist cause.

No wonder Donald McLachlan, when appointed first editor
of the *Sunday Telegraph* thought of offering Utley the job of
television critic! But he's blind,' they pointed out. 'I can't see
that's any objection', Maclachlan said. 'It will help to give him
a balanced view'.

His admirable wife, by whom he had three children, was of Anglo–Irish descent, the former Brigid Morrah, whose brother Dermot was occasionally employed by the *Telegraph* to supply heraldic information to the 'Peterborough' column I was so often accused, not without reason, of parodying in my own. Dermot Morrah, an elderly man with a loud, harsh, plangent voice, worked in the College of Heralds and sometimes appeared in the *Telegraph* office in full regalia, wearing a tabard with the Royal Arms and, for all I knew, carrying a silver trumpet. I was going up in the lift with him once when he was thus glorified; a negro workman who got in at an intermediate floor was so amazed at this apparition that his jaw dropped and I thought he was going to fall to his knees. Instead, he shuffled out, gibbering with wonder, at the next floor.

The Theatre of the Absurd occasionally changed its venue, usually to a strange establishment, long demolished, at the corner of Fleet Street and Chancery Lane, called 'Peel's Hotel: Founded 1347' (can this be right?). It was immediately opposite El Vino's and sometimes the overflow from that famous place, which closed at eight in the evening, would spread across the road and coalesce with elements of the Theatre of the Absurd. The bar at Peel's had a large pipe running diagonally across it from floor to ceiling and there were many packing cases and barrels standing untidily about; it resembled part of the lower deck of a ship, very satisfactory to people like myself who were fond of illusions of departure, though here I had to supply the vibration of the ship's engines from my own imaginative resources. The landlord and his family were Italian and as Stephen Daneff, who knew Italian, discovered, were still strong supporters of Mussolini; he claimed he had seen the aunt, Zia Maria, giving the fascist salute and had established the name of their Alsatian dog by a process of elimination: when he said 'Duce' softly, it rolled over and waved its paws in the air.

Here, one memorable evening, there was a gala performance, with several journalistic notabilities from El Vino's such as the witty and melancholy Philip Hope-Wallace, instantly greeted by Weston with harsh cries of 'Poofter!' and 'Jew!', the latter term certainly inappropriate. Peter Duval Smith also appeared, as well as the critic John Raymond, sometimes called 'Raymond Revuebooks' because of his habit of carrying round piles of books he was reviewing and leaving them in unexpected places, a man of irascible temper, with Weston's own peculiarity of passing from sober affability to furious drunken rage in mid-sentence. There was a man with a blocklike wooden-looking head who claimed to be the inventor of fish fingers. He also claimed he could sing a song about any kind of fish you cared to mention. But after 'herring' and 'haddock' had been disposed of, his rendering of 'a swordfish song', no doubt a *tour de force*, was lost in the general uproar. The evening ended when the landlord closed the bar and threatened to call the police. The shouting mob spilled out, some elements drifting down the street to the Kings and Keys, to resume the performance.

Such was the Fleet Street Theatre of the Absurd, famous in its day, deserving to be remembered for ever in the annals of serious drinking. A lifelong serious drinker myself, I was both participant and observer and, being a cautious drunkard as well as a cautious amorist, got blind drunk almost as seldom as I fell blindly in love. It was good to know, as I toiled away upstairs in the *Telegraph* building, that this resource and catalyst was always or almost always at hand when I needed it. Immersion in this anarchic riot undoubtedly helped me to construct, in my column, dreams of ideal beauty and hierarchical order.

So, perhaps, did my personal or private life, so much at

variance with the steady respectability of the *Telegraph* that Constantine called it a 'horror comic'. In the background was Kate's commitment to a lifelong love affair (the crisis at the end of our French holiday had long passed away and so had many subsequent ones); my own uneasy complaisance, once initial jealousy had faded, alleviated by occasional rather meaningless affairs of my own; and my determination, which Kate, for all her vagaries, undoubtedly shared, to bring up Jane as well and decently as possible. Jane was my reason for not leaving Kate; or so I told myself and others assumed; yet I had, after all, left my first wife and child, though they were perfectly blameless, without qualm or hesitation; so it is reasonable to infer that I still had enough attachment to Kate to find living under the same roof with her not absolutely intolerable.

Nor was it; she was still what is repulsively called a 'fun person' and for me a valuable link with other people, sometimes a purveyor of friends I might not have made for myself. For all her egotism, her innumerable deceits and broken promises, for all our ferocious rows, for all her 'infamous war on reality' she was (to use another repulsive term) 'on the side of life'; more than that, I sometimes felt she had heroic stature. I admired her ferocious clinging to the man she loved without hope of marriage; and although I had reached the point of being merely amused at reports which reached me of their stormy relationship – Michael ffolkes told me he had seen them in a restaurant and witnessed a really outstanding bout of food throwing ('When the Food Began to Fly') – I sympathised and perhaps even envied it a little. The time came when Kenneth, desperate at his predicament, would come to me and ask my advice. What was he to do? What was I to say? Of course I could not help him; I did not even feel the sense of ironical triumph which the circumstances seemed to dictate; only sadness, impatience and a certain guilt. The only upshot of such meetings was that we both became extremely drunk.

This manner of life was to last another three years, but it was ten years before I left Putney and twelve before our divorce and my own re-marriage. Thus the 'horror comic' went on for a very long time, but though often comic it was not always horrible. In 1961 and 1962 we spent several holidays in Cornwall. I had never been there before and was intrigued to find the Celtic past still underlying the holiday present. Besides, it was the first time I had ever had a seaside holiday. After an unfortunate experience with a flea at St Anne's on the Lancashire coast when I was three, my mother, I was told, had banned seaside holidays and thereafter we always went to the Yorkshire Dales. It was a new experience for me to be able to watch the sea for hours on end, a new method of auto-hypnosis and a new source of pantheistic feeling. As an old man who lived by the sea once told me: 'You never get sick and tired of it'. Nearing fifty, I played at sandcastles for the first time in my life.

It was about this time that we acquired the last and best of our au pair girls, Dixie von Pilati, whose family *schloss* in Austria lay among forests on the Czech border, almost within sight of the Iron Curtain. She was a pretty girl in her early twenties, but of neurotic temperament, which was not surprising considering the circumstances of her upbringing during the war and afterwards, with a father taken prisoner at Stalingrad and returning home crippled and soon to die. It took me some time to realise that Dixie, who was not, of course, without English admirers, had taken a fancy to me. But although one day when we were alone I made my customary opening gambit, 'What a funny girl you are,' we were interrupted and the opportunity never occurred again.

It was in the early summer of 1962, when we were on holiday at an *auberge* on the banks of the Dordogne, not far from the little town of Martel, that Kate told me she was pregnant, and not by me. This did not make much of an impression on me at the time except as one more ingredient in the 'horror comic'. We were sharing our holiday with the military historian Correlli Barnett and his wife Ruth, friends I had for once made for myself and afterwards introduced to Kate. A lively, amusing and intelligent man, 'Bill' Barnett shared my reactionary views, though later on he became well-known for his thesis declaring that the decline of England had been due to the cultural ideals of Matthew Arnold, 'the public school ethos' and the neglect of science and technology, a view abhorrent to me. Neither he nor Ruth shared our fondness for drinking and staying in expensive hotels. So there was a certain amount of latent friction on the journey by car to and from the Dordogne, when the Barnetts' preference for economy threatened to interfere with our enjoyment of good living. There was no open quarrel, but it is a well-known fact that the surest way for two married couples to ruin their friendship is to spend a holiday together.

Back in England I began to digest Kate's news. I went so far as to consult my old army friend Stuart Daniel, now a barrister, whose acquaintance we had taken up again, often visiting him and his wife in a delightful little house they had in Hampstead. He referred me to a divorce lawyer with a reputation for aggressive methods. I did not care for this brisk, matter-of-fact Jew, who told me brusquely to leave Kate at once and then come and see him again. That was probably why I did not do so. A more sympathetic lawyer would have made a better impression and might even have induced me to take action which would have changed my whole life.

As it was, I did nothing. Passive and lacking in initiative as always, or almost always, I let things be. In my column, I noticed, I had written, without realising its meaning at the time, an item in my parodic 'Nature Diary' about a preposterous bird, the dotterel, which could never make up its mind whether to migrate or not. There was a strong subjective element in my writing. Why did my sad, defeated man of letters, Julian Bird-bath, who lived at the bottom of a disused leadmine in Derby-shire, constantly dream of going to 'glittering' literary parties?

That autumn was the time of the celebrated 'Cuba missile crisis', when for a week the 'nuclear holocaust' – which had haunted everybody's dreams for so long and brought the legions of CND walking each Easter to Aldermaston, to sit down in Trafalgar Square and generally try to put other people's nerves on edge as well as their own – seemed near fulfilment. Kennedy and Khrushchev, both equally preposterous in their contrasting ways, gobbled on the television set we now, to my disgust, possessed like everybody else; sinister warships slid across the grey Atlantic waters. Most people looked apprehensive, some looked frightened. Our two old friends from Mick's Café, Peggy Duff and Pat Arrowsmith, the stalwarts of CND, actually fled to Western Ireland. This struck me as very amusing. Should they not have been at their posts, waiting with righteous indig-nation to the end, to be vaporised and turned to shadows by the horror they had warned us against for so long?

For myself, I was not in the least bit afraid. I knew with absolute certainty that the time was not yet, and would not come for another thirty years. Was this certainty due to my reading of the apocalyptic literature which so many kindly read-ers sent me? Whatever the reason, I felt calm as few people in London must have felt, apart from the Jehovah's Witnesses. Normally cowardly by nature and a confirmed worrier, I saw with satisfaction how much I was surprising friends and

EVENINGS IN FLEET STREET

acquaintances by my reassuring words. Kate obviously wondered whether I had taken leave of my senses. But I think I
helped her (she was, after all, seven months pregnant) to keep
calm as we carried on with our normal life. In fact it was not
quite normal. For some reason I never discovered I had been
put on the complimentary list of the Sadler's Wells Opera and
two tickets arrived for every production. So almost every night
we went to the opera, a thing I never did before, or have done
since, finding it difficult, with my part-West Riding soul, to
accept, any more than my mother could, the obviously 'dotty'
conventions of this musical form. Afterwards we had champagne
suppers and even went dancing. In the mornings I smoked
cigars, greatly enjoying this 'role-playing' as a man-about-town.

The Tunnicliffes had invited us to spend a weekend with
them at the Metropole Hotel in Brighton – the same hotel,
then an apparent paradise of luxury, where I had stayed with
my parents in the golden autumn of 1922 – savouring for the
first time the mysterious smell of the sea, coveting the cream
cakes in the lounge of the hotel and watching on the pier-
cinema a newsreel of the burning of Smyrna by the Turks.
Now the sea was grey and sad, and the hotel had fallen into
decay – that ancient glory gone forever. As the tension mounted
we walked by the sea, drank a great deal, ate lavishly, visited a
casino where rouged and extravagantly-dressed old women with
terrible greenish faces, who looked as if they had been exhumed,
sat staring at the cloth with eyes gleaming dully like paste jewels.

From time to time I had to reassure my companions when
they spoke of trying to enjoy our last hours on earth: 'Please
do not worry. Nothing is going to happen.' It was my finest
hour except for the even finer hour on Sunday evening, after a
day when the smell of fear was everywhere, as the news came
through: Kennedy and Khrushchev had come to an agreement.

139

The crisis which for me had never been was over. 'How did you know?' asked Joe Tunnicliffe with gratifying wonder and respect. 'Oh, I just did, that's all,' I said. But I could not resist the temptation of telling him that I had to go up to our room for a moment to transmit a message. The old jokes, as everybody knows, are still the best.

That winter Dixie suddenly decided to leave us. She gave no reason but Kate, I noticed, showed signs of unusual discomfiture. Not long afterwards I had a letter from Dixie, telling me how she had gradually become disgusted with 'what was going on', how much she sympathised with me and how she strongly advised me to protect Jane by sending her away to school as soon as possible. I did not reply to this opening; much as I liked Dixie, I did not think she was a girl with whom I ought to get involved; so she became one of my long list of might-have-beens. Years later she came to London in the company of her protector, a rich Munich businessman, and on her suggestion we met briefly for drinks at Claridges where they were staying. It was an awkward meeting. Dixie had changed, grown more worldly and cynical; her friend was intensely German in the worst sense of the word, with most of the bad qualities of that race and few of the good. We had little to say, and I took my leave awkwardly, realising, not for the first or last time, what a mistake it is to meet old friends or acquaintances after a long interval: they have always become different people as I have become a different person.

At Christmas, which unusually we did not spend with my mother in her gradually degenerating cottage at Amswick, Kate went into hospital at Royston in Hertfordshire and on 27th December her baby was born, a girl she called Victoria. It was intensely cold – a blizzard had been raging and the country was under deep snow. I stayed by myself in Putney; Jane, now ten years old, had gone to stay with the Foster-Melliars at their cottage in Allen's Green near Sacomb's Ash, which was now occupied by strangers. Meeting Jane at Sawbridgeworth Station, Andrew Foster-Melliar found it was impossible to reach their cottage because of deep snowdrifts. He and Jane had to spend the night at the pub where the FitzGibbons had once ruled. For Jane, it was an adventure she never forgot; the snow, the silence, the unaccustomed supper they ate in the pub by candlelight because the electricity had failed. If she should ever write a book herself I think this adventure will figure in it.

It was about this time that I learned that the Granada Television programme '*What the Papers Say*' had voted me 'Columnist of the Year'.

5
A Nasty Turn

Ever since I had had an attack of the horrors in a lonely house in the Berkshire woods ten years before, I had been subject to intermittent feelings of uneasiness and dread. They were now getting more frequent and more intense. During a visit with Kate to the valley of the Loire, I had a particularly nasty attack when confronted with the Château of Chambord. I have always disliked French château architecture, and the low, open landscape of the Loire, with a wide river running between pebbly, sandy shores, often dividing into separate channels, then reuniting, does not appeal to me. Looking at Chambord – the monstrous size of the thing, the unreal feel to it – like painted scenery – I felt a powerful dread, an overwhelming desire to escape. At the restaurant which faced this alarming building I rushed into the lavatory and swallowed with difficulty one of the small white phenobarbitone tablets which my doctor had given me. This somewhat reduced my terror; but I still felt I must get away from Chambord and the Loire as soon as possible. Grumbling slightly, though she understood something of what I was feeling from her own experience, Kate drove us northwards to Normandy; this brought immediate relief.

What was the meaning of this experience? Why should Chambord, a show-place visited by hundreds of thousands of people every year with evident pleasure, have set off in me this feeling of intolerable dread, this glimpse of the Void from which our ordinary daily lives are so thinly separated? In fact it was not Chambord which was to blame. As an experiment, I visited the place with my third wife many years later. There was the monstrous building just as before, the restaurant, the crowd of visitors. As architecture, I found it just as unpleasing as ever. But now it was just a French château I did not like. There was no fear; I could even laugh at the fear as I tried to describe my experience to a woman who, having a mind free of phantoms, had never known it. Had Kate been the cause of the fear? By no means; the cause was neither in her nor in the château; nor in the park, the fields, the trees, the empty sky; it was in myself.

As the year 1963 went on, I had a deepening feeling of depression and more frequent recourse to the doctor's pills. My ability to write was not impaired; indeed my inventive powers had never been better since I started work on the column, sometimes producing complex and elaborate fantasies which made ffolkes, when I read some effusion over the telephone for him to illustrate, exclaim in alarmed appreciation, 'You're going mad!' This should have been a warning. But I was on a path from which there was no straying. And after all, wasn't I 'Columnist of the Year'? Perhaps because of this award, I was approached by a publisher to produce an anthology of the column, using material which had appeared since the last anthology in 1958.

Dr Donald Johnson was no ordinary publisher. He was a medical doctor who had been a GP in the North and then, entering politics, had become Conservative MP for Carlisle. He was a tall, shambling, ill-dressed man, then about sixty, with traits of eccentricity which I found endearing. He had founded a small 'family' publishing firm, but up to that time seemed to have published very little apart from a satire on Parliament which he had written himself, a booklet on the menace of Chinese opium imports into England and a book of Conservative essays by T. E. Utley, the blind *Telegraph* leader writer. Dr

Johnson lived with his second wife, formerly a nurse and in her own way almost as eccentric as he was, in a villa in the south London suburb of Sutton, which also served as his publishing headquarters. He had another office in Stanhope Mews off Cromwell Road. It was approached by a steep staircase where there was a powerful smell of fish from a neighbouring smoked haddock and kipper store.

If the approach to his office was unusual, the office itself was even more so. It was one of the most untidy rooms I have ever seen. Piles of books and papers lay everywhere, under layers of dust. There was no room at the desk to write. A half-eaten sandwich on a plate was balanced on the telephone. Perhaps deceived by the smell on the staircase, I thought I caught a glimpse of a kipper on a shelf of books. In this strange den Dr Johnson transacted his business with me. I was obliged, of course, to get Sir Colin Coote's permission for the publication. This meant that I had to bring Dr Johnson to see Sir Colin in his office. It was evidently not the first time they had met. If he wished to be ungracious Sir Colin was not lacking in the talent to be so; his face expressed sardonic suspicion, as much as to say, 'Well, Johnson, if you want to take this on, that's your funeral'. The interview over, we shambled awkwardly out. I invited Dr Johnson for a drink at the Kings and Keys next door. He drank a half pint of beer, listening uneasily to the background noise through which the snarling voice of Philip Weston could be distinctly heard. It was early in the evening and he had not yet 'gone critical' – by the time I had seen Dr Johnson out and taken leave of him, he had. 'Poofter!' croaked Weston. 'I suppose that's your new protector!'

The work of choosing about three hundred items from the previous five years' output for the anthology, was considerable. But it was welcome at that time; routine work, the counting of

words, the compiling of lists, is always soothing, a great ally in
the struggle – no, not the struggle, because if you regard it as
a struggle it is already lost – in the avoidance of *angst*. So when
I was not writing the column itself I spent a great deal of my
time on this task, paying as little attention as possible to Kate,
the new baby and the mother's help who came in daily. At this
time Kate was carrying on with her freelance journalism. At
the beginning of spring she had a commission from some maga-
zine to write a series of articles on hotels in different parts of
the South of England which catered especially for children. So
off we all went for long weekends, Kate, myself, Jane and the
tiny baby in her carry-cot, to stay at these various places.

These trips seemed to bring on attacks of dread within a
deepening cloud of depression. I had powerful feelings of unreality at an hotel at Sandbanks, a suburb of Bournemouth, a
town I had not seen since my first marriage at its register office
on the day the Spanish Civil War broke out; I peered into the
Void at an hotel at Battle in Sussex, as the rain poured down
on the field of Hastings; and dread was hovering about as we
drove through Norfolk on our way to an hotel at Cromer when
an event occurred which put a temporary stop to those excur-
sions and to my fears as well.

We had stopped for a cup of tea near Wymondham and then
were making towards Norwich when, as we approached a minor
road on our left, a dark green van came towards us, hesitated
and then turned across our path. I saw that a collision was
unavoidable, braced myself, cried out a warning, and then came
a jolting, jarring, glass-shattering crash. My injuries were small:
a cut on my forehead where I hit the windscreen and a triangular
tear in my left knee, bleeding a bit and spoiling a new pair of
check trousers, where I had hit the edge of the glove compartment. Kate was knocked unconscious. In a few seconds, she

145

came to; in the back seat, Jane was shocked but unharmed; while the baby had been jerked right out of her carry-cot and had landed on a pile of baby-food tins on the floor. As in the way of babies, she was the only one of us who seemed entirely composed.

We staggered out into the road, dazed and cursing. The van driver, a middle-aged teacher-like man who confessed he was in the wrong and, what was more, was a drama organiser for the county council, was apologising and dabbing at a gash on his head. He helped us to separate the locked vehicles and push them on to the verge. The side of his van was bashed in and so was the nearside wing of our car. Someone telephoned the police and soon a police car arrived and took us all to the police station in Wymondham ('Could you please be careful not to bleed over the new upholstery?' a policeman said nastily as we went along). After some time an ambulance took us all to Norwich General Hospital, where my leg was stitched and bandaged and we were all examined. A kindly nurse hung the baby upside down to demonstrate her amazing indestructibility.

The Barnetts, who by chance lived in a village a few miles from Norwich, gave us beds for the night. When we woke up, we found ourselves bruised all over and almost unable to move. But as it happened the Barnetts had a friend and neighbour, Calvin Wells, a retired doctor who devoted himself to research on palaeonosology, the study of diseases of past times as revealed by the examination of bones; in this unusual branch of learning he was a distinguished expert. More to the immediate purpose, he was an expert in getting insurance companies to pay damages to people involved in motor accidents (he had recently got Ruth Barnett £250 for being run into from behind). As I had never been involved in a motor accident before this form of alleviation had not occurred to me. But good Dr Wells arranged everything. 'Get you at least a thousand pounds for this,' he chuckled as he took us in his car to Norwich to be x-rayed. Our car was a 'write-off'. Supplied with a new one by the garage which collected it, and still somewhat bemused, we drove off back to London.

I was away from work for a fortnight. Whether or not the accident had really worsened my mental state (Dr Wells's cheerful, matter-of-fact contention that it had was a help to us later on, to collect the £1000 he promised) I cannot say. In theory, it might have had the opposite effect, the physical pain jerking me out of my melancholia. But whatever the reason, things got worse. I had just reached my fiftieth birthday, a notoriously bad time, when the futility of life becomes apparent and the possibility of change for the better recedes. Many factors contributed to my gathering depression, my ever-deepening sense of unreality. It came to a head at the beginning of July just before we were due to go to Brittany for a fortnight's holiday. I had been invited to spend a weekend at Waterstone with Constantine and his dark, shadowy second (or third) wife. As it happened, Kate, Jane and a woman friend had arranged to go camping that weekend at Long Burton in Dorset, not very far from Waterstone, and were to drop me off on the way.

Our connection with that part of Dorset went back a long way. We had stayed several times at a pub in Buckland Newton which Kate had discovered during some journalistic assignment. It was a great pub for serious drinking. The landlord, a Dorset man who verged on dipsomania, was often at odds with his wife, who was from Lancashire and had pretensions to refinement, including an 'improved' accent of great phonetic interest. She was anxious, since custom was not brisk, to bring in more trade by selling ice-cream to weekend visitors. This the landlord resisted; he felt, rightly, that to sell ice-cream was an affront to his manhood. This was a man out of an older, still rural England. In his youth he had been a carter, visiting places as distant as Salisbury Plain, the memory of which he described most movingly: miles of rolling downland which had never known the plough, let alone the war machines of the army, when Stonehenge was still a solitary wonder and the neolithic barrows were undisturbed. This unlettered man knew what poetry was. He knew the poems of William Barnes, Hardy's friend, well, and could repeat some of them by heart. He was the wreck of the strong man he had once been and the phantom of the poet he might have been. In his cups he raged against the ignoble present. It was no wonder he wanted nothing to do with ice-cream. But his wife prevailed, and soon the cheap plastic symbol of the ice-cream future sat above his doorway. He did not long survive it, but died as he swore he would. Nor did his widow long remain at the pub where we had drunk and talked so pleasantly into the small hours. She sank into a state of melancholia and was soon a sedated inmate of Charminster Mental Hospital. Thomas Hardy might have made something of their sad story.

He could have made nothing of my weekend at Waterstone. I have a faint recollection of struggling against a feeling of unreality which grew ever more powerful and irresistible. We went, I think, to several parties at rather grand houses in the neighbourhood. Crichel Down may have been one; Cranborne another (the name of Pitt-Rivers surfaces through dense fog). On the Sunday we certainly lunched with the engraver Reynolds Stone and his family at their house at Litton Cheney and afterwards walked in their water-garden. Did they notice my increasing anguish, my efforts to keep it under control? Or did they think I was always silent and found it hard to understand what people were saying to me, let alone reply? We returned to

Waterstone, where Kate, though barred from entering the house, was to pick me up in the car that evening. I took a long time to pack my things, finding some relief in this routine activity. It was a fine July evening as we drove east towards London. I had had a good deal to drink, but with no more than an anaesthetising effect; one kind of non-feeling seemed to be superimposed upon another. At Salisbury, where we stopped for supper, I had more drink. I became garrulous, revelling in fantasy, piling on more and more absurdities ('you were in really good form'). At home in Putney I fell into bed, dog-tired, and slept.

But I woke early in the blank, ominous summer morning. The full horror had come upon me: a deadly sense of non-existence; pervading terror; coldness of the extremities and the genitals; convulsive trembling. It was like the affliction I had suffered ten years before, but worse. Trying to recall that experience as 'a queer turn', as I had facetiously named it in an attempt, hitherto successful, to defuse the horror, I told myself: it will pass. But now this hitherto useful formula was not working. I had sunk beneath the level of words into pure unfeeling. It was Monday, a working day. But I was obviously incapable of work, indeed of any activity. Kate sent for the doctor. He gave me a sedative, then arranged for me to go as a voluntary patient into a mental hospital he recommended, Halliwick Hospital at Southgate in North London. So all day long I waited while people came and went, until the time came for Kate to drive me there. I checked in, was shown to my bed and given an injection which put me into a dreamless sleep for thirty-six hours. I woke and for a few seconds had an overpowering feeling of relief and happiness until the leaden burden of nonentity came and weighed down on me once more. I had become a mental patient, and for all I knew, was doomed to be one for the rest of my life.

Halliwick was no ordinary mental hospital, though it had the standard appearance of one, with its long range of grey stone Victorian buildings and its tall tower set amid a dull garden of shrubberies and pebbled paths. It had a wing for 'serious' cases, some violent, but the part of it I had been assigned to was devoted to cases of 'mild clinical depression'. Although it belonged to the National Health Service and was free, it had a high proportion of middle-class patients, many of them from places like Hampstead. I found out later that the writer Maurice Richardson, an occasional member of the FitzGibbon circle, had been an inmate for a time, suffering from a mild attack of mania; so had my old friend, coeval and former colleague at the BBC, David Thomson, who was to suffer from schizophrenia for the rest of his life.

He had been on a trip to Tanganyika, as it was then called, in connection with some BBC programme, when he was suddenly seized with violent, highly-coloured delusions and was flown home to England and Halliwick. He had quite enjoyed his stay there, he told me, when we exchanged reminiscences later. As therapy he was given large sheets of paper and some bright colours to paint with; he began painting huge figures of naked women amid tropical vegetation and became so absorbed in this work that he used up all the hospital's supply of paper and for that reason, if for no other, was reluctantly discharged. Other people from similar backgrounds as Richardson, Thomson and myself had been inmates, I believe, of this 'sick bay of Hampstead'; later I suggested having a special Halliwick tie designed, but nothing came of it. And in the course of time, no doubt, the privileged status of the place was done away with and it became a National Health hospital like any other.

I was heavily dosed with coloured pills and no longer felt the acute horror which had brought me there. But I still felt that everything about me was unreal and some things, like my shaving-brush, were tinged with evil. I had a room to myself but fed, when I had any appetite, which was seldom, in the communal dining-hall, a bleak, institutional room with separate tables in whose hinges lurked an uneasy feeling. I was sent to a psychiatrist for interview. He was a young Scotsman who made no particular impression on me, nor I, perhaps on him, for he referred me to a senior consultant, Dr Silver, a stocky, powerful-looking Jew who made a strong and very unpleasant impression. He was clearly interested in my case and may even have known of my profession; if so he gave no hint of it.

I was told to report for occupational therapy. This consisted of basket-weaving. I was so superlatively bad at this, producing after much effort a tangled mass of straw, that the instructor made it clear that he regarded me as hopeless and wished me elsewhere. Unlike David Thomson, I was given no paper, paint or other therapeutic material, but was left very much to my own devices. I walked the pebbled paths under the menacing summer sky with its slowly moving clouds and felt the presence of the Void. Applying my own therapy, I sat on my bed and tried to write some sonnets, choosing for the sake of difficulty the strict Italian form. I completed several, metrically correct but probably without any other merit. I do not know what became of them.

In the afternoons I went to the large patients' lounge, comfortably furnished with armchairs but with a noticeable absence of books (in any case Kate and Michael ffolkes, who also visited me, had brought me books which I tried to read, but finding them meaningless, desisted). In the lounge I got talking (this was a good thing) to a sad woman of my own age from Hampstead, called Wendy Porter. She lived alone and had fallen into a mild depression after the death of her dog, whom she had loved in a way I could not understand until, late in life, I kept dogs myself. With her I played innumerable games of Scrabble and exchanged symptoms, gaining some slight momentary relief.

So the days passed. I was allowed out in the morning after breakfast to buy newspapers and cigarettes. It never occurred to me that as a voluntary patient I could simply decamp; I had no will to do anything so positive. I read the *Daily Telegraph*, in which my holiday relief, Colm Brogan, was writing the column; it meant nothing to me whatsoever. I had several interviews with Dr Silver, and at each one he seemed to become more hostile. I began to implore Kate, when she visited me, to get me out of the place. Dr Silver, I gathered, was strongly against the idea. He believed 'I would benefit from further treatment'. Since, apart from great quantities of pills, I was not having any treatment, I have no idea what he meant.

After ten days this living death came to an end. My deliverer was Desmond O'Neill, whom Kate had called upon to help. Dr Silver put up a good deal of resistance; but as a psychiatrist himself, and a distinguished one, Desmond was in a position to overrule him and secure my release by undertaking to treat me himself. What he proposed was that I should undergo a course of electro-convulsive treatment in his own house in St John's Wood, one of our refuges during our nomadic period and scene of many enjoyable parties. I agreed. I was not much in favour of having an electric current passed through my head in order to shift and jumble up the pattern of depression which had seized on my brain circuits. This is, roughly, the theoretical basis of this kind of treatment; I have heard young doctors refer to it crudely as 'a bash of the box' or 'plugging 'em into the mains'. But anything seemed better than the state I was in. 'The most important thing,' said Desmond, 'is to get you back to work as soon as possible.' In this he was undoubtedly right, and for this I am everlastingly grateful to him.

What followed jumbled up not only my depression but also my subsequent memory of everything to do with that period of my life. To compensate somewhat for the loss of the Breton holiday, Kate had rented a cottage at Ash, a village near Sandwich in Kent. I see myself, between the electro-convulsive sessions, standing in the untidy cottage garden with Jane, and Victoria in her pram; sitting in the car on the way between Kent and London; visiting some Kentish village pub where I was allowed to drink only one half pint of beer; looking out over a calm sea at Sandwich; meeting the Phillimores for a vague dinner at an hotel at Winchelsea, where we had driven over circuitous roads; or, back in London, being led out of Desmond's house in the afternoon, with a blinding headache, to nearby Lords to watch a few overs in the sun. Kent had always been the part of England I knew least, being in the opposite corner of the country from mine, in the extreme south-eastern and most civilised corner of England; because of the unpleasant associations it collected at that time it is still the part of England I know least and the part I have never wanted to know better. Now that it is cut up and destroyed for the sake of the Channel Tunnel, the epitome of everything I detest, it is doubly lost to me.

Of the electro-convulsive sessions I remember little, except lying down on the couch while Desmond and his assistant arranged the apparatus; the prick of the anaesthetic needle; oblivion and waking, for a time unable to tell who I was or to recognise my surroundings. Kate told me (she may of course have invented this) that once I came to and asked her who she

153

was, and when she told me, said, 'You can't be. You are beautiful'. I felt that the treatment, apart from the headaches, was
doing me good; at least it was making me feel different, even
making me feel as much alive as I was then capable of feeling.
So, after I had been away for five weeks, Desmond advised that
I should return to work. On a morning in mid-August I took
the train from Canterbury to London and sat down at my desk
again. The first column I produced with a brain which had
been electrically deprived of its previous pattern of thought was
not a distinguished one. I had also been deprived of the pattern
of thought which produced the column. Perhaps it would have
been better for me if it had never returned, so that I might have
got some more sensible work to do. But gradually it did return
after an uneasy period when, Annabel told me later, she had
grave fears for me.

It was necessary for me to find out what had been happening
in the outer world while I had been 'under the weather' – a
very apt description of my state of mind during those five weeks
of my absence before that dismal feeling began to retreat or I
to move out of its influence; the matter could be put either way.
A great deal had been happening, as I soon discovered. The
Profumo Affair had exploded while I was in hospital: the War
Minister, convicted of lying when he told the House of Commons that he had had no 'improper association' with the
delicious call girl Christine Keeler, had resigned, and the reper-
cussions of the matter were still sounding away in the courts;
such characters as Mandy Rice-Davies, Dr Stephen Ward,
'Lucky' Gordon and Christine herself filled the newspapers and
were continually talked about.

These matters in fact offered little for my column. I was
more affected by the death of Louis MacNeice, though I cannot
say exactly why. I had not known him well, and though I had

once or twice got drunk in his company I had always been wary
of his dark horse-face with its slightly sneering expression and
threat of a possible nasty bite, and of the black notebook which
he would often take from his pocket to write down a phrase or
line. Unlike 'Bertie' Rogers, whose alliterative poems seem to
have gone permanently out of fashion and even sunk without
trace, MacNeice will live. His wonderful poem on the fire-blitz
on London, 'Brother Fire', would alone be enough to ensure
it. So it was sad to hear of his death. This happened, I was told,
when he got soaked to the skin while on a BBC assignment in
a cave and developed pneumonia. He was taken to the Middle-
sex Hospital where his request for a bottle of whisky was
rejected. He was accustomed to heavy drinking and this foolish
piece of hospital routine probably cost him his life.

Gradually, as I recovered, I picked up the threads of my
working life. Seeking guidance, I looked at the columns I had
been writing before what Constantine, in his American style,
called my 'crack-up'. The very last one, suggestive of mounting
hysteria, contained a piece in which I found myself, while 'working on a research project on alcoholism in a Fleet Street bar',
suddenly producing 'Tibetan-type thought-forms' of the columnar characters:

General Nidgett peering forcefully through his glinting spectacles, Shri Swami Ron J. Bhattacharya, Ted Bloke and Eric
Lard, 'Redshank' the nature writer, babbling of badgers and
of dotterels' nests among the watercress, Mrs Dutt-Pauker
and even Mrs Dutt-Pauker's late husband with his snowy
locks, Stalinist pipe and blood-red knitted woollen scarf of
Revolution. So real were they, these forms, so far beyond
even Tibetan psychic skill, that they could react on each
other, I found, without my interposition. Soon Lard and

'Redshank' come to blows and Nidgett, ever susceptible to feminine charm, began absently stroking Mrs Dutt-Pauker's *Daily Worker* Bazaar Roumanian raffia-work handbag, as he talked on, stimulatingly, of service, initiative and leadership. Bemused by the din, I let my attention wander for a moment – the production of thought-forms is extremely tiring – and when I looked again the whole lot had vanished. Only a vague diminishing murmur of voices seemed to come now from the lamplit streets, now from the clouds.

There was a certain poetic imagination at work there, I thought – as well as an unmistakable unease – and now it was my task to recover it and even, if possible, turn my unpleasant experiences to the service of the column. It was perhaps at this time that I began to think of the column not merely as something which provided me with a living, but as something to which I was going to devote the rest of my working life. Or was it that the column itself, exacting this daily labour which sometimes seemed a burden not to be borne but sometimes gave me pleasure in creation, had become a monster, making me its slave? In my old age, when it already seems forgotten, super-seded by more violent, obscene and outspoken writings, I have come to dislike it and to lament – God help me! – that this is all I have to show for a lifetime's work. It is far removed indeed from my youthful dreams of becoming rich and famous. I have succeeded in neither.

Slowly I recovered, not without setbacks. Desmond had laid down a 'regime' of pills I was to take – some green and white, some red – respectively 'uppers' and 'downers' as they came to be called later on when taking drugs became more and more common among people like myself who were being driven mad by the egotism laying waste themselves and the technological progress laying waste the world. Which was worse? Obviously the former. What is a 'nervous breakdown' but an extreme form of self-regard and therefore deadly sin?

While I was taking these pills, Desmond told me, I should not drink alcohol. For a time I followed this advice quite strictly, avoiding the pub and even taking a masochistic pleasure in passing the door on my way to the bus-stop, receiving a momentary blast of enticing noise as my former drinking companions shouted their heads off within. I took a solitary lunch, preceded by one glass of campari and soda – a bitter drink I disliked then and have disliked for its associations ever since – in an Italian restaurant, long defunct, at the lower end of Fleet Street. I never asked Annabel to accompany me, either at that time or later. I felt instinctively that although I liked this beautiful, amiable and intelligent girl we had nothing much to say to each other. She must have got only an impression of austerity and gloom radiating from the other end of the little room we shared four days a week for eight years.

On the fifth working day of the week, Friday (there was no column on Saturdays) I went to the BBC to attend to the part-time job I had cunningly retained of reading short stories; I was still treated by the BBC administrative machine as a member of the staff, with the normal four weeks holiday a year and regular increments in my salary, which at its highest reached £12 a week. During my prolonged absence, which I counted as an official holiday, a huge pile of these short stories had accumulated; this had been noted by some busybody, and my friend James Langham, the producer of 'Morning Story', had had some explaining to do. He had managed to pacify his immediate superior in the Talks Department (everybody in the BBC had an immediate superior, a thing which delighted my hierarchy-loving soul), but, as he told me, I was under suspicion

A DUBIOUS CODICIL

of not being sufficiently conscientious about my work; mental illness was not regarded as a valid excuse unless officially certified.

Some months later, when James retired, another member of the Department, a very conscientious woman who succeeded him and who had had her eye on my job ever since suspicion fell on me, managed by a series of elementary intrigues to annex it to her own. The day came when I was summoned to the office of a high-grade administrative official in the lofty heights of 'B.H.'. There was a re-run, to me most satisfactorily ironical, of the interview I had had with one of these 'greymen' five years before. It was not the same 'greyman', but he used much the same words: 'reorganisation of the Department ... rationalisation ... necessity of retrenchment ... sorry that the time has come for a parting of the ways ... very grateful for the services you have rendered ... ' I looked at the 'greyman' as he spoke his piece, and a feeling of genuine pleasure and amusement came over me such as I had not felt for months.

For a moment I thought of making a scene: bursting into tears, going on my knees, kissing his well-polished black shoes, begging him to think of my wife and five small children, now threatened with starvation and beggary. But I was no Peter Duval Smith, and did no such thing. Instead I got up, looked out of the window and said 'What a wonderful view you have from here'. Perhaps this was more effective than tears. He certainly looked nonplussed as I took my leave, smiling hideously to myself as I descended in the lift, already composing a request to the *Telegraph* to increase my salary as I passed through the heavy bronze doors of 'B.H.' into the street.

Thereafter, except for one occasion in the Eighties when I was interviewed about my autobiography for a radio programme – how changed was the studio, crammed with elaborate, incom-

158

prehensible machinery, technicians and girl assistants, whereas in my time the producer would have been alone except for one engineer – I never passed through those doors again, except sometimes late at night when Kate and I and some companions would 'go on' after an evening of heavy drinking to the BBC's underground all-night canteen. We were never challenged when we entered this delightful place, where the 'buck rabbit and chips' was legendary and the kindly manageress, a Welsh-speaker, could sometimes be persuaded to sing 'Bugeilio 'r Gwenith Gwyn', my favourite Welsh folk-song.

We also used the services of the BBC duty officer, who lived in a room to the left of the central lifts and was said to be able to give the answer to any enquiry. Once in the small hours we telephoned to ask him to supply a missing line in the song 'Home on the Range'. He did so without hesitation. How heartrending is the decline of the BBC into barbarism since those days! Its marble foyer – where once a special subsection of pious women had the duty of arranging flowers in enormous chaste white urns beneath Eric Gill's bas-relief with its noble Latin inscription – is now disfigured by a platform where an official presides over security, while posturing rock-stars with fantastic hair-dos and strange, barbaric leather costumes impatiently await a degenerate breed of obsequious producers. And cracks are appearing in the walls.

Desmond had told me that attacks of depression often came in series, and I was aware during the next few months how precarious, though gradually strengthening, was the balance of my mind and how near I often was to falling once again into the pit. We had arranged a boarding school for Jane, who was now ten; it may be that if I had been in a normal state I might have been against the idea of sending her away from home so young. But I remembered Dixie's advice and made no objection.

A Catholic school in Dorset, Leweston Manor, a few miles from Sherborne, had been recommended. Run by a teaching order of Belgian nuns, with the redoubtable Mother Eleanor as head, it was a former country house in a large and beautiful park surrounded by woods, not far from Kate's former camp-site at Long Burton.

Jane's first departure for school from Waterloo Station was the model for such repeated leavetakings, with floods of tears on both sides. Worst still was the first weekend when we were allowed to take Jane out on Saturday afternoon. It was raining heavily, of course, so the only place to go was the cinema at Yeovil, where we saw a terrible epic film, *El Cid*, and then took Jane to a tea-shop in Sherborne before returning her, with more harrowing scenes, to school. It was the first of such experiences, which gradually grew more bearable as time went on and she progressed at the school, marked out by Mother Eleanor as a potential head girl until she became not just normally rebellious but excessively so, thus missing that eminence. Mother Eleanor, a shrewd woman, had realised that all was not well between Kate and me. She soon began to show a marked preference for me. I am easily frightened by nuns, particularly strong-minded ones, and soon began to behave towards her in a sycophantic, Uriah Heap-like manner which Jane noted with derision; this naturally made me exaggerate it to the point of caricature.

It was not long before I began to disregard Desmond's recommendation about not drinking alcohol. Soon I was taking his pills and alcohol as well. This did not seem to have bad effects at first; in fact it seemed to improve my ability to write the column. But it did make my behaviour more erratic. For a time I was convinced I was in love with Liz Hogg. This was not particularly surprising; I had always thought her delightful, both for herself and for her knowledge of 'Celtic' matters. However, my pursuit of her, such as it was, cannot have been very convincing. When drunk, I would drop in on her at the Hoggs' house in Woodlands Road in Barnes, a pleasant shambles of children and musical instruments, liable to be invaded by various neighbours we called collectively 'the Woodland Folk'. Among them was the elderly and eccentric retired Admiral Sir Caspar John, son of Augustus John, and his even more eccentric wife, who when he was Chief of Naval Staff must have been a continual source of worry at official functions.

Sir Caspar himself, a handsome, majestic man, had fallen into a state of melancholy in his declining years and was liable to appear in the Hoggs' house declaring in a deep and sombre voice, 'I am the Mayor of Casterbridge,' while Lady John, a small, lively, sparrow-like person, jigged about and tried to persuade everybody to dance. Other people who belonged to 'the Woodland Folk' were Christopher Wordsworth, a critic whom we had come across earlier on, among the English settlers on Clough Williams-Ellis's estate in North Wales, and Basil Davidson, a marxist and almost single-handed inventor of the history of Black Africa, which he peddled so persistently that many people actually came to believe in it.

My courtship of Liz Hogg virtually ended, though we remained friends, when the Hoggs asked me to spend New Year's Eve with them. I got very drunk in the Kings and Keys and arrived in Woodlands Road long after midnight when they had long given me up and only let me in, reluctantly, after I had thrown several snowballs at the window. My courtship of Martin Jameson's wife, for whom I suddenly took a violent fancy in the same pub, having known her for several years without showing any interest whatever, was even briefer. My courtship of a young and attractive Scots girl, Morag MacMunn

– whom I had met in some Fleet Street pub with an acquaintance of Stephen Daneff whom we had nicknamed 'Gimli the
Dwarf' (it was the time of the great vogue of Tolkien's *Lord of
the Rings*, which I was reading in bed, a chapter a night, giving
myself stupendous, partly drug-induced dreams) – was more
protracted.

Morag was a friend of the dying poet Brian Higgins, a protégé
of the wild-living George Barker; both were thoroughly disreputable. Things between Morag, who was about twenty years old,
and myself became difficult when she declared a passion for
me which soon eclipsed mine for her. Very drunk, I took her
to a party given by some respectable friend of the Worsthornes,
probably Kenneth Bradshaw, Clerk at the House of Commons.
We were not well received, so retired and went to bed in her
very unrespectable room somewhere in Bayswater. I crawled
out into the street in the early morning, wandered about in the
fog and at last got a taxi to Putney. But for all that I was at my
desk in the *Telegraph* by noon that morning settling down to
write the column for the day.

Such unseemly goings on could not be sustained. I arranged
(or Kate arranged, I dare say) a week's interlude when I took
the column to Rome, Kate accompanying me to help write the
copy, with ffolkes to do the drawings. We stayed (courtesy of
the *Telegraph*, of course) at an excellent hotel, the Inghilterra,
and visited the sights; the Colosseum, Keats' death chamber,
the Café Greco; the English tea-house below the Spanish Steps,
the gardens at Tivoli, Hadrian's Villa.

It was the time of the crucial Vatican Council, though I don't
think any of us, Catholic or not – and ffolkes was a 'militant
atheist' of an unthinking kind, which many people would be if
they were honest with themselves, and could not understand
why anyone should give any religion a second thought – had

any idea how crucial it was. What I witnessed in St Peter's was a scene of almost unbearable splendour: the Swiss Guards marshalling us, together with the faithful and unfaithful of all nations, to watch the white-robed Pope, triple-crowned, borne along in his golden chair past the black barley-sugar *baldacchino*, while the cardinals of the whole world – white, brown, yellow and black – applauded, like a theatre audience, with cries of 'Viva il Papa! Viva!' Organs and choirs thundered; censers swung, releasing clouds of incense; my head swam; facile tears streamed down my cheeks. 'I'm getting out of here,' muttered the indignant ffolkes. And in fact he and Kate almost had to drag me out of this quasi-religious orgy into the Sistine Chapel for some more sober art appreciation (I was surprised by the smallness and brownness of the celebrated ceiling).

I found it difficult to adapt the column to writing about a foreign country, far from the safety of my desk, and the administrative arrangements, which I had to look after as well, were formidable. I never attempted such an enterprise again. This was a pity, for the *Telegraph* would gladly have been the means by which I could have visited any place I chose. So in the end I got nothing much out of it except a living and a little doubtful pseudonymous fame.

After we had spent the four columnar days in Rome, we flew bumpily over the Appenines to Venice, where we put up at the most expensive hotel I have ever stayed in, the Daniele. It was full of Americans, the cheapest drink cost about £4 and the air-conditioning, a thing I have always hated, ensured that I got scarcely any sleep at night. Venice in October, misty, dark and slimy in its maze of canals and alleyways, dangerously lowered my spirits, such as they were. Only later did it occur to me that the sinister unreality of the place was at least partly due to what ought to have been a prime attraction: the absence of motor traffic. Venice, in the state I was in, was not for me. I have never been back there, or felt the least inclination to risk a better state of mind by another visit, or try the test I passed on my second visit to Chambord. On being told, as I have often been, that I must surely love Venice as all civilised people and partisans of beauty love it, I have to keep silent or, with a groan of anguish, explain my sad predicament.

Back in London, Sir Colin asked me in his sardonic way if 'I had enjoyed my holiday', which was how, perhaps rightly, he regarded it. I had not enjoyed it, if only because the concept of enjoyment was not at that time part of my confused universe. Under Desmond's watchful eye, I had many narrow escapes from total relapse. Feeling in particularly low spirits one winter morning, and oppressed by the lurking hell of unreality, I went to see him for a consultation. I found him sitting in his consulting room, a big transparent plastic box of many-coloured pills beside him which would have delighted children. 'As it happens,' he said, 'I've just had a new anti-depressant drug sent in from America. It has to be injected. Would you like to try it?' I hesitated. 'I'm going to try it myself,' he said. I could hardly refuse. So he injected us both, and within a few seconds we were laughing together in a powerful state of euphoria and exchanging childhood reminiscences. I have no idea what the drug was, but the subsequent let-down was formidable. It was some help to learn that it had been as bad for him as it had for me.

The child Victoria, who naturally became known as 'Vicki', was now in her second year, and I began to grow fond of her. She was an engaging, lively and mischievous child, pronounced 'wick' (or lively) by my mother, who liked to come out with Yorkshire-dialect words, when we took her to Amswick in the spring of 1964. There, in the sitting-room with its fragments of

Dresden china and other relics of the splendours of Harrogate, looking out across the dale to the limestone scars, Vicki learned to take her first steps, as Jane had done ten years before in that very same room. My mother seldom approved of girl-children. She did not approve of women in general, always maintaining that in matters of courtship and marriage it was women who 'chased' men and that if any of them caught me, as occasionally happened, I 'must have encouraged her'.

With these prejudices it was quite surprising that she took to Vicki as she did. It was an accolade indeed; when we took Vicki over to see Emma, my brother's widow, settled ever since his death in her native Swaledale, she pronounced the child an 'elf' or 'changeling' and for once my mother did not condemn this fancy talk with her customary 'silly woman!' Did they realise that Vicki was indeed a changeling? And was this for them, as it may have been for me, part of the child's unusual charm? Even her extreme naughtiness, only intermittently checked by Kate, a loving but careless mother, and scarcely at all by me, was irresistibly attractive. When, later on, we began to take her with us on visits to Jane, she got herself barred for life from all the tea-shops in Sherborne; in a tea-shop in Cerne Abbas, the place of the giant, she unravelled all the rolls of lavatory-paper in the washroom, so that paper came cascading down the stairs and out into the street. We thought this most amusing, and so did she, thereby spurred on to even greater feats of disruption.

It was in April, a bad month for the depressed, that I came nearer to falling once again into the pit. To struggle with this black woe of non-feeling was merely to add terror to it. One evening, while Weston and Jameson were performing in the Kings and Keys, I felt such despair – how could I go through all this again? – that Kate unwillingly hurried me to Desmond's house. He kept us waiting, as psychiatrists necessarily do, a very long time, while glasses of white wine – he was a very understanding doctor – appeared regularly for our refreshment. In his consulting room he listened, then advised another course of electro-convulsive therapy. He arranged a first instalment for the very next evening.

There was no reason, he said, why I should not carry on with my normal life and work – indeed he strongly recommended it. Only I was to eat nothing in the meantime, and drink only a little water, while taking my customary pills. I obeyed his instructions and next morning sat down at my desk, perhaps staring at Annabel more portentously than usual. I tried to write about whatever came to mind at that time – immigration, 'Mods and Rocker' riots, aggressive trade-unionists, who can say? – but could get down no more than a few disjointed sentences. Suddenly a miracle occurred – a paradoxical idea! I wrote it down; the cloud lifted from my mind, and when at lunchtime Kate came in to see how I was getting on in preparation for my ordeal I told her I felt better. 'Good,' she said in her masterful way. 'Ring up Desmond and tell him you don't need the treatment, and come out and have a drink!' So that is what I did.

It was about this time that Sir Colin Coote retired from the editorship, resplendent in years and honour. There was a farewell luncheon at the Savoy Hotel, the first of many such luncheons I attended in the days when the *Telegraph* was generous with its money – even 'Zed', the Literary Editor, got a luncheon at the Savoy when he retired, and L. Marsland Gander, the aged radio (and, I suppose, television) critic, got a hilariously comical one at which recordings of early radio stars like Wilfred Pickles and Henry Hall were played between the speeches. Sir Colin was succeeded by Maurice Green, an economist from *The Times*, a very different sort of person who, though fairly suspicious of my column and apt to worry more than the robust Coote about possibly libellous material, was amiable and cordial and even, unlike his predecessor, occasionally relieved our evening sessions by laughing at things I had written or complimenting me on being in good form. In fact the ten or eleven years of his editorship did find the column (which he always quaintly called my 'notes') at its zenith, if it ever had one.

However, it was not long before he complained that he could not get on with Colm Brogan, who looked after the column when I was on holiday. Green could not understand a word Brogan said in his admittedly ferocious Glasgow accent; whatever he might actually be saying, Green complained, he always sounded as if he was swearing, and it was beginning to get on his nerves. I explained that Brogan was really one of the kindest of men and could not help it if, when Green asked, for instance, what the time was, he seemed to be making ferocious threats. It was no good. Brogan, who badly needed the money, had to go.

His departure was no credit to me; I felt remorse because I had not defended him as strongly as I might, and for all his phonetic and facial ferocity, he was not good at defending himself, or at any rate at looking after his own interests. He was one of the most lovable and honest men I have ever known. He was also capable, when he forgot to be irascible and was mollified by alcohol, of being extremely entertaining and amusing. I sometimes visited the gloomy flat in Bloomsbury, where dark brown was the predominant if not the only colour, in which he lived with his wife and daughter Mary, who worked on the *Telegraph*'s women's page. She cooked terrible brown meals of Irish stew and offered Guinness and Irish whiskey. Colm would play alternate records of Irish 'rebel' and Orange songs, delighting equally, as I did myself, both in 'The Battle of Aughrim', that wonderful dirgelike song of defeat, and 'The Old Orange Flute', that wonderful, rollicking song of preposterous bigotry. He used to say that he was the only man in the world who was both an Orangeman and a Sinn Féiner. A universal nationalist, I had much the same attitude to the 'Irish problem'; but as a Scots–Irish Catholic he was more directly concerned.

Towards the end of his life the most undeserved misfortune fell on this truly good man. He became a modern Job. First he fell ill with an ulcer, requiring a serious operation; then his wife, who with her cheerfulness and patience had been his faithful support and safeguard, fell ill with cancer and died within a few months. This was both shocking and amazing. I had always assumed, as some doctors believe, that only unhappy, introverted and selfish people die of cancer. Mrs Brogan was the very reverse of this: happy, at least to outward view, extrovert and unselfish. After her death, Colm soon became ill again, undergoing another operation, and although his daughter looked after him as unselfishly if not as cheerfully as his wife had done, she could not replace her. He was reduced to shuffling about, with rueful anger, by means of a walking frame until he died. He never lost his faith.

Colm was succeeded as holiday relief by Anthony Lejeune, a clever man of suitably reactionary views not leavened, like mine, by a certain tendency to self-mockery which, however despicable, was necessary to put them across in an acceptable way. Lejeune was also a tremendous snob and extremely knowledgeable about gentlemen's clubs and the habits and diction ('U and non-U') of the upper class.

His attitude to me was rather patronising, and after a year or two I became tired of this and of his somewhat wooden and uncharitable attitudes. An inaccuracy in an item which demanded a correction when I returned from holiday gave me the opportunity of dispensing with a deputy altogether. Henceforth when I was away, the columnar space was filled with other material, usually short articles, and apart from occasional contributions from Colm Brogan, Charles Herring and Michael Green – and even those gradually fell away for different reasons – I wrote the column by myself.

The anthology had had some success; Dr Johnson published a new edition, with some supplementary matter, and proposed to bring out a second anthology in 1965. He even gave a party in the upper room of a pub in Sutton. It was a joint party; the other publication to be celebrated was a book of poems by an elderly Australian woman who had probably paid for publication herself and may have been a relation of Dr Johnson's by marriage. Michael ffolkes, who, apart from the host, was the only person I knew at the party, was impressed by the extreme dimness of the arrangements. There was nothing to drink except beer and British sherry and nothing to eat except potato crisps and peanuts. There was a general air of bewilderment. What was it all for? As we came out into the rain ffolkes said it was probably the worst party he had ever attended.

I was inclined to agree; but the very hopelessness and obscurity of this parody of a 'glittering' publisher's party appealed to the masochistic side of my nature, a certain instinct for self-abasement inherited from my father, so strongly that I was almost hysterical with amusement as we made our escape from Sutton and fell into some brightly-lighted restaurant in the West End. I thought of the worst party in English literature: Giles Winterbourne's party in Hardy's *Woodlanders*. But apart from underlining my failure to become rich and famous, this party in Sutton had done me no harm; it had not, for instance, like poor Giles's debâcle, lowered me in the eyes of the woman I loved.

It was in the summer of 1964 that I found a woman who for the first time in my life offered the promise of a strong, steady mutual love and at once began to alleviate, if she did not entirely remove, my neurotic fears. Susan was thirteen years younger than myself, a painter, partly Swedish and in all ways appealing. She was a devout Catholic, and it was another ten years before we married. Before that, Jane had graduated at Bristol University and I thought myself free of the duty (though by a typical wish to have my cake and eat it, not entirely free of the inclination) to go on living at Putney. Even when, in 1965, Kate had had another baby, not, of course, by me, I did not leave. The 'horror comic' continued, and Constantine was able to quote the familiar saying about history repeating itself, the second time as farce. In fact, because of my new attachment and frequent absences, there was less horror, less verbal abuse; fewer plates were smashed and fewer handbags or briefcases flung from the windows of taxis in motion. Kate and I visited Jane at Leweston just like respectable parents (were we, in fact, less respectable, had the truth been known, than many of the other parents?). We went on foreign holidays together. In that same year, 1964, we spent a fortnight in the Minho. Jane, who was now in her twelfth year and very beautiful, innocently captivated a susceptible young Portuguese.

For the voyage back to England we took a boat from Vigo, in Spain, to Southampton. It had brought a cargo of negroes from the West Indies, part of the flood of alien people who were invading and part-colonising England, transforming it in ways which nobody, certainly nobody among the easy-going mass of the indigenous population, could possibly anticipate. We ourselves, of course, had no idea at that time of what the appearance of these people was going to mean; we looked at them with surprise as they came up on deck from the lower depths of the ship, some hesitant, some compensating for their own bewilderment by an overbearing attitude. We looked at them and thought no more of it. If we – the indigenous population – had taken thought then, could we have prevented the tragic consequences? Was this fatal loss of our racial homogeneity due to human error on the part of our rulers, to their stupidity – or to a deliberate conspiracy against England, the one country in Europe spared for centuries from invasion, occupation or revolution, the one country, therefore, whose destruction must be brought about if the final ruin of European civilisation were to be assured?

Signs of such a conspiracy were all around us: the importation from the vilest gutters of America of degenerate sub-musical rubbish, of drug addiction, pornography, aggressive feminism, aggressive homosexuality. Even worse in principle was the inversion of values by which the 'media' welcomed these evils as signs of human liberation, collectively called 'the permissive society'. Perhaps there was no conspiracy and no need for one; perhaps the people of England were unconsciously conspiring against themselves. Perhaps Satan, the spirit of evil, was loose in the world, as some of my readers believed. Perhaps, as I explained in an ironical 'note', I objected to these things only because I was getting old, jealous of young people and out of touch. But I do not think so.

At any rate there was plenty of material for my column, evils which I could either rail against or satirise, or sometimes both; this way of treating them often produced the most satisfying results. And while I railed against the 'permissive society', I was living, as I always had, what the famous crusader against that society, Mrs Whitehouse, would have regarded as a 'permissive' life. There was no hypocrisy in this: I was not promiscuous, I did not listen to rock music or take drugs or enjoy pornography.

I led two separate lives: one based on Putney, with Kate and her family; one with my friend and companion with whom, whenever possible, I travelled about England and Wales, exploring the vanishing countryside – and twenty-five years ago there was still a lot that had not vanished.

At midsummer we stayed at a delightful hotel in Savernake Forest and walked in its still enchanted glades; in autumn we travelled in Northumberland or in North Wales or in the limestone dales of Derbyshire; in March we once saw genuine mad March hares leaping and boxing on the Wiltshire Downs.

As for my life in Putney, it was good to see the children growing up and revive, vicariously, my own lost sense of wonder; it was good to visit Jane at Leweston and observe her progress in the intervals of toadying to Mother Eleanor. It was good to visit my mother in Yorkshire and to get drunk, as Kate and I often did, with the Tunnicliffes, either in their capacious bungalow, hidden in trees above the now forgotten Minoan Ball Ground, or in various pubs and hotels in that part of Yorkshire. They lived what John Braine thought of as 'life at the top' but with an element of raffishness and high spirits which made it irresistibly attractive. When their second daughter, Patricia or 'Trish', married the young scion of another West Riding industrial dynasty, they gave a splendid party with vast marquees and red carpets in the garden of their big house in Wharfedale; we went on drinking until the small hours, to Jane's alarm, though we were able to allay her anxiety when she telephoned from Amswick for news.

The pleasure of those days is best summed up in a shared fantasy we had of buying a mysterious, derelict mansion called Oughtershaw Hall, in Langstrothdale, not far from the sources of the Wharfe. This house was a piece of romantic Victorian mediaevalism, originally built by the Woodd family, friends of

Ruskin; it was buried in shrubberies; its furthest walk over-looked a gloomy waterfall which in winter must have permeated the lives of all who lived there with its ceaseless boom.

Of course our fantasy of living there came to nothing. In later years, when this period of our lives was long over, I often passed that way, to find the house just as mysterious and more decayed, with signs of occupation by squatters or wandering people. But 'Oughtershaw Hall' has remained a symbol of the unattainable, a Yorkshire version of Alain Fournier's lost domain.

There was a reverse side to all this: boredom, inertia, occasional attacks of *angst*, though never of great severity or long duration, which made certain places where these inexplicable afflictions broke the surface of my mind into places I have always subsequently avoided. Orford in Suffolk was one place where I suffered one of these 'queer turns' lightly attributed to 'bad vibes', while ascending the castle tower on a day of dismal rain. Deep breathing, together with one of Desmond's green and white pills and a large gin-and-tonic, brought relief.

Simple loneliness could also be an affliction when, as some-times happened, both sides of my life failed and I was left to myself. A low point of middle life: I was returning from Fleet Street to Putney on a dismal autumn evening when there was nobody at home. As though by a masochistic instinct I entered the most depressing pub in Putney High Street, ordered a bottle of beer and a portion of pure cardboard pork pie and sat down at a small table, swimming with liquid and covered with the abandoned plates of previous eaters. As I began this miserable repast with Gissing-like lassitude a rough-looking young labourer sat down at the table opposite me. We did not speak, but I discerned in him an additional, satisfying element of boredom and menace.

There was a kind of perverted pleasure in this humiliating situation; even a mystical sense of freedom, hard to explain, but analogous to an experience I had years later on a wild road in the mountains of Galicia when returning from a pilgrimage by car I made with my third wife to Santiago de Compostela. We had lost the way – it was still blissfully possible to lose the way in those days, as innumerable pilgrims must have done before us, before the tourist signs appeared for the tidy regulation and direction of travellers – and quarrelled over my reading of the map. Losing all patience, she drove away, leaving me sitting on a large granite boulder by the wayside in this totally deserted place.

My anger left me; and what came over me was an overpowering sense of freedom. It was not freedom from my wife; there was 'nothing personal in it'; I still loved her. It was the 'absolute' freedom to go anywhere I pleased. I had my passport and enough money for my immediate needs; I could as soon walk away in one direction as another: return to England, my job and responsibilities; take a ship from Vigo or Coruña to the ends of the earth; or remain in Spain, find a small town and settle there to await whatever might come. I did none of these things; the moment of illumination passed; my wife, her temper recovered, drove slowly back, and we resumed our journey in silence. I did not try to explain what had happened to me until long afterwards, and even then I am not sure she understood. But any life must contain such inexplicable moments of illumination in which it seems all may be changed for ever. Perhaps, like so much else in life, the ecstasy of physical love included, they are anticipations of death.

6

Some Reactionary Causes

Bringing to an end what he called 'thirteen years of Tory misrule', Harold Wilson won the General Election in the autumn of 1964. The election-night party which Lady Pamela Berry and her husband (later to become a life peer under the name of Lord Hartwell, converting her into Lady Hartwell) gave at the Savoy Hotel was a much less triumphant affair than the previous election parties I had attended; as the results flashed up on the big screen and the coming Labour victory became unmistakeable, the champagne-swilling guests showed signs of unease, which naturally made them swill champagne at an even greater speed.

Dr Johnson decided to call his new anthology 'Peter Simple in Opposition'. This was misleading because I was always in opposition, scarcely more so when there was a Labour Government than a Conservative. I am quite incapable of understanding 'the economy', 'the trade gap', 'the balance of payments' and so on, which everyone on the *Telegraph* said would be more seriously mishandled by the Labour Party; indeed, I have never been able to understand what 'the economy' is, and when I asked people like Colin Welch, who evidently did, for enlightenment I came away none the wiser. They could not answer my fundamental question: how did money originate, and if, as appeared to be the case, the world economy was ruled by a system of manipulation of imaginary money by credit, who ultimately controlled the system? It may be that these questions led us on to quaking ground. They were fully explained by

175

Major Douglas, inventor of Social Credit and patron of my friends the Greenshirts; but unfortunately I could not understand his explanation either.

In everything which really interested me and which I thought I *could* understand, there seemed little to choose between Labour and the Tories: neither seemed concerned with the moral degeneration of England; neither seemed concerned with the flood of unassimilable alien immigrants who were altering the character of entire cities to the dismay and anger of the indigenous population, which were eventually suppressed by law and by the monstrous growth of the Race Relations Industry (a term I invented about this time); neither seemed concerned by the infiltration of every government department and every sizeable institution by people who, whether they were Communists or not, had no loyalty to the State and in many cases were actually working to overthrow it.

Dr Johnson, unlike myself, was a party politician and naturally regarded the advent of the Labour Government in 1964 as an unmitigated calamity. However, he was (it was one of his many admirable qualities) a man independently-minded to the point of eccentricity. During what he rightly thought were humbugging goings-on in the Commons and behind the scenes which accompanied the Profumo Affair and the advent of Sir Alec Douglas-Home as Prime Minister, he had frequently declined the whip and during an important debate openly declared he was going to play golf instead of attending. This annoyed his constituency association as much as it delighted me, and he was forced to resign his seat as MP for Carlisle. At the consequent by-election he stood as an Independent Conservative and lost, but succeeded in splitting the vote and letting in the Labour candidate. Henceforth his name was mud in the Conservative

Central Office, and although I think he tried, he never managed to get nominated as a candidate again.

The later history of this lovable man was even more curious. He and his wife bought an hotel at Woodstock in Oxfordshire, but soon contrived to alienate the staff. One morning they all concertedly walked out on him. Later he maintained that they had been taking cannabis and, more serious, had introduced cannabis or other 'substances' into his and his wife's food, who found themselves acting so strangely that they were both certified insane by (he believed) corrupt doctors and committed to a mental hospital. They were released after a short time; but the case caused quite a sensation. Years later, when I happened to be having a drink in this hotel, I noticed on the wall a crude comic drawing showing Dr and Mrs Johnson staring aghast as a procession of their staff made their way out of the door and into the street.

It may have been a mark of Dr Johnson's eccentricity that he went on publishing anthologies of my column at intervals until the last one appeared in 1973; henceforth they were published by the *Telegraph* publications department. Johnson Publications had only meagre sales arrangements and no money for advertising, so the books' sales were small; but at least they looked like books; the *Telegraph*'s productions, cheap-looking affairs printed on grey paper and with the appearance, as one friendly reviewer, Dick West, complained, of 'samizdat publications', did not. But perhaps it was right that these books, which purveyed unfashionable opinions and got away with them because they were supposed to be funny, should have a clandestine air about them.

It was in 1965 that I was presented with a cause after my own heart: the declaration of UDI by the Rhodesians after prolonged negotiation with our own Government had driven them into a corner, giving them no other option. I wrote a 'note' entitled 'Compelled Romantics' which explains why I became such an enthusiastic supporter of this most unfashionable cause. The Rhodesians, I explained,

> can hardly be called a romantic people. Yet their cause must surely appeal irresistibly to those like myself who instinctively support the weaker side . . . Here is a group of British people like ourselves – only more so, since they represent a simple, rather suburban attitude to life which is vanishing in our own country – with almost the whole world against them.
>
> They face the fanatical power of black nationalism; tongue-tied themselves, they face the supremely vocal, embattled Left-wing moralisers of the world, the daily propaganda which seeks to persuade us that their mild paternal rule is one of the most vicious tyrannies the world has ever seen. These simple farmers, shopkeepers, tennis-players and devo-tees of afternoon tea are trapped in a situation – a truly heroic role – which does not suit them and which they are only just beginning dimly to understand. The most unromantic of people, they may soon acquire the romantic dignity of all those who, though their cause seems lost to start with, resolve to stand and fight.

So unfashionable was the Rhodesian cause that my colleague Kenneth Rose, an excellent writer but somewhat given to snob-bery, told me incredulously: 'You really oughtn't to support these people, Michael. They're – well, terribly common, you know. None of them has ever read a book.' I was aware of this, but did not see how it justified people recommending their black subjects to cut their throats. Among 'Hampstead thinkers',

of course, there was a large element of snobbery in their fanatical loathing of the white Rhodesians. In my column, Mrs Dutt-
Pauker condemned them for talking about 'afternoon tea' and
'serviettes' and saying 'pardon?' If they had read books and
possessed a symphony orchestra and an opera house, the tone
might have been different. This snobbish attitude was to surface
again in the loathing of English intellectuals or would-be intellectuals for the white South Africans and Ulster Protestants
and is a minor reason why I have always been on their side.

The Rhodesians in London, whom I met after the declaration
of UDI and who often asked me to their wonderfully boring
parties at Rhodesia House, were not entirely happy about their
new friend. One middle-aged lady with an outsize flowery hat
actually said: 'Mr Wharton, I sometimes think you must be a
repressed intellectual,' clearly a term of serious reproach. But
I went on supporting them through the fifteen years of their
amazing and heroic struggle against terrorism and organised
mendacity, whose final act I witnessed at first hand when I went
to Rhodesia to write about the fraudulent election of 1980,
when Mrs Thatcher's Conservative Government was forced,
probably if not certainly against her own inclination, by its
American overlords to betray them.

The end of white-ruled Rhodesia (it had already been
renamed 'Zimbabwe-Rhodesia' in an absurd attempt to placate
the international bawling for racial equality and 'a commitment
to black majority rule' which temporarily elevated the pathetic
Bishop Abel Muzorewa) was both tragic and farcical. 'Fair and
free elections' had been promised under the auspices of Lord
Soames, created 'Governor of Southern Rhodesia' for the purpose, and the two rival black terrorist groups, led by Robert
Mugabe and Joshua Nkomo, had agreed to participate in these,
mainly because the former, the more astute politician of the

179

two, had been privately assured he would win. The fairness and freeness of the elections was supposed to be ensured by the presence of British observers at points where the black terrorists, who for years had been raiding the country with growing ferocity and with increasing quantities of weaponry supplied by the Communist empires, were required to assemble and give up their arms. Many but by no means all did so. The observers were supposed to prevent intimidation of the voters. Intimidation took place on an enormous scale, but when the Rhodesian officials reported this to Soames, he ignored their complaints.

It must have been odd to be a Rhodesian at that time, vaguely realising that power in your own country, the country which had been wholly created by white people and ruled by white people with at least as much justice as most countries in the world, was being mysteriously and furtively taken away from you without your being able to do anything about it. There was, to be sure, talk of a military coup. I asked General Walls, the very intelligent and efficient Commander-in-Chief of the Rhodesian Army, if he had considered this. He smiled at my romantic notion and said, perhaps implying that he had, that it could not succeed. The fate of Rhodesia had been decided, he said, when the South Africans withdrew their support; his forces could have gone on fighting indefinitely so long as the southern frontier remained open for supplies. Without that, Rhodesia could not hold out for long. There is a myth, one of those Left-wing myths like the myth of the innocence of Alger Hess, that the 'war' in Rhodesia ended in the defeat of the white Rhodesians by the black 'Freedom Fighters'. This is not true; the Rhodesian army was never defeated in the field and the black terrorists never occupied or even entered any urban centre. The myth has now, of course, become accepted as historical fact.

The *Telegraph*'s correspondents in Salisbury (such people are admirably capable of looking after themselves) were based at Meikle's Hotel, an excellent, well-run hotel of the old-fashioned kind, and there I stayed while I carried out the week's programme they had arranged for me. There were times when I felt as I had felt on my journeys round India forty years before; but then I had been in uniform and subject, however tenuously, to army rules and regulations. Here in Rhodesia I was one of a horde of visitors: journalists, politicians, observers from all kinds of bodies from the League of Proportional Representation to the Association for the Advancement of Human Rights. Among all these people I must have been one of the very few who had any sympathy at all with the white Rhodesians as they saw their country being filched from them in the name of various hollow abstractions. Every evening officials of Lord Soames's secretariat gave press conferences at which they spouted soothing disinformation, and every evening the press turned up in great numbers to absorb it; when questions were invited they all came from journalists who were plainly dissatisfied because the Rhodesians were not being punished enough for the crime of existing.

I went to see a farm about thirty miles from Salisbury where a white farmer whose ancestors had been in Rhodesia for two generations ruled over a domain larger than many landed estates in England. There were portraits of his forebears on the walls of his large, cool bungalow; unlike most Rhodesians he had bookcases too; among the books I saw some of my own, and was sorry that I could not live up to the image of the writer he cherished. However, he and his wife (his sons were away, serving in the army) made the best of it. They led me to their paradisical garden, with lawns, beds of enormous flowers and trees decked with red and purple flowering creepers. From the shade, to complete the picture, emerged two fine yellow labradors, looking at the stranger with mild, sad eyes. What more could anybody want? And who would not fight for such a place?

This farmer, who grew mainly maize and tobacco and also had herds of cattle, showed me over his well-tended lands, defended, as all such places were, by a perimeter of electrified wire, its current now cut off for the truce. There was a simple hospital, and a school for his black workers' children. It was a Sunday, so the school was empty, and I could glance at the neatly-ranged desks, the neat exercise books with sums or spelling corrected. A group of small black girls in their Sunday best, white-socked and pigtailed, watched me curiously from a distance. In the workers' village, with its neat, one-storeyed houses, a witch-doctor did a statutory dance as we drank horrible but reputedly very intoxicating Shona beer. And all seemed prosperous, happy and contented under the iron heel of the colonialist oppressor who at that very moment, in the pages of the British press, was lashing out with his whip at his miserable starving slaves and setting his dogs on them.

Another day I went with a *Telegraph* correspondent to a press conference given by Mugabe himself, in the grounds of a capacious villa which had been put at his disposal for the election. We were made to take off our shoes for inspection before we could approach him; his men had evidently heard of the possibility of concealing sharp knives or other weapons in the toe-caps of European shoes. Then we sat in a crowd round a table where the great man presided. He made a short speech in a quiet voice about his confidence of victory, then answered questions. Many of the questioners seemed to be Canadians. They were intensely respectful. Among themselves they always referred to Mugabe as 'Bob', but when one Canadian girl, who got as near to him as possible so that she could gaze yearningly into his face, actually addressed him in this way there was a shocked silence and subsequent rebuke.

This formidable Jesuit-educated Marxist who was soon to be Prime Minister and thereafter president of the new state of 'Zimbabwe', named after mysterious ruins in the south of the country which were considered of great importance because they were the only stone buildings in Africa attributed to black builders (the current joke among the less devout was that they were polling-booths for some prehistoric 'fair and free' elections) – Mugabe, though shiny black, did not have pronounced negroid features; he had a reptilian, even saurian look, a hint of Nilotic origin. He was obviously very intelligent; what he thought of his white adorers, whose powerful combined delusions, compounded of a perverse hatred of their own kind and a genuine sympathy for those they thought oppressed, would soon bring him to power, it was impossible to say.

I retired thoughtfully to my hotel; later that evening I had dinner with my colleagues and watched a curious scene. There was a resident pianist at Meikle's, an old white man called Jack Dent, a general favourite, who must have played his piano for innumerable Rhodesians, both in the days of peace and in the days when they came on leave from the war in the bush, where they had built up a formidable spirit of cameraderie as only men who are consciously defending their own can do; now he was playing the last notes of the old order in Rhodesia. At a table not far from ours sat Lord Soames and his party of ladies and gentlemen from Government House. A large dinner consumed, he rose with his partner, all paunch and jowls, and danced to the tunes, loaded with sweet nostalgia, of wartime England: 'These Foolish Things', 'Don't Fence Me In', 'Begin the Beguine', 'You Must Remember This'. At the time we had not thought that war, with our illusory victory, was being fought to reduce our country to a cypher, to destroy our Empire and hand over the Crown Colony of Rhodesia to a gang of educated, power-seeking savages. Ponderously danced this fat, smiling politician; he danced the end of what, for all its faults (and it had fewer than most) was a country decent and just and well-managed enough; with jowls and belly quivering he danced deceit and calculated surrender of the better to the worse; the triumph of all that was false and silly in distant England. I watched him dance; and a powerful feeling of disgust welled up inside me.

I was still swallowing it down as I flew back to England (a seemingly interminable journey of thirty-six hours, owing to compound failure of air-flights, an overnight stay in Johannesburg, a long doze jammed in a narrow seat relieved by whisky and the sight of dawn creeping up the south-western edge of Crete); and next day as I wrote rapidly, and in great excitement, in my room at the *Telegraph*, an elaborate dithyramb, which somehow fell into the four movements of a symphony, for inclusion in the last columnar space that week; soon I heard the news that Mugabe had won the elections 'in a doddle', as Ian Smith himself had predicted in his irremediably 'common' parlance.

Smith was now out for good, to the concerted cheering of all the liberal thinkers of the world. No more would Janet his wife open garden fêtes for the denizens of the Rhodesian suburban paradise; no more would Desmond Lardner-Burke, a highly respectable solicitor and 'rebel' minister for internal affairs, described in the British press as 'the Himmler of Rhodesia', sign terrorists' death-warrants; no more would Rhodesia's citizen army parade with home-made weapons, or the 'crack' Selons Scouts on their swift grey horses (hated as few bodies of men had been hated since the Waffen SS, with whom they were constantly compared in the *Observer*) remorselessly pursue the terrorists in the mountains and forests; no more would Smith himself, asked by the band at some exaggeratedly old-fashioned English function if they could play his favourite tune, unhesitatingly choose an anthem of the ruefully unpretentious: 'Side by Side':

> Ain't got a barrel o' money, may look ragged and funny,
> But we're marching along, singing this song:
> Side by side.

If he had chosen something by Mozart or better still, Schoenberg, would the *Observer* have forgiven him, and Rhodesia survived?

Back in 1965, the year of UDI, Rhodesia had involved my column in its first and only libel action (though in the early days the newspaper had to pay Lady Chatterjee, widow of a Parsee lawyer, damages of £100 when I used the title 'Lady Chatterjee's Lover' for a fictitious book – but even so she was good-humoured about it). While the uproar about Rhodesia was going on in the United Nations, and that fraudulent body was discussing what measures could be taken to bring the Rhodesians to heel, a left-wing Labour MP, Lena Jeger (afterwards Lady Jeger, a life peeress) said in the House of Commons that she 'saw no objection to the presence in Rhodesia of troops of the Red Army wearing the blue berets of the United Nations'. For this I described her as 'an unconscious fifth columnist', and she immediately sued. The *Telegraph* decided to defend the case and a long drawn-out legal process began. I prepared a statement defending my remarks, describing the record of the

Red Army and its atrocities in Eastern Europe at the end of the War – which are, even now I suppose, largely unknown to people in England – and explaining the mentality of people like Mrs Jeger, who even twenty years after the war still had a vestigial admiration for Stalin and 'our gallant allies' which no revelations of the truth about them would ever entirely dispel. It was reasonable, I wrote, to describe such people as 'unconscious fifth columnists' on behalf of the Soviet Union, then our potential enemy.

Legal processes, I was now to realise, take a very long time. It was three years before a date was fixed for the hearing at the Law Courts: 21 August 1968. Our dispositions were made: I had discussed everything with the *Telegraph*'s admirable solicitor, Richard Sykes, a man so huge that I thought of him as Quinbus Flestrin, Gulliver's 'man mountain'; I was keyed up for my appearance and cross-examination, a considerable ordeal for one who has always disliked public appearances. Then, barely a week before the hearing was due, Mrs Jeger, without any explanation, suddenly dropped the case.

On 21 August, the Red Army, with contingents of the Warsaw Pact forces, invaded Czechoslovakia and ended the 'Prague Spring' of the unfortunate Mr Dubcek. I was relieved in a way, but also disappointed: in the circumstances we could hardly have failed to win. But what were we to make of Mrs Jeger's withdrawal?

That year, 1968, was the year of the Paris students' uprising, celebrated by Paul Johnson, in his romantic Leftist phase, in lyrical articles in the *New Statesman*. 'A spectre is haunting Europe – the spectre of student power', he wrote, fatuously parodying the opening words of the Communist Manifesto. There was plenty of mileage for the column here: it was only too easy to comment that the spectre which was really haunting

Europe was 'the same spectre which had haunted Europe for fifty years – the spectre of the Red Army'.

There was plenty of mileage, too, in the students' demonstrations and sit-ins in the London School of Economics; in the demonstrations in Park Lane, where a small mob tried to build a barricade – so inefficiently that it took only one policeman to remove it – and then, in its frustration, tried to invade the Bunny Club and the Hilton Hotel and set them on fire. A good example of the misunderstandings I often met was when a 'right-wing extremist', Lady Birdwood, told me how horrified she was at this behaviour; I said it was a pity they didn't succeed, thus adding puzzlement to her horror. A great demonstration against the Vietnam War in Grosvenor Square that autumn was followed by a huge procession through London which took in Fleet Street and passed the *Telegraph* building, where, to my delight, the modish horde raised banners with slogans against the 'Fascist Peter Simple'.

It was the heyday of the weird American activist Ralph Schoenman, secretary to the aged Bertrand Russell and, it was thought, organiser in his name of such ludicrous stunts as the trial for war crimes of President Johnson *in absentia*. I had a fantasy, which may have contained some truth, that Schoenman was holding Russell a prisoner in his house at Penrhyndeudraeth in North Wales, where Schoenman acted as 'works manager' of his 'peace factory'; I devised a plan for rescuing Russell by means of a parachute drop and hiding him in a place of safety in the columnar territory. Schoenman greatly resented these fancies and telephoned me several times, ordering me not to write anything about him in future without discussing it with him first. But it was not long before this most bizarre of Sixties 'fun-revolutionaries' became the subject of scandal and dropped out of public view.

187

While these stirring public events were going on, Kate and I, with her growing family, were having trouble in 'Chartfield', as our Putney house, swelling in fancy to a large country estate, was commonly called. The agreeable dog-loving family which had been living above us moved to the outer suburbs, while almost at the same time the Prings, the quiet and respectable middle-class couple below us, moved to the country. The Prings were succeeded by a strange married pair of disparate age and valetudinarian disposition; the top flat was occupied by a gang of stage-Australian students whose most senior member, distinguished by his coffin-shaped, rat-trap face and nasal whine, was known to the others, evidently as a mark of respect, as 'Mr S.' He was the quietest member of the gang, but that was not saying much; they often spent their nights playing a kind of Rugby with what sounded like a tin can, booming and roaring overhead so that it seemed our ceilings would come down.

We were going through a strangely cosy domestic phase at that time, sometimes retiring to bed in friendly chastity with mugs of hot chocolate or, if we had colds, hot whisky and lemon, and even reading the novels of Elizabeth Taylor aloud to each other, so the rowdy antics of the Australians were very trying. Complaints brought some alleviation; but they soon relapsed and reverted to their normal behaviour. There was poetic justice in the situation; we were now on the receiving end of the punishment we had meted out to the Uhlmans in Downshire Hill ten years before. But I do not think this irony occurred to us. Our torment ended when the Australians went too far; one evening two of them were leaning out of their window, as was their custom, and scanning the street, when Mr S. approached. 'How are yer, big prick?' one of them roared. This led to general complaints from the neighbours and threats to call the police. Perhaps realising they were not wanted, the

Australians left soon afterwards. 'Are yer glad we're going?' said Mr S., when I met them in a group in the street. I smiled but made no answer, every inch a po-faced, whingeing pom.

It was about this time that Annabel, who had been sitting opposite me in my little room for over eight years, patiently typing my column, repelling madmen on the telephone and enduring my gloomy countenance, decided to leave. She had published a novel which I could not read, though that was no reflection on her literary talent, and was going through a difficult phase in her private life, or so I judged, and wanted a change. She had been ill with glandular fever earlier that year, and had been absent from the column for three months. For a temporary replacement I naturally applied to the Utley Secretarial Agency, which supplied a delightful blonde – an attractive and intelligent girl called Jenny Dale. She was of 'genuine working-class origin', a fact reflected in what I at first thought of, in my instinctively self-defensive way, as 'pretty but blunt, plebeian features'.

Her father was a lifelong Communist; Jenny had the statutory left-wing views of the time, but she had won a scholarship which had taken her to a famous girls' public school and given her a small, rapid, breathless, upper-class way of speaking which was at variance with everything else about her. She had nice grey eyes, wore the mini-skirt, à la mode at the time, which suited her slight figure, and she had good teeth, though they were without any tendency to my preferred 'goofiness'. This was perhaps just as well, for I found her very attractive and, incorrigible, often repined at the difference in age between fifty-four and twenty-seven. She was deaf in one ear, perhaps as a result of a blow in childhood, for, as she related in a very well-written, clearly autobiographical novel she published many years afterwards, she had had a tough, motherless childhood at the mercy of a sadistic grandmother. I could never remember which was her deaf ear, but was often near to going up to her and shouting into it: 'I love you'. But I might well have chosen the wrong (or right), good ear; and what would have happened then?

When Annabel announced that she was leaving, I would have liked to secure Jenny as my permanent secretary. But she was not available, because she had got a highly-paid job with a monstrous American-Jewish bestselling novelist whose private life was disordered to the point where he had actually been accused, falsely for all I knew, of murdering his wife. So the Utley Secretarial Agency supplied another girl, a friend of Jenny who had graduated with her in English at Keele University.

She was a pleasant girl but no substitute for Jenny; nor did she seem to know much English. I was amazed to find that she had never heard either of Mrs Gamp or Mrs Grundy; when I used the word 'quisling' in the column, she asked me what it meant. In my explanation I said it was unfair to the Norwegian leader Vidkun Quisling that his name had become a synonym for traitor, and if she did not know it there might be a chance that it would drop out of common parlance. This probably did not endear me to her; nor did my rebuke, which I could not repress, when she said she thought Brigadier ('Skipper') Thompson, the admirable and dauntless Defence Correspondent of the *Telegraph*, 'inherently funny'. My mutterings about 'making fun of them that guard you while you sleep' must have seemed Blimpish as well as incomprehensible.

She left next year and with some misgivings I gave the job to Claudie Worsthorne, who thus resumed it after an absence of nine years. Our relations were difficult at times; older and more sophisticated than Annabel, and moreover, wife of Peregrine and frequenter of 'glittering' social circles to which I had no entry, she was disinclined to take the role of secretary seriously. Her English spelling was sometimes erratic; but another reason for my frequent impatience with her was a typically base one: my resentment at her superior social arrangements, at first conducted on the telephone until my obvious annoyance – or even direct veto – caused her to spend a lot of time in neighbouring vacant rooms so as to carry them on undisturbed. I then had to answer the telephone myself, sometimes finding to my chagrin that the caller wanted to invite Claudie to a party and would be awfully grateful if I would give her the message.

There was a certain element of masochistic pleasure mingled with my rage, which when I had been drinking at lunchtime sometimes discharged itself in violent scenes in which I would curse Claudie and ineffectually try to sack her. This behaviour, as well as being noted with amusement by our neighbours along the corridor, put me firmly in the wrong. As far as Claudie herself was concerned, of course, I was always in the wrong by definition; no woman, in a disagreement with a man (or, for all I know, another woman) will ever admit she is in the wrong. When her friends asked her why she put up with my ineffectual bullying, she would say in her amusing French accent, 'Poor boy, 'e cannot 'elp it' or, more charitably, 'I stay because I enjoy watching 'is creative mind at work'. She was herself 'creative' in her own way, writing such long letters in French and English that I called her 'the last of the world's letter writers'. One day, I hope, these letters of hers will be published.

As time went on we established a *modus vivendi* and grew, I think, to like as well as hate each other, the liking on my part at least gradually supplanting the hate. There was much to like about Claudie: her liveliness; her vivid gossip which sometimes seemed extravagantly malicious but was not – it was gossip for gossip's sake, an art form; her courage – she had faced danger fearlessly both in war and peace; her gift for mimicry – she could take off other members of the staff without any pretence of phonetic accuracy but presenting, by means of their physical foibles, an amazingly accurate impression of their characters. Her imitation of myself was particularly good, even better than my own; it usually consisted of speaking inaudibly into a telephone. Enjoyable, too, were her 'Claudieisms', part genuine, part contrived, as when she said of some dupe, 'So you see, 'e 'as swallowed the 'ole trick, bell, hook and stinker'. Or did I improve on that one?

In the late Sixties I began to see more of my son Nicholas, who had taken a Ph.D. at Leeds University and was doing postgraduate work there before taking a post as lecturer in philosophy at Reading. His first marriage, to the high-born Dinah Livingstone-Learmonth, a leftist poetess, who bore him two children, Tom and Zoë, had predictably collapsed. He was now in search of a second wife, presenting me with one or two candidates who, though agreeable enough, did not seem suitable. Elated by the triumph of Jewish arms in the Six-Day War and no doubt for other reasons, he had reverted to his and my original name of Nathan and although hardly more than one-eighth Jewish by blood, declared: 'I look Jewish, so I might as well *be* Jewish,' – an argument scarcely worthy of a philosopher. I was not in favour of this, though I did not, as I was at first inclined, 'cut him off with a shilling' but became reconciled to what I thought perverse eccentricity.

When he declared he was in love with a half-Jewish girl and intended to marry her, I strongly advised him against thus reinforcing the Jewish element in his prospective offspring. I met the girl, Alex; she was delightful, attractive and intelligent as well as good-natured, a fine linguist and pianist. Alas! But not, no thanks to me, alas in the event. They married and had two sons, Max and Isaac, both amiable and highly intelligent, the younger inheriting her musical talent. What is more, they have, as far as I can judge, one of the few marriages I have ever come across which seem to be genuinely happy.

Towards the end of 1968 I was idly looking through a copy of *Country Life*, one of the publications supplied to me by the bounty of the *Telegraph*, when I suddenly came across an article, illustrated by photographs, which almost brought me out of my chair and to my feet. It was about a 'threat to the Eden Valley' and described a scheme which for sheer horror I could not have invented in a nightmare. In my time at Hoff, in Westmorland, where I had lived before the War and during the first year of it, we could see, out of our front, eastward-facing windows across the valley, a wonderful prospect: the line of the North Pennines from Merton Pike and High Cup Nick in the south to Crossfell in the north. There, below the line of the hills, an entrepreneur was now planning to construct what would today be called a 'leisure park' covering acres of beautiful country centred on the woods of Flakebridge, once part of Lord Hothfield's Appleby Castle estate, but already sold off by his eccentric heir. There was to be an hotel, a casino, a marina or glorified boating lake, nature trails, a night-club, shops and all conceivable delights for the too-many. Merton Pike itself, one of the conical outliers of the main Pennine range, was to be turned into an artificial ski-run with a chairlift. Several sheep farms would be incorporated, with large sums of money offered to the farmers in compensation.

The article said that local people and national bodies like the Council for the Preservation of Rural England (it had not yet

changed Preservation to the more defensive Protection) were
organising protests against this plan; local opinion was divided,
some councillors believing that the project 'would provide work
in an area of high unemployment' (a standard parrot-cry in
such cases); the Vicar of Appleby was said to be in favour,
perhaps believing that the project would 'inject new life into
the area' (another standard parrot-cry); Appleby shopkeepers
were also said to be in favour for reasons of their own; whilst
the Conservative MP for Westmorland, Mr Jopling, was non-
committal.

I cared nothing for all this. If I have ever dreamed of an
earthly paradise it is of the Valley of the Eden, suitably glorified,
that I have dreamed. Now the landscape I had looked at daily
through changing seasons with unchanging delight was in
danger of defilement, indeed destruction for ever. In a state of
excitement and anger I sat down to write what I felt in a 'note'
of about four hundred words and put it at the head of next
day's column. Within a week I had a strange, rambling letter,
written in a firm, spiky hand on yellow lined foolscap paper,
from a Mrs Ruth Rose who lived at Keisley House, in the very
middle of the projected outrage. She told me how glad she and
her husband, Major Rose, would be of any help in repelling it;
she also invited me to stay at Keisley, adding, by a sure instinct,
that they could not only offer me home-brewed ale but that
there were half a dozen bottles of whisky, collected by a grateful
public, awaiting me, stored in a grandfather clock.

Who could resist such an invitation? I accepted, but before
I could make any further move, Ruth Rose herself appeared in
London, on a mission to gather support from anybody she could
think of. One evening, waiting for me in the 'Lodge', was a
woman in her forties with wiry black hair and a lined, humorous
face which had once been very good-looking and was still

attractive. She was eccentrically dressed in makeshift clothes, the most remarkable part of which was an army-issue khaki pullover. She had an individual way of laughing, deep, loud but melodious. She was one of those beings who are completely themselves, without selfconsciousness, and always the same whatever class of people they are talking to. We became friends and allies at once, and would have done so, I think, even if we had not had in common the urgent cause of repelling this attack on my paradise and her home.

We went into the pub and drank a great deal of Guinness as we discussed what might be done and what influential people (she seemed to think I was one) might be enlisted in support. She told me that her husband, Jimmy Rose, had just retired from the army, that she herself was an army wife who had lived with him in many postings in the distant lands of our receding Empire – Borneo, Malaya, Burma and lastly Arabia, where he had fought in Aden and the Yemen. They had returned to Keisley, the only home they had, only a few months before. It had originally been a shooting-lodge and then a place to stay in the holidays, belonging to her father, Dr Boddy, a well-to-do physician in Middlesbrough. It was a wonderful place, she said, apart from being their home. It must be saved. I fervently agreed. She was staying that night with friends somewhere in south London and returning to the North next day. She was in an even more frenetic state than usual, she explained, because her car had just been run into from behind by a madman. But she would give me a lift wherever I wanted to go.

I could not see any evidence of damage to her car, a solid old Jaguar, the only sort of car I could imagine this delightfully forthright, vigorous and eccentric woman driving. We had a confused and hilarious meal at an Indian restaurant in Putney; I noticed that although she drank a good deal she ate hardly anything, explaining this by the fact that her false teeth did not fit. She demonstrated this. We parted after I had promised to pay a visit to Keisley 'for a top-level conference' the very next weekend. I could get a train from King's Cross. She would meet it in her car at Darlington.

I thought about the Valley of the Eden, and about this remarkable woman who lived in it, a good deal during the next week. In the Kings and Keys one evening I ran into John Chisholm, the *Telegraph*'s architectural correspondent, and told him about the threat to Keisley, with some vague idea that he might be able to help. This was only about the second time I had met this man who was to become a close friend. He was from Lancashire, Wigan-born, and spoke with the attractive accent of the area. He was a strongly-built man with a pale though healthy-looking face and the general appearance of a Baltic stevedore.

He tended to wear bright blue shirts, drawing mechanical shouts of 'Poofter!' from Weston. I soon found, on closer acquaintance, that although he claimed never to have read a book he was both intelligent and witty and that his cast of mind was not unlike my own. He was intensely musical. He was married, though uneasily, to a formidable half-Jewess from Manchester, Judith, and lived in Hampstead. When I told him about the trouble which was agitating me he undertook to do what he could to help. I arranged for him to come to Keisley; he could not come with me in the first place, he said, but promised to get there as soon as he could manage later in the weekend.

So on a dark night at the beginning of December, I found Ruth waiting for me at Darlington station with what seemed a perfectly intact Jaguar, though the story of how it had been damaged tended to recur, part of a whole saga of inter-twining stories, mainly drawn from army life, which if related by anybody else would have been boring. But I did not find this saga boring when it came from Ruth, at least not then; I was caught in a spell in which my old love for the numinous countryside of Westmorland, now powerfully revived, and my love for this curious woman seemed to be combined. She drove fast and expertly westward through Barnard Castle, where we stopped for a while by mutual consent to drink Guinness, and her loud, melodious laugh astounded the regulars in the bar; then by the Roman road across wild Stainmore into the Eden Valley. It was typical of her that nearing Keisley she took a wrong turning, leading us to open moorland where the road turned to a stony track. When we reached Keisley we had long been expected.

A flagged path leading to a strong square whitewashed house overshadowed by sycamore trees whose branches dripped big droplets on our heads; tall lighted windows with frames painted, in the Westmorland fashion, dark green; dogs barking at the door; and a great noise of people within. Major Rose, Jimmy as everyone called him, came to meet us and led us into a big, long room with log fires burning at each end. Bookcases crammed with books covered two walls up to the ceiling; Persian rugs and other trophies hung on other walls; there were sofas, armchairs, and camel saddles covered with sheepskins which served as footstools. The Major was a big, strongly-built man of about fifty, with a military moustache and a military bearing; he stood among his guests like some ancient chieftain in his hall, laughing, talking, dispensing hospitality.

The guests were of all kinds and conditions: one or two sheep-farmers and their wives and sons from neighbouring farms; another retired soldier, Brigadier Heelis from Milburn, one of a string of villages under the Pennines; Dr de Latt, the doctor from Appleby; Mr Bunney, the architect from Kendal, who lived at Hwith, near Ravenstonedale, not far from Uldale, the farm where my dead elder brother had presided over his strange ménage. And all these people, in their different ways, were determined to repel the invasion by a citified fun-fair of what still remained in those days an entirely rural place, with rural thoughts and rural ways of living. I had a sense of glory and privilege because such people as these thought me a person with enough influence to help them.

The Major put an extremely large glass of whisky into my hand. 'Hope you'll stay with us as long as you like,' he said in a deep voice without accent. 'I can offer you some rough shooting. No fishing at present. A bit of rabbiting with ferrets with Tom Dargue here – hey Tom?' he gestured at a man, about his own age, with an oaken squareness and strength. I demurred feebly, explaining quite truly that as I got older I got less and less inclined to kill creatures of any kind. Not surprisingly, he looked a bit disappointed at this. 'You'll be a strange sort of guest,' he said, and for a moment I was afraid I had got myself, as with the Rhodesians and the hangers and floggers, into a misunderstanding.

But I need not have worried; we became great friends, all the more so, perhaps, for having little in common except a fondness for drinking and card-playing, a love of the country and of history and a humorous, curious turn of mind. Isn't that enough for any friendship? Beneath his military exterior and bluff manners, Jimmy had a lively, imaginative, unconventional nature. He was also, as I found, a man of infinite generosity and patience. I came in time not only to love and admire him but almost to revere him.

Some of the guests began to leave. But there must have been a dozen at the long table in the dining-room next door. Jimmy himself, who was an accomplished cook, had prepared a huge and magnificent curry. Everything in this house seemed to be on an heroic scale – the host, the guests, the food and drink, the good old Westmorland voices talking of sheep, country pursuits, neighbours' disputes, the vileness of councillors and all officials. Within was the chieftain's mead-hall; outside the lighted house a thick, starless, soundless night.

The guests had all left and my host, after giving us both several more drinks, went off to bed, taking with him his two big yellow labrador dogs, Leo, the noble-looking male, and Ready, the softer bitch (short for Ready About, a name acquired on some aquatic adventure). Ruth declared she was going to have one last drink, and so was I. So there we sat into the small hours by the log fire, this woman of extraordinary energy telling me her life history: how she had been coming to this house ever since she was a child, and had come to love it more than any other place on earth; how her three brothers had all been killed in the War, flying in the RAF; how her mad, boring sister had married a man who was a bore but not even mad; how she had taken a degree in biology at St Andrew's; how she had been a despatch-rider in the Blitz and later joined the Wrens; how she had married Jimmy, probably the only man in the British Army who had been, in the course of his career, both a sergeant-major and a major; how he had fought in the North African Desert, been captured by the Germans and escaped; how he had served in the Far East, where, when it was possible, she had served with him; how she had taught English to Malayans and later to Arabs in Aden; how she had lost her baby at five months and was now childless; how they had come back to Keisley to live, and how it was now threatened.

At four o'clock I staggered to bed and woke the next morning to find that the Major, this man of iron, was planning to drive up the track beside the ravine of High Cup Nick in his Land

Rover, with a neighbour, a former comrade in the army with the strange name of Derek Import. For what purpose I never discovered. Would I like to come? I was exhausted and had a considerable hangover. But after my failure with the country sports I felt I had to accept his suggestion as a chance of rehabilitating myself. Was it a test of my character? I never discovered, though I suspect it may have been. In the event I passed, though only just. After driving in the Land Rover up the stony, deeply trenched, pot-holed and in places almost vertical track, wrenched this way and that, we got out and began to walk, well above the cloud-line, across the moor towards the upper end of the famous geological prodigy, High Cup Nick.

As I did my best not to fall behind in my heavy black Crombie overcoat, Jimmy, who during the summer months, I learned, worked as a warden of a nature reserve at Ravenglass on the coast of Cumberland, pointed out a buzzard, a peregrine falcon and other notable birds. I asked if there were any dotterel, rare birds I had introduced as comic creatures in parodic nature notes in my column. He gave me a keen look and said there was a nest of dotterel at the top of Crossfell and he would be delighted to take me there. As Crossfell, the highest hill in the Pennines, was about ten miles away and at least a thousand feet higher than our present position, I declined.

Back at Keisley, we found Ruth busy organising the Resistance, as I was beginning to think of it. She had got over Mr Howard of Greystoke, an important landowner in Cumberland, to discuss matters; since he had had to cope single-handedly with, and repel, a similar project led by the same entrepreneur not long before, though on a smaller scale, he was most sympathetic and helpful. So, in their different way, were the local farmers we canvassed later that day. Many of them could expect large sums in return for the use of their land; some, whose land would be bought if the scheme went through, could expect to become rich, enabling them to retire and live in Morecambe for the rest of their lives (these were the days when the newly affluent were not yet buying properties on the Costa del Sol). Their angry rejection of these prospects was heartening to hear. So was the reaction of some of the younger farmers who gathered at Keisley in the evening.

It was the time when Welsh Nationalists were blowing up pipelines as a protest against 'England's theft of Welsh water'. These young Westmorland men spoke, not altogether jokingly, of blowing up the fun-fair installations if they ever got built. 'If t'Welsh can do it, we can do it – and better,' said one. My own pleasure at this remark warned me against giving way to fantasy. I would have to be entirely serious about this campaign if I were to help. And yet both Welsh Nationalists and Westmorland farmers were in rebellion equally against the 'modern world' and the newly-emerging attitudes which measured everything in terms of money, the quantifying cost accountancy which both political parties stood for. Labour Ministers were already telling small farmers like these that they were fools to work their guts out as their forebears had done when they could make more money and have an easier life by 'diversifying' into the bed-and-breakfast trade and selling ice-cream and souvenirs to tourists.

Later on Conservative Ministers were to tell them the same thing more persuasively and seductively, and with greater success. It is not easy for a poor man to stand against the times. Twenty years later the odds against the small farmers and their 'way of life' – a term which had become disgusting because it was favoured and constantly used by the very people who were doing their best to destroy it: the executives of the hideous 'tourist industry' – were to become overwhelming. Yet these small farmers, in so far as they still survive, are almost the last truly independent-minded people remaining in this country. What sort of a country will England be when there are no such people left in it? It was reflections like these, as well as my desire to preserve a place I loved and stop this beautiful part of England from being changed into something other and worse, which drove me to devote so much time and energy to this campaign.

All that afternoon Keisley was at cloud level and it was impossible to see more than a hundred yards or so from the front windows which looked across the valley. But towards nightfall the cloud lifted and I could see beyond Appleby and Hoff to the hills which concealed the small tributaries of the Eden – Lyvennet, Leven and Lowther – to the Lake District hills in the west and in the south the Howgill Fells and Wild Boar Fell where I had wandered idly and usually alone during my vacations at Uldale. I was looking out from the place I had looked at daily during my life with my first wife and child in our cottage at Hoff before the War. This was a strange sensation, as if the self of today stared at the self of thirty years before, and that lost self stared back.

Next day we were to meet John Chisholm off the London train at Oxenholme Junction, on the Kendal road from Appleby. But first I was to go to Appleby Castle at the invitation of the present proprietor, who was a reader of the *Telegraph* and, Ruth implausibly maintained, an admirer of my column. I had always wanted to visit the Castle, indeed I had always had the ambition of owning it. It was a real castle, with its main gate at the top of Boroughgate, the main street of Appleby, balancing, in a paradigm of Church and State, the parish church of St Lawrence at the bottom. In my time at Hoff, Lord Hothfield had lived there with his estates still intact, including the now endangered pheasant-woods at Flakebridge; he was a figure of legend:

tall, stately and as well as being lord of the castle, he was the perpetual Mayor of Appleby itself, towering, as was only right, over the puny councillors at the mayoral procession during the annual assizes. Now many of these councillors were in favour of the Flakebridge Horror; Lord Hothfield was dead and his eccentric son had sold the estate and, it was said, converted to Islam, and perhaps worse, worked as a casual labourer.

The present proprietor was a Mr Coney (it was odd how these rabbit names kept cropping up – there was Mr Bunney the architect, and two of the local farmers were called Warren and Burrows). He was a large, affable man, with a leg in plaster from having lately fallen down the stairs; he had made a lot of money from the West African trade and had been captain of Southport Golf Club, a distinction which did not impress me as much as it evidently should have done. Placing in my hand a very large gin-and-tonic which he took from a trolley that a white-gloved servant had wheeled into the enormous drawing-room, he himself took one of the same dimensions and showed me round his tapestried halls, bidding me look out of the windows at the swimming-pool he had lately installed in the courtyard and then, turning to the interior, at the elaborate new electric lift which brought up food from the vast underground kitchens to the vast mahogany and crystal-infested dining-room. He led the way back to the drawing-room, handing me another even larger gin-and-tonic and taking one himself.

This fulfilment of my old dream was not turning out quite as I had expected. Perhaps sensing my slight disappointment, he asked if I would like to have a look at the tower, the old Norman keep, by far the oldest remaining part of the house. He handed me a huge, ancient iron key and another large gin-and-tonic, not forgetting to take one himself. With difficulty I unlocked the door of the tower, which stood at some distance

203

from the eighteenth-century range where we had been, and, balancing my drink as best I could, made the perilous ascent of the dilapidated staircase, emerging at the top to look out over broken battlements towards the little ancient town in whose pubs I had sat drinking beer so many years before, playing dominoes with anonymous men or meditating alone on time and chance.

In my altered circumstances I meditated on them again, and with good reason, before making the even more perilous descent. The large gin-and-tonic Mr Coney handed me in exchange for the key and my empty glass was just what I needed. Ruth, who had been about some business in the town, was already chatting away to him in her enviably easy way and was also holding a large gin and tonic. I had the impression that both she and Mr Coney had had at least one of these each while I was up the tower.

Taking leave of Mr Coney, whose hand was already moving towards the trolley, we drove out of Appleby on the road I knew so well, past the New Inn at Hoff, scene of so many pleasant evenings thirty years before (it would have been foolish to stop there, even though it did not seem greatly altered from those days); past the end of the lane which led to our old cottage, still rough, stony and apparently unchanged (I resisted another foolish impulse) and through the woods to the limestone-flagged uplands already beginning to be plundered for the rockeries of Surrey. Ruth had an alarming way of driving rather too fast in the middle of the road, talking incessantly and sometimes with only one hand, or none, on the wheel. When I asked her why she did this she said it was because it was easier to see traffic coming in the opposite direction if you drove in the middle of the road.

We reached Oxenholme Junction a few minutes before John

Chisholm's train was due. So we had more drinks in the neighbouring pub, emerging to find the train had already come and
gone. We peered this way and that and eventually saw his blue-
shirted figure, wearing a formal suit and carrying an architect's
portfolio, walking in the wrong direction and looking remarkably
out of place in the grey Westmorland village street. He and Ruth
immediately got on well. Although the pub was just closing, she
persuaded the bewildered landlord to give us more drinks by
saying we were two VIPs who had just got off the train from
London.

We were to call on Mr Bunney the architect at his house
which he had built himself, Hwith, in wild country near Ravenstonedale. It was difficult to find, and my whistled inquiries for
Hwith had Ruth in fits of laughter. We were still laughing,
since I for one was decidedly drunk, when we found the quiet,
serious Mr Bunney in his house and persuaded him to write a
statement for the public enquiry. He was just as angry about
the Flakebridge project as we were (he was very active in what
would now be called conservation and as a Friend of the Lake
District) and took very little persuading; I borrowed his type-
writer and typed his statement on the spot. He also said he
would write a letter to *The Times*.

It was dark when we reached Keisley. Brigadier Heelis had
arrived with others for drinks in this house of plenty. John, who
had an instinct for outrage, caused a sensation by saying he was
a pacifist and had been a conscientious objector during the
period of National Service. Jimmy playfully threatened to expel
him from the house. The Brigadier put him on several charges:
(1) being improperly dressed; (2) speaking to Ruth with a cigarette in his mouth; (3) dumb insolence; (4) ordinary insolence.
To my embarrassment, Ruth said I had held the rank of
lieutenant-colonel during the War. I admitted this, but

205

explained to the Brigadier that I had not been a 'proper lieutenant-colonel', but only on the General Staff. This caused a good deal of amusement, as the Brigadier himself had reached that rank only as a staff officer.

More guests arrived: Brian Doe, an Arabic scholar at Cambridge and an authority on the archaeology of South Arabia, who had served with Jimmy in Aden; Tom Dargue the man of oak and his son Edwin the shepherd, a younger version of himself; the Harker brothers and their wives, sheep-farmers from Merton, famous for their silver cup-winning Swaledale tups, and other farmers who had 'heafs', that is, grazing rights for certain numbers of sheep, on the common land where the projected ski-run would be. Another evening of serious drinking was under way. Tom Dargue offered to show John, a fairly hefty man much younger than himself, the art of wrestling, Cumberland and Westmorland style. This involves the two antagonists putting their arms round each other and staying like that for a very long time until one of them gets a minute momentary advantage in posture. But it was no more than thirty seconds before John was on the carpet. Later he challenged one of the Harker wives, a bold, good-looking blonde woman of thirty, to a fall. He was on the carpet in twenty seconds, amid wild rustic cheering. But Ruth, who had, unexpectedly, a marked puritanical streak, was also a delightful snob and easily offended by what she believed to be breaches of protocol, later rebuked him for this.

I left for London next day, leaving John, already a firm friend of the house, behind to do further work for the cause. I was in a state of great excitement; I had fallen in love with Keisley and everybody and everything in it and about it. I wrote another 'note' about this threatened paradise. When John returned that week, he made this 'threat to the environment', as it would now be called, the subject of his weekly article. A correspondence was starting about it in *The Times*, and the *Telegraph* itself printed a letter from Mr Bunney. In the Kings and Keys John and I began to converse in the accent of Westmorland – I from what I remembered of this way of talking from my previous life there, he from an astonishing facility for picking up English accents, even this unusual and rather difficult one. This private joke, for once, baffled Weston, and after a few shouts of 'Poofters!', and 'If you want to talk in that stupid Welsh accent, go somewhere else!' he gave up.

As in all such cases, the people in the Appleby neighbourhood who were in favour of the scheme argued that it was what the local people wanted and that it was opposed only by a handful of the 'selfish middle class'. Appleby was technically in a 'depressed area' of 'high unemployment'. I had seldom been in an area which seemed less depressed. It was, however, necessary to counter these misleading arguments.

Ruth suggested that Tom Dargue, Edward Harker and two or three others whose land was threatened should write a short letter to *The Times*, submitting it to me before sending it there. They duly produced one. It was movingly written but in the sort of unnatural, 'educated' style they thought suitable for such a letter. But when I had finished with it, it was in simple, direct language and really sounded like the voice of down-to-earth, honest Englishmen. I have seldom been so pleased with anything I have written as the letter from the sheep-farmers of the North Pennines which duly appeared in *The Times*. I had given them better words than their own and expressed their real thoughts as they could not express them for themselves.

I felt, in a strange way, that what I was defending in them was what I was defending in the Rhodesians – their admirable determination to stand up for what they had got against those who wanted, for whatever reason, whether profit or abstract theories of equality, to take it from them. Add to that the new friends this cause had brought me – not only Ruth and Jimmy Rose, but also John Chisholm, that talented, funny, lively yet melancholy man – and the glimpse of an enchanted life in Keisley – and it was no wonder I was lifted for a time out of my customary miasma of boredom into a euphoric state, like being in love. The *Telegraph* people, however, began to grumble about 'the Westmorland lobby' which was filling the paper; John was ticked off and told that his job was to write about architecture, not scenery or the lives of reactionary sheep farmers.

The public enquiry called by the Ministry of Works, as it then was ('the environment' had only just been invented as fancy jargon for what I preferred to call 'the Creation', and there was no Ministry yet in charge of it) was duly held in Appleby. I could not attend myself, as I was occupied with my column, and in any case could hardly have given evidence to the effect that I just wanted to stop a beautiful part of England which I was particularly fond of from being destroyed. But Ruth and several farmers and outside experts spoke against the scheme. According to John, Ruth made a particularly good impression on the inspector from the Ministry. So now all we could do was wait for the Minister's decision. We had good hopes of Greenwood, one of the more civilised Labour Ministers.

But there was some danger that the scheme would go through on the grounds that the site was not part of the Lake District National Park. Had it been, of course, there would have been no question of allowing such a development. Yet the fate of the Lake District has not been less tragic because of its favoured status. It has escaped serious disfigurement but suffered intensive planning which has not saved it from being overwhelmed with visitors and has imposed the additional blight of tasteful schemes of 'interpretative' and 'educational facilities', turning it into a 'museum of scenery'. It is no longer a place which anyone who knew it before this fate overtook it would wish to visit. But at least it has done a service to the Eden Valley by attracting hordes of people who might otherwise have turned their attention to the less spectacular scenery next door. The 'tourist industry', now supplemented by the 'heritage industry', is perpetually seeking new places to exploit. The Eden Valley is now in greater danger than ever.

During the period of waiting, John Chisholm and I made several visits to Keisley. There was an excellent train which left St Pancras at about eight o'clock in the morning and proceeded slowly through the Midlands to the North by way of Sheffield, Nottingham, Leeds and Settle to arrive at Appleby at about three o'clock in the afternoon. This meant that we could start having breakfast in the restaurant car as soon as the train left St Pancras and go on having breakfast until it merged into lunch, so that we were pleasantly drunk by the time we arrived. Or we would vary this by taking the Glasgow train from Euston, enjoying a similar session, with different scenery, until we arrived at Penrith in the afternoon, when Ruth would meet us in her still mysteriously functioning Jaguar.

These journeys were often very entertaining, offering insight into the workings of the higher échelons of British Rail. On one such journey we noticed that, as we approached Preston, the stewards were getting themselves into an unusual state of readiness, dusting down a certain table, obsessively arranging and rearranging the cutlery and side-plates and even placing a statutory vase of railway flowers on it. At Preston they welcomed aboard, with many a nod, wink and antic gesture, a cheerful, rubicund man who looked as if he had already lunched well but was not averse to having a second luncheon. Relieving him of his briefcase and furled umbrella, the head steward ushered him to his seat, unfolded his napkin, placed before him a large glass of brandy and ginger ale (or 'B.G.A.') and took his order. He got through the soup satisfactorily but when the entrée was placed before him his head fell forward onto it and he remained there, breathing heavily and producing rather beautiful fluted patterns in the mashed potatoes. 'It's the district manager,' the steward explained. 'Is he always like this?' 'Yes, sir, always. We'll have a job getting him out at Glasgow, I can tell you.'

Kate was inclined to be scornful about my infatuation with Keisley and its inhabitants. She had met Ruth on one of her visits to London but was not entertained by her tales of lost teeth and damaged Jaguars. Nor had Ruth's visit to the Kings and Keys been a great success. As she insisted on wearing her khaki pullover and other military memorabilia, Stephen Daneff maintained she was a thought-form I had projected (was there some truth in this?) while Weston, I could see, was trying hard to think of some way of insulting her. He eventually gave up in disgust and retired to the far end of the bar, from which his croaking roar could be heard for the rest of the evening. But Ruth made a good impression on the only genuine old soldier present, Mac the commissionaire, a man of great charm who habitually got so drunk that in winter he often spent the night wrapped round one of the boilers in the basement below the rolling presses.

In the spring, after Jimmy had left Keisley for his nature reserve on the Cumberland coast, I persuaded Kate to visit Keisley and bring her two children, Vicki, now aged six, and Kit, aged three. John Chisholm, his wife Judith and their two children, both boys and a bit older than Kate's, were also there. I have never stayed at Keisley without enjoying it. Kate,

however, soon decided, and said, that it was 'not her scene'.
She had come up against a woman who liked to be the centre
of attention just as much as she did, and although there were
no disagreeable episodes, we were continually on the verge of
one.

The children all slept in an improvised dormitory in a big
room over the old stable, where Vicki, who had a good deal of
her mother's leadership qualities (sometimes called 'bossiness')
soon established her domination. On the first morning she
dared Kit to release the two beautiful, fierce white ferrets which
lived in a cage under the dormitory, and only one of them was
recaptured. Some of the guinea-fowl were reported missing.
Ruth had arranged for the girls from the nearby farm along the
fellside to bring some ponies for the children to ride, but Vicki,
already a promising horsewoman, was disappointed with hers,
a mild beast with a tendency to go to sleep standing up in a
corner of the paddock, unresponsive to her wild shouts. John
did his best to help by mounting another pony and immediately
sliding off under its belly.

Ruth, who for all her unconventionality held to strict rules
of behaviour as an army wife, did not like Kate's bad language,
fairly usual among our acquaintance in London, and liked
Vicki's language, which was almost as bad, even less. As for
Kit, he was only just beginning to develop his talent for objur-
gation. After a few days at Keisley Kate cut her visit short and
left with the two children, driving stylishly away in her new
white convertible. When I got back to London, I found she had
jaundice and so was in low spirits, angry, too, that she would
be confined to the house for several weeks. It was the beginning
of the end of our curious ménage and of the 'horror comic'.

One day news came from Keisley that the Minister had
turned down the Flakebridge plan. Keisley was saved; John and

I, after an evening of inebriation in the Kings and Keys under Weston's scornful eye and with some sarcastic comment from the *Telegraph*'s features editor ('Can we really hope for the winding up of the Appleby Lobby?') went to stay at the beloved place, now liberated from the threat of destruction. We all agreed that for once we must be grateful that we had a Labour Government and a civilised minister in charge of planning. There is not much doubt that a so-called 'Conservative' Government, keen on profit, the tourist industry and thrusting, dynamic businessmen, would have been more likely to approve the plan. There is not much doubt, either, that this odious project will be put forward again, this time, perhaps, by a more dynamic and thrusting entrepreneur with more money behind him; and who can say what will happen then?

Meanwhile Keisley was saved. We could look out every day over the unsullied woods and fields rolling down to the Eden, with the lost country round Hoff beyond it, rising to the distant fells and the long line of High Street on the far side of Hawes-water. For me this is the finest panorama in England. I would not like to count up the number of hours – it would probably run into weeks – I have sat on fine days on the narrow flagged terrace in front of Keisley employed mainly in looking at this vista, either alone or with John, Ruth and other friends. I have sat there through all seasons, even with snow on the ground and muffled in my good black Crombie greatcoat, watching the changing light, the flight of birds, noting the occasional car on the lane beyond the paddock which Jimmy called 'the Keisley motorway', and sinking into a mystic trance to which the abundant drink available at all times may have contributed something but not all. If anything is imprinted on my memory, perhaps to present itself at the moment of death – or even afterwards – it must be this well-beloved scene.

In the summer, when Ruth joined Jimmy on his nature reserve for short periods, I sometimes visited them there, finding a whole new body of myth which insistently demanded to be turned into fiction. Some of it found its way by the back door into my column. I made copious notes, too, and wrote innumerable beginnings of 'the novel' I had been trying to write for most of my life, seldom reaching more than one or two thousand words before running into the sand. During the six months he worked as warden of the reserve, Jimmy lived in a well-designed caravan, large enough for us to fit into for a prolonged session of serious drinking during rainy weather. He must have been alone there for weeks on end. But he was one of those men who can cope perfectly well with solitude. As for the hardship of a cramped life with monotonous meals he cooked in a caravan which in windy weather rocked like a ship at sea, what was that for a man who had seen service in desert and jungle and, escaping from a prison camp, had killed German guards with his own hands? He had the run of the sand-dunes, with their vipers, natterjack toads and rare butterflies; he had the great flocks of migratory birds to observe and, as part of his duties, to report on for the distant bureaucracy of the National Conservation Council or some such body; and he had the wide sweep of sand by the sea-shore to walk along, from which in clear weather the Isle of Man could be seen, a seemingly enchanted island where, perhaps wisely, I have never yet set foot.

Spring at Keisley; summer; autumn; New Year, when once we were snowbound for several days – an experience which, if there is plenty of time, food and drink and good company, everyone should have at least once in a lifetime: so many sequences of days run together. At the end of August we always went to Dufton, the nearest village, for the annual Show –

jocularly known as 'the Royal Fellside' – where for several years Jimmy was, as the saying goes, a popular President. There were sheep-dog trials, groups of sheep and cattle in their pens – John and I had a plan to buy a noble Swaledale tup with curved horns and keep it in Fleet Street – and numerous tents for the vegetable and flower competitions as well as the arts of cookery ('best three ginger biscuits', 'best group of carrots') and for writing, drawing and photography. A magnificent photograph taken by John, which showed the view from Keisley through a pint glass of Jimmy's home brew, magically suffused with the golden light of autumn, was never exhibited; it would certainly have won first prize as one of the great photographs of all time.

And in this place, that broad field between the Pennines and the lower valley, there was not a single thing which was not wholly of Westmorland and England. It was the quintessence of what I wrote for, though well aware I wrote in vain. All this which had endured so long and was now for the time being reprieved, was yet condemned to death. It was some consolation to know that the megalopolitan horror which would succeed it – within a few years it was beginning to creep unmistakably in – was itself, like everything on earth, under sentence of death.

Through all those years Ruth had gradually grown more and more eccentric. Eccentric she had been when I first met her, but eccentric in a lively and attractive way. Now it was as though her hold on life began to fail. She had put all her vital force, which must have been immense when she was young, into the task of saving Keisley; now, that task accomplished, it seemed to drain away. She drank more; became repetitive in her conversation; became vague and unreliable. She had always been unpunctual; now she began to carry unpunctuality to the point of lunacy. One summer evening, when Jimmy was away on his reserve, Mr Bunney, the architect of Hwith, who had done such good work for the great campaign, invited Ruth, John and myself, as well as Major Doe the Arabist, who was also staying at Keisley, to a dinner-party at his house. Owing to several long telephone conversations, her inability to find the right clothes, some necessary preliminary drinks and various other reasons, Ruth, who was to drive us in her Jaguar, was ready to leave only at about the time we were expected to arrive. Since the journey would take about forty minutes, we were already late. We had not gone more than a few miles before we met some farmers on the road. Ruth felt she had to talk to them. She talked for about twenty minutes. A few miles further on the car ran out of petrol. So in the end we were more than two and a half hours late for Mr Bunney's dinner-party. He was not pleased.

Another time, in the winter, Ruth proposed that she drive John and myself over to Longsleddale to see the Lunesdale Hunt. She had promised to attend the meet. But what with one thing and another, it was one o'clock before we left Keisley. Our route lay near the Shap Wells Hotel, a place of which I had always been fond, partly because of its singular situation in a hollow below the Shap granite works, partly because of the oddity of finding what looked just like a railway hotel in such a remote place, and partly because during the war it had been the administrative centre of a German officers' prison camp whose Commandant had been billeted at our cottage at Hoff in the winter of 1940 while I was away doing my primary military training at Topsham Barracks, Exeter. I was unwise enough to tell Ruth all this and we had to stop there for a drink. We had several drinks; then Ruth took it into her head to ask for a glass of the mineral water which had been the reason for the attempt, which came to nothing, to establish a spa there. It was obvious that nobody had asked for this mineral water for a very long time, perhaps not within living memory. But Ruth had to have it, and after a long, rambling conversation about the history of the Spa, she got her glass of water, and plain ordinary water was what it probably was. Dusk was falling as we reached the head of Longsleddale; hounds had just killed and the hunt was over.

This sort of rambling behaviour was not to everybody's taste. Gradually Ruth's friends began to fall away. The big room at Keisley, which had made such a deep impression on me on my first visit, began to be empty of guests. And Ruth, though she talked as much as ever, seemed to be losing heart. She began to fall ill, though of no definable illness, and, more and more, to take to her bed, on which the two labrador dogs took to sleeping at all times, growing fat and heavy as she grew thin and pale. It was sad to see this woman, once so full of life and energy, take on the rôle of confirmed valetudinarian. When we took her food on a tray, she did not eat it, but left it for the dogs, who thus grew fatter than ever. She had the doctor from Appleby to see her. He prescribed some treatment, but Ruth, convinced it was the wrong treatment, told him and others that he did not know his business. Thus she lost another friend and, when she absurdly threatened to report him to the General Medical Council, gained an enemy. She sought more doctors, only to discard them. After a time, it seemed that all the doctors between Penrith and Kirkby Stephen had become characters in this valetudinarian saga. Ruth was able to see the humour in this, but that did not help her to bring it to a conclusion. She had lost the will to live, and there seemed to be nothing we could do to help her.

The neighbouring farmer's young wife, a perfect woman of a breed almost extinct, looked after Ruth's immediate needs.

But when Jimmy came over from his work on the reserve all the responsibility fell to him. Never had this great-hearted man seemed more admirable than now, when as well as running the day-to-day affairs of the house and maintaining good relations with his neighbours he became both cook and nurse to a wife whose slow, inexorable decline must have filled him with sorrow and gloom and sometimes with impatience. But I never heard him utter a single word of complaint. 'She's all I've got!' he would say ruefully, as he sawed logs, or carried coals or cooked one of his magnificent curries or took up books she asked for to her bedroom. I do not think she read many of them, not even Burton's *Anatomy of Melancholy*, which she asked me to get her. Sometimes, when I was there, she would come downstairs for a while and drink a terrible concoction of brandy and Cyprus sherry which must have gone ill with the multifarious pills she was taking on the prescriptions of several different doctors.

The coal-black hair she had inherited from her Welsh ancestors, including the genius and false bard Iolo Morgannwg (she hated the Welsh anyhow) turned grey; her cheeks hollowed and the bones of her finely-structured skull protruded. Death was unmistakably hovering. She suffered, Jimmy told me, a slight stroke which confined her permanently to bed. And then, one morning in December, twelve years almost to the day after my first visit to Keisley, I was in my room at the office when the telephone rang and Claudie answered it. I lifted my own telephone at once and knew from Jimmy's broken voice that it was over. Claudie looked at me enquiringly. She had often shown curiosity about my eccentric woman caller with the distinctive laugh. 'You won't be getting calls from Ruth Rose any more,' I said.

7
Blank Misgivings

It was time for me to leave Putney – or Chartfield, as we called our establishment, giving it, as part of that 'infamous war on reality' in which both Kate and I were such strenuous warriors, the status of a country estate, with all the longed-for splendours that went with it – the cedared lawns, terraces, walled gardens, avenues, lakes, a noble park and a home farm, with a staff of dozens of servants to run it from Venables the butler and Mrs Brewer the housekeeper – this one borrowed from Kate's own mythologised childhood home at Mountbeacon, near Bath – to the humblest groom or gardener's boy. I had a place to go to, a small flat high up in Prince of Wales Mansions, in Prince of Wales Drive in Battersea. There was no make-believe about this flat, though it overlooked Battersea Park which, from the front window, I could imagine was my own property. Prince of Wales Drive is one of those London streets, like certain streets in Chelsea, Oakley Street or Redcliffe Gardens, of which it is said that everybody has lived there at one period of his life and some people twice, 'once on the way up and once on the way down'.

It had taken me something like twelve years to prise myself away from Putney, and the actual leaving, which took place in September 1971, was not easy. Jane had left school and was studying at Bristol University, living at Bristol for part of her vacations and otherwise doing odd jobs. One of these summer jobs involved looking after an amazing collection of delinquent children from Glasgow at a gloomy, mock-Gothic Victorian castle in Galloway. It was managed by a strange tartan-clad dwarf and his tall wife, figures who were later to appear quite often in my dreams. Invited to visit them with Jane when I was in the neighbourhood, I suffered an affliction to which I am occasionally prone – uncertainty about my own identity and inability to think of anything to say or, when addressed, to answer. This may have been one among many of the painful experiences which later led Jane towards the study and practice of psycho-analysis.

I had nothing, in principle, to detain me in Putney except old habits, habitual inanition, a settled belief that any change must be for the worse, a residual attachment to Kate and a fondness for her children, particularly Vicki, who was now nine years old, a remarkably lively and attractive child, with a mind open to wonders of every kind, from the naming of the stars to the observation of butterflies: these were particularly plentiful that fine late summer, when I carefully released a magnificent peacock trapped in the nursery window. Vicki had the intense love of animals which a child of her age should have; she kept white rats in the cellar, to Kate's alarm, and once nursed a pigeon with a broken wing down there among the waste paper and bottles, releasing it when healed to almost certain death from a prowling cat or the wheels of some heedless motorist. But she had the right instinct not to grieve too much.

I had bought the essential furniture and household necessities for the flat. But it was a melancholy place in which to be alone, which out of necessity I often was, in the period before I could get a divorce and a dispensation from the Catholic Church to marry. The procedure for securing this was curious in the extreme. Since Kate was a Catholic by birth, however lapsed, the Church regarded my marriage to her as null and void because of my first marriage, dissolved in 1945; it was only this marriage that the Church was concerned with. To make *that* null and void it was necessary to show that it had not been a marriage at all, and since there was a child of the union, my son Nicholas, this could only be on the grounds that I had not been in a state of mind at the time which made me capable of marrying. In other words, I had to have been so irresponsible as to be barmy. I needed two witnesses who had known me at the time, as well as my first wife, to prove this to the satisfaction of the Church. I chose Con FitzGibbon, now living in Ireland, and Eithne Kaiser, formerly Wilkins, who with her husband Ernst had returned to England from Rome and was lecturing in German Literature at Reading University. On their arrival in England they had not unnaturally asked for the return of their borrowed furniture. This set off a truly comical set-piece explosion of moral indignation in Kate and a new source of masochistic feeling in me: I had to give back my desk to them. So all were satisfied.

Con and Eithne composed moving statements testifying to my disturbed state of mind in the late Thirties, and in due course, after I had been interviewed by several priests, the Church, on the authority of the Vatican itself, declared my first marriage dissolved, leaving me free to marry, if I wished, in a Catholic church. Surprised at this outcome, I asked the priest who had been dealing with the case, a pale, ill-looking man attached to Westminster Cathedral, whether all non-Catholic marriages like my own first marriage, where neither party had been a Catholic, were regarded as valid by the Church, and therefore a bar to any subsequent marriage. Yes, he said, they were. I could not resist asking what happened, say, if a Muslim who had divorced four wives wished to marry a Catholic girl. Did only his senior wife count? And would a Nazi pagan marriage, solemnised by the mingling of blood and leaping through a bale-fire, be regarded as legitimate? Wisely, he merely smiled a wan smile.

I had found a number of new friends in Fleet Street, notably the journalist and writer Dick West, a man of admirably reactionary opinions who liked to lead a wandering life in dangerous places like Vietnam and Central America; Christine Verity, a very amusing and intelligent blonde Yorkshire girl who because she had a Cambridge degree in Law was regarded with some awe by the ordinary run of semi-literate journalists; and Celia Haddon, a journalist, animal-lover and perfect woman who later married the fortunate Ronnie Payne; I spent a lot of weekends with these new friends and others at Ron Hall's electronic house in Hampstead, which I had named 'Klingsor's Magic Garden' because it had glass doors at the back, operated by a switch in a central keyboard and opening to reveal, beyond a terrace so narrow as to be two-dimensional, a mysterious, illusionary wilderness.

But Ron had no other resemblance to Klingsor. With his wife Ruth, a fine harpsichord-player who was also good at my own favourite Yorkshire charades ('She should never have had that clock, Edie' – 'No, and if you'd been half a man you'd have seen I had my rights' – 'He was hardly cold in his grave when Alice was in there, picking up whatever she could get', etc, etc), he gave a famous New Year Party every year at which all or most were welcome. So much so that even after Ruth had died untimely and he ceased to give the party, little groups of people used to turn up at his house on New Year's Eve and, finding no party, hang about incredulously. Perhaps they still do.

Apart from such diversions I led a life of routine boredom while in London, taking a masochistic pleasure in keeping to a strict timetable which favoured efficient work at the *Telegraph*

office. Roused by my alarm-clock at 7.30 a.m., I sprang out of
bed immediately, groaned a few times, took a bath and, defer-
ring shaving, prepared an unvarying breakfast of fresh orange
juice, cereal including bran, bacon and egg, toast and tea. I
then shaved and dressed, walked down six flights of stairs to
the street and then two hundred yards to the No. 137 bus stop
in Queenstown Road; on this bus, often delayed, I travelled to
Sloane Square, where I bought a copy of the *Telegraph* and took
a No. 11 bus to Fleet Street, where I arrived by 11 o'clock. I
found these very slow bus journeys conducive to composition,
and on a good day would have large parts of the day's column
already written round the edges of the paper even before I got
to the office. The grotesque quarrels between passengers and
conductor that often occurred during these journeys sometimes
provided the germ of a 'note', as well as more writing time
when, as might easily happen, they brought the bus to an
indefinite standstill.

By half past two I would usually have almost all the column
ready for Claudie's typing. I would then go to the Kings and
Keys and drink two large brandies and ginger ale with my
luncheon, invariably one thick corned beef sandwich without
mustard. I seldom spoke to anybody during this performance,
though various journalists, mostly very boring ones, occasionally
came and stood beside me, talking of whatever interested them
without seeming to require me to take much notice. Kate,
perpetually active in her freelance work, occasionally dropped
in, and we had more drinks in a friendly spirit, talking of old
times and random fancies; sometimes we went on drinking at
a neighbouring restaurant which Kate, in her enterprising way,
seemed to have taken over so completely that some people
believed she owned it. On these occasions I was apt to get back

perilously late to the office. Claudie, who was highly intuitive, invariably guessed or rather knew the reason.

If I was not otherwise occupied in the evening I returned to Battersea by a different combination of buses, such as a No. 9 to Hyde Park Corner, then a No. 137 the rest of the way.

Sometimes, on my way home I would call at the launderette in Pimlico Road to collect the laundry I had left that morning. Here, as often as not, I found one or two odd socks missing. Then the kindly manageress would bring out the Great Bag of Socks, a collection, continually augmented, of all the odd socks which had turned up in the machines since time immemorial. Great was our satisfaction, even triumph, when we found a sock to match a bereft companion in my own day's wash. I grew quite fond of this homely ritual (another subject for Spitzweg). Once, when I called just as the shop was closing, I found the manageress playing Snap with her two small children, and was glad to take a hand. This might have been the start of an unusual friendship. It was my loss that it was not.

Back in the flat I scared away, in vain, the pigeons which infested the back balcony with their disgusting detritus. I took nothing more to drink except iced lime juice and water and set about preparing my evening meal. This invariably consisted of grilled fish fingers, normally five, mashed potatoes and frozen peas, followed by an apple. I ate rapidly, usually listening to music on my transistor or occasionally to science programmes edited by John Maddox, a friend of the Worsthornes, which because of their smug certitude I often found unintentionally amusing. I then washed up, read and went to bed by 11.30, sometimes reading in bed until the small hours without any noticeable effect on my ability to get up next morning and resume this almost unvarying routine.

If I have described this routine in what may seem insanely

boring detail it is in order to present the background to a state of melancholia which gradually came over me. It would be surprising if it had not. This mere sadness was not like my former 'breakdown'; there was little terror in it, or if there was it could be dispelled by the 'Tibetan' methods of deep breathing I had half-unwittingly learnt. There was no morning when I woke to find I could not go on. There was a dead feeling, just bearable and usually relieved by the company of friends. Yet I could not allow it to persist. I went to see my former deliverer, Desmond O'Neill, with whom I had lost touch. He had sold his house in St John's Wood, to one of the Beatles, I believe, and now lived and had his consulting room in a large house on the edge of Regent's Park which belonged to the uncle of his patient or ward, whom he had married. I found him sadly changed. He had himself suffered a severe 'breakdown' and was, I judged, on a 'régime' of drugs which meant that he was in a far worse state than I was. How bad it was I did not then realise. The man who had saved me from Dr Silver and his minions in dismal Halliwick and set me on the road, if not to full recovery, at least to a hopeful and sometimes reasonably contented life – this noble, talented and friendly man could not save himself. A few years after our last meeting he fell into such despair that he took his own life by hanging. How great must have been the self-hatred and anger in him that he, a doctor with recourse to so many ways of suicide, should have chosen this most brutal way! Peace to his memory; of him I can most sincerely say: Requiescat in Pace.

Though nobody could take his place, I found another admirable doctor, recommended by Claudie, who was not unacquainted with 'nerves' herself and therefore sympathetic to occasional 'queer turns' and other manifestations. Dr Raymond Rowntree, a tall, grave, yet humorous man whose consulting rooms were in Knightsbridge, knew himself, I think, what it is to peer into the Void, a necessary qualification for any doctor of mine. He prescribed various kinds of treatment which kept me going. But what really saved me, oddly, was a physical illness. Here I proved for the second time in my life the truth of Groddeck's theories. Georg Groddeck was a German psychiatrist who maintained mental pains could take physical form in some malady affecting an appropriate organ or part of the body – a thing universally acknowledged, of course, in common parlance. Thus 'pain in the neck' or fibrositis, indicated that the sufferer is carrying a burden of worry and indecision. In my first experience twenty years before, the symptoms of fibrositis had vanished immediately when I decided, after long hesitation, to marry Kate. Now, after I had divorced her and before my new marriage, a manner of life which I 'could not swallow' expressed itself in the form of a pharyngeal sac, brilliantly diagnosed on the spot by Dr Rowntree when I consulted him about an apparent swelling in the throat, assuming I had cancer.

This sac was a small pocket which had developed in the pharynx, causing food to lodge in it, with feelings of nausea and loss of appetite. An operation was indicated for this disgusting condition. Dr Rowntree sent me to Mr (later Sir) Douglas Ranger, a hearty, ebullient, confidence-inspiring New Zealander regarded as the best otorhinolaryngological surgeon in England. After he had explained matters, I asked him what would happen if I did not have the operation, a complicated one which had become feasible only quite recently with the general advance of surgery. 'Well,' he said in his reassuringly loud and cheerful voice, 'you could always stand on your head after meals and try to bring the stuff up – I mean down – that way'. Shortly afterwards, on this endearing man's advice, I entered King Edward VII's Hospital for Officers, a splendid establishment where, since I had reached the rank of lieutenant-colonel in the War, I automatically got a private room.

In any case this was a hospital where, by definition, only patients who were at least honorary members of the middle class were admitted. This was such blatant class discrimination that I occasionally wondered why the hospital had not been suppressed by egalitarian fanatics: as I went through the various stages of the operation from the bliss of the pre-operation shot in the buttocks to waking with a tube up my nose, another attached to the incision in my neck and another attached to my wrist for an intravenous drip – I am told I looked like a witch-doctor – I was thankful it had not. I was in the hospital for a fortnight and, once I had got over the pain in my throat enjoyed my stay there so much that I was rather sorry to leave, acquiring a dangerous taste for hospital life, or at any rate life in this particular hospital. I even liked the process ('nil per mouth') of being fed through the nose by the tube, which, ordinarily taped to my forehead, would be hooked behind my ear for a feed of soup. I asked a doctor if it would be possible to send whisky down; he said it would, but there were more efficient ways of inducing euphoria.

This operation, which as Mr Ranger told me in his amusing way, was 'tricky' and, as it involved by-passing all the main life passages of the body, carried some risk of death, did me a lot of good. So did my long-delayed marriage to my companion of ten years. We were married in the Catholic church in Cirencester and spent our honeymoon in the Budock Vean Hotel, near the Helford River in Cornwall. There was a most auspicious conjunction of Jupiter and Venus at the time; it was also the time of the much publicised predicted arrival of the Comet Kohoutek. But this, as we scanned the skies in vain, was a sad disappointment. And the year was not altogether happy.

Time had caught up with my mother at last. She had stayed in her cottage at Amswick until she was in her nineties, still evasive about her exact age and sometimes saying 'It's not right' or 'I don't *feel* old' and reminiscing as she had always done about the splendours of her early married life, which became more extravagant as her memory grew more confused. My elder sister Kathleen – who had come back to England from Rhodesia in the sixties after her divorce, to live in a cottage in a neighbouring village bequeathed by her mother-in-law (the formidable Alsatian dog-breeder) – did what she could to attend to our mother's needs but was apt to grow impatient at reminiscences of the mythical past. She had always preferred the company of her mother-in-law, whose passion for dogs she shared. As she got older herself she could no longer cope with Alsatians; so, by an interesting exchange of large and fierce for small and whimsical, took to breeding Pekingese instead.

The obvious solution to my mother's problems would have been for her to share her daughter's cottage. But this she steadfastly refused to do, clinging fiercely to an independence which she was less and less able to support. Her cottage grew ever more ramshackle and neglected; her remaining treasures went undusted; in heavy rain the spring in the hillside opened and flooded her back kitchen, swirling round the antique mangle and the mouldering flower-pots. My sister and I made some improvements and would probably have made more, but my mother, who had always had some of my own ingrained resistance to change, was obstinate, set in her ways and obstructive to all suggestions. 'It'll see my time out', she would say, and there she was right. A time came when for her own safety she could stay in the cottage no longer. So the heart-rending business of moving her began, at first to her daughter's cottage and then, after a little while, when that did not suit either of them, to an old people's home not far away.

It had been the mansion, built in mid-Victorian times, of a West Riding magnate: a big, solid, square-built house of stone set in a fine park where cattle grazed by an ornamental lake. From the terrace there was a pleasant view of woods and beyond them a group of small, conical hills, outliers of the Pennines. It would have looked, to a casual eye, like an ideal place in which to end one's days. But my mother, though she often said she was ready and even anxious to end her days, was really no more willing to do so than most if not all of humankind. She hated this place, asked repeatedly when she could go home and once, setting out to make her way there, for she remained surprisingly active, was apprehended at the lodge gates and led back uncomprehending to the only home she had.

Extreme old age seemed to come on her all at once, as though to make up for being so long delayed. Soon she was confined to bed, no longer able, even had she wished, to sit amongst the dismal group in the big, comfortably-furnished common room before the ever flickering but scarcely heeded television set. True to her old ways and lingering delusions, she shunned her fellow inmates, sometimes with a ferocious rudeness that used up some of what little energy remained. Did she repeat her old sayings: 'I can't abide waste in any shape or form' or 'I've got a rooted objection' to this, that and the other? In this way she may have puzzled and irritated those who looked after her. How could they know or care about whatever life she had lived or its strange vicissitudes before she came to this final place?

To be three-quarters deaf, with failing sight, disfigured by baldness and the growth of facial hair: this was the end of this being who had borne me and given me far more love than I ever gave her. I was at her bedside on a summer evening just before she died, to hold her small, arthritic hand and to observe, as I looked intently at her face in an effort to communicate – what? – a single tear start from her fast-blurring eye.

Soon we had a new editor at the *Telegraph*. He was William Deedes (later, as a life peer, Lord Deedes), a man of the same age as myself, but with little else in common. He was an affable, humorous man, always known as 'Bill', rightly popular with everybody and in some ways a contrast to Maurice Green, the outgoing editor. Green had been cautious in his columnar policy, inclined to worry about 'pressure groups' such as the 'family-planning' industry, whose financial and propaganda machinations I had been concerned to expose in several 'notes' under the general heading 'That Hideous Strength'. But in spite of his worries he never succeeded in inducing me to apologise to these repulsive people or to go further in placating them than allowing that some of them genuinely believed they were doing good in propagating 'the contraceptive mentality'. I believe this is one of the worst contemporary evils, substituting the techniques of the laboratory for the honest congress of the sexes. The most brutish copulation is preferable to the technology of Eros. Where Green had been cautious, Deedes was easy-going, even indulgent to my vagaries; indeed I sometimes thought he was inclined to pass things I had written which I myself feared might attract legal action; but they never did.

We spent a fortnight in Germany just after Deedes took over; Nicholas, who had now moved from Reading to the University of East Anglia at Norwich, was doing a six-month exchange with a lecturer from the University of Munich. So, taking Jane with us, we stayed in agreeable lodgings in the centre of Munich after crossing by sea to Ostend and then driving in my wife's blue mini-car, almost as crowded as Kate's Singer had been, by way of Trier, Heidelberg, Mannheim and Ulm. Jane was now working in London in a school for 'difficult' children; she had emerged self-cured from a period of mysterious malaise, involving homoeopathic medicine, an operation for appendicitis and even hypnotism, under the ministrations of various doctors, to buy her own flat in Battersea not far from mine and to find her first vocation in a difficult branch of education: child delinquency.

Once she had moved out of the shadows of the past, this remarkable girl, who had some of her mother's energy and determination directed into different channels, seemed to grow in moral stature every day. As an armchair psychologist I thought the origin of her troubles might have lain in the trauma of being fostered, in Redhill of all places, during the first twelve months of her life. I remembered how, after we removed her from her foster-mother because we had at last found a place to live, she seemed in a state of total shock, physically healthy but quite impassive, showing no reaction to her surroundings or to the people round her, not even to Kate and myself. It was only when her cot, bedding and other familiar objects were restored that an amazing change took place: from being a tiny zombie or, perhaps, contemplative Buddha, she suddenly turned into a living baby. Our relief was extreme; and so must hers have been.

Jane did not like Germany, but I did, though not unequivocally. It was the first time I had been in this country which still, thirty years after the War had ended, seemed under an evil spell. In their dealings with us foreigners the people were polite and correct but inhibited and ill at ease. I had a pervasive feeling that the territory of West Germany, contracted by the victors of the War, was not big enough for their bursting energies. It was late March, cold with persistent snow-flurries and

occasional heavy falls; but the wintry landscape was disappoint-
ing. Where – amid the brand-new factories and the stage-
scenery restorations of ancient cities and towns demolished
during the last months of frenzied, vindictive bombing by the
allied air-forces – was the fabulous landscape of the German
forest I had come to see? The sense of something lacking and
of something latent intrigued me. This was the country from
which my paternal grandparents had come. I felt a tenuous link
with it, difficult to grasp; even a perverse sympathy for the
Third Reich which led me to dwell on its terrible and violent
end and to speculate on the real rather than the assumed
attitudes of its survivors.

I noted, at the entrance to the nave of the huge rebuilt
cathedral of Ulm, a single red rosebud placed at the exact
centre of the pavement. Was it secretly replaced from time to
time, a war memorial more moving than any monumental statu-
ary? Memorials to Hitler's forces hardly existed; those that did
were hard to find. I found one in the centre of the untended
square of grass in front of the derelict Alte Residenz in Munich.
A rough slab of stone covered a small underground chamber
where lay the bronze effigy of a dead or sleeping knight; on the
walls were bas-reliefs of armies, with angels bearing crosses
and the inscription 'Our fallen shall rise again'. There were
one or two unkempt and furtive wreaths in memory of those
who in the end had fought alone against the whole world with
its weight of technological weaponry, and had fought against it
for so long when all hope of victory was gone.

However vile the Nazis were (and who from Stauffenberg
down doubted their vileness?) there can be no doubt of German
heroism. With such forbidden thoughts in my mind I looked at
this unpretentious war memorial, so carefully hidden away; soon
a couple of urchins rushed into the underground chamber,

whooping and scrambling over the recumbent warrior. This had a painful symbolism of its own. Nobody rebuked these children; they had probably been taught at school that Germany had no history between the rise of Hitler and his end. But this unprecedented voluntary self-censorship cannot endure forever. There are unmistakable signs that the Germans are breaking free from their guilt. Will it turn into pride? Who can predict the chances and changes of history? If there are any Germans (or any other people) in Europe a few hundred years from now is it utterly unfeasible that Hitler and his followers may have turned, by a strange twist of fate, into legendary heroes? Or will a World Government ensure that all legends are forbidden apart from its own, intolerably flat and boring as they will be?

We wandered around Munich; walked in the English Garden; saw the Isar rolling in wintry flood; visited the splendid art galleries in the only surviving buildings of the Nazis' preferred monumental style; saw the Nymphenburg and the silvery Amali-enburg; travelled from the spotless railway-station, infested with dangerous-looking Turkish migrant workers, on a spotless, impeccably punctual train to Regensburg and the house of Kepler alongside the rushing Danube; drove over the Austrian border to Salzburg, where from the castle's battlements I looked towards Berchtesgaden and indulged in some more of my per-verse and wicked thoughts; saw a relieved Jane off at the airport on her way back to England, then sank into a tea-room where on buying a newspaper I found it was the eightieth birthday of Ernst Jünger, the greatest living German writer, and a hero of mine: holder of Germany's highest military honour, the Knight's Grand Cross of the Iron Cross, in the First War, and in the Second, preserver of Laon Cathedral and its Merovingian manuscripts during the German advance in 1940; diarist of the Occupation and of the weird life of the *haute collaboration* in

Paris; naturalist; aesthete; scorner of the Nazis; author of at least one strange masterpiece, *On the Marble Cliffs*; protector of animals and of the weak; himself the epitome of the strong.

When the time came to leave Munich we set off northward to spend a few days in the Franconian Forest, which promised something of the Urforst of German legend. But here again I was disappointed; it was a small square of hilly woodland, heavily signposted with coloured marker for graded walks and interspersed with sour streams. We stayed at Muggendorf, a grim village inhabited by grim country people, not particularly friendly to the English (and why should they be?). One evening in our hotel there was a meeting of local farmers to discuss some matter or other, big, thick-set men whose fathers must have supported the Nazis fervently; from the next room the deep, harsh drone of their voices came intimidatingly. Before we left Germany, on the *autobahn* north of Ingolstadt (a small brand-new ancient town about the size of Skipton, on the Danube, where the restored buildings had a particularly unreal and uneasy feeling about them), we had a curious encounter. We had stopped in a forest lay-by to eat our lunch. I was sitting in the little car while my wife took some photographs when I became aware that a big old-fashioned Mercedes had drawn up behind us. Presently a huge man, about sixty, loomed over me. 'English?' he said unnecessarily, with an ogre-like smile. There was something ogreish and larger than life about him altogether. 'I go to England soon,' he said, 'England, Scotland, perhaps Ireland. I am going to look at your English gardens. I am a gardener.' I told him the names of a few famous English gardens. We talked desultorily. 'It must be funny in England now,' he said at last. Indeed it was. Harold Wilson was Prime Minister. 'It depends what you mean by funny', I said cautiously.

233

But he only smiled in his ogreish way and began to walk back towards his car.

Snow, which had been falling in intermittent flurries, began to fall steadily. The brown-black forest began to look as a German forest should. I noticed that on the radiator of the ogre's car were fixed two small metal letters, 'R.A.': Republica Argentina, notorious as the refuge of 'war criminals'. Was he a 'war criminal'? If so, would he be likely thus to advertise the fact? Was he really a gardener (he might, of course, be a fugitive Nazi leader as well)? Or was he a genuine German ogre, perhaps the Erl King himself? He faded away with the forest as we resumed our journey. I immediately began to regret it. I have regretted it ever since, certain that this encounter was one of the great lost opportunities of my life. It would have been easy to exchange addresses, ask him to look me up when he came to England in search of gardens. It is a strange paralysis of the will, an instinct for the negative which is at the root of such folly. Here, perhaps, was the secret of the German forest; it had been offered to me, as in the best fairy stories, by a chance encounter on the road; and I had rejected it. It would not, I knew, be offered a second time.

Back in England, I entered the third decade of my columnar service. Colin Welch, who had become deputy-editor of the *Telegraph*, resigned when he realised he was not going to achieve his ambition of becoming editor, and took up freelance work. Dr Johnson found he could no longer afford to publish two-yearly anthologies of my column; so the next two anthologies were published by the *Telegraph* itself. Soon Dr Johnson had a severe stroke which paralysed one side, and died not long afterwards. I had regular news from various sources, of Kate's love-affair, which had now continued for twenty years; after all that time, in my own newly-settled state, I began to take a benign attitude to what was clearly going to be one of the great love-stories of the twentieth century.

8
The End of Fleet Street

The years passed in my tiny office on the third floor; for four days a week, week after week, allowing for the six weeks' annual holiday and rare absences through illness, I sat at the same desk while Claudie sat at the same desk opposite me. Behind me was the door which led to the fire-escape, marked 'Fire Escape' in large red letters. It had a complicated locking system which in the case of fire might have caused trouble; the door was as difficult to close as it was to open, and sometimes in windy weather it would swing wide, leaving my back exposed to the elements and my papers blowing around the room. Our desks often tended, through the vibration of Claudie's vigorous typing, to move together, causing my own desk to vibrate with increasing force until I invariably said, in the muttering tone she imitated so well, 'I think we've got a bit of osmosis'. Apart from the desks with their trays and blotters, there was little furniture. There were two small tables, one holding a file of the *Telegraph*, the other a file of *The Times*. There was a dull green filing-cabinet with four drawers. One contained very little except the remains of Miss Thompson's filing system with its neat, pink cards, virtually abandoned when she left in 1957, a mouldering monument of efficiency which I kept for superstitious reasons; it was of no practical use whatever. Claudie's own filing system was simple: she put almost all correspondence into the waste-paper basket as soon as she had answered it, retaining in a green folder, for a few weeks only, such letters which she thought interesting or important, then putting most of these into the waste-paper basket in turn. In our early days I used sometimes to complain about this system; but after a time I became reconciled to it. After all, in its rough and ready way it did prevent the room from filling up entirely with waste-paper.

The two middle drawers of the filing cabinet were largely empty except for my 'personal files' and details of publications; the lowest and largest drawer contained a pair of Claudie's shoes, a carton of cigarettes and one or two other personal possessions such as unwanted Christmas presents of talcum powder or children's books. It also contained a bottle of vodka with only a teaspoonful of liquid in it, together with a small cheap drinking-glass, relics of some forgotten party. As with the column in general and everything that concerned it, there was a strong feeling of immemorial custom about this filing cabinet and its contents. If Claudie ever felt any inclination to clear it out, and I doubt if she did, she never acted upon it. We understood each other.

The only other notable piece of furniture in the room was a tall, antique hat-cum-umbrella stand, surmounted by antler-like extrusions and possessing for me an almost sacral character. There was a hanging bookcase on the wall on my left, opposite the window, containing a fine collection of books sent in by readers, almost all of them unreadable and carefully kept by me for that reason: some were volumes of execrable poems published at the authors' expense, but most were works of 'conspiracist' literature such as *Kissinger – KGB Agent, Commucapitalism* and *Wall Street and the Rise of Hitler* – this an alarmingly persuasive book which suggested that Hitler had been, whether wittingly or not, a tool of international finance in its plans for world domination. It was certainly 'calculated to make you think', as the left-wing BBC programme-makers said of their own productions. But its weakness was that it explained everything too convincingly.

On the fourth side of the room, facing me, behind Claudie and next to the door, was a wide shallow steel cupboard with sliding doors, painted dark green. It contained a mass of stationery – boxes of typing paper, carbon paper, writing paper, plain or with the *Telegraph* heading, envelopes of various shapes and sizes, paper-clips and rubber bands, mingled with certain readers' letters and sometimes with magazines Claudie had secreted for her personal use, all in a state of indescribable confusion. It was difficult to slide the doors open; they often jammed on protruding boxes or other items; and when Claudie had to move her chair back into the narrow space between it and the cupboard after I had complained of 'osmosis' it was difficult to get at the cupboard at all. This was part of our system of office management. Irritating though it might seem, I regarded it as traditional, 'given', part of the eternal order of things. To alter it in the slightest would have brought my whole way of life to an end.

On the wall above the cupboard were two framed maps, one of Europe and one of Great Britain, the latter with its ancient counties intact and with proper pre-metric measurements; both were turning yellow. I would have liked a map of Europe as it was at the outbreak of war, or even a map of the Europe of Hitler's New Order. But that, as well as being hard to obtain, would have offended Claudie, a commendable French patriot, to such an extent that she might well have torn it down during my absence. I would have been too passive to restore it.

The decorative scheme of my room was suggestive not so much of the rich eccentricity and nostalgia I might have gone in for if I had followed my inclinations according to my public 'image' as of neglect and decay. It was the only room belonging to a senior journalist on the paper which had no carpet but retained its original brown linoleum. Offered a carpet by the kindly functionary who dealt with office furniture, I declined it. I obstinately retained my uncomfortable high-backed chair until, returning late from the Kings and Keys one night, I fell asleep in it, some time later plunging backwards and waking with a start to find a cleaning woman looking at me with disgust as I lay on the floor amid the chair's irreparable ruins. Though unwilling, I had to accept a modern cushioned swivel-chair instead. Believing 'all change was for the worse' – this was by way of being a columnar motto – I resisted change even in the most minute particulars. I felt a superstitious dread that if there were even the slightest change either in my surroundings or my routine I would be unable to continue my obsessive work on this column which by the early Eighties had reached a total of something like four million words.

Locked in this unvarying manner of life, I thought it must go on unvaryingly for ever, or until death or imbecility supervened. As with my life as an undergraduate at Oxford or my life in the army, I began to feel there was no life conceivable outside it; that the organisation which upheld it – the *Telegraph* with its unchanging ways of working, its hierarchy from the Proprietor and Editor-in-Chief, Lord Hartwell, downwards through the Editor, 'Bill' Deedes, the leader-writers, feature-writers, columnists, correspondents, sub-editors and reporters, and the printers on the 'stone' with their punctually thundering presses, their inviolable privileges and age-old customs and practices – I thought this whole self-contained world in which I had so unexpectedly found myself a special, personal, self-contained niche must also go on, unchanging and for ever. But now the first signs of possible change began to appear.

For some time there had been talk of 'the new technology',

a thing by definition quite as abhorrent to me as it was to the printers whose ancient way of life it threatened. Because of the special, personal nature of my job on the paper (it was simply to write about one thousand words a day on any subject I liked and, within obvious limits, in any way I liked) I had been free of the conferences, meetings and departmental discussion groups which had plagued and bored me so agonisingly at the BBC. Apart from making sure through the sub-editors that my writings were printed – I had gradually and insensibly phased out my evening meetings with the editor, probably to his relief as much as mine – I had no connection with the rest of the paper, making a running columnar joke out of my daily defence of the columnar territory. Then one day came a summons, signed by Lord Hartwell himself, for all 'heads of departments' to attend a meeting on 'the new technology'.

It was about the new electronic techniques which were going to revolutionise the production of the paper, substituting computerised word-processors for composing and printing machines and eventually enabling journalists to produce the paper themselves. We listened sceptically. The general view was that the present system would last out our time and that we need not worry about these fancy innovations. As for the printers, secure in their union power, their closed shops, their ability to bring the paper to a stop at a cost of millions of pounds a week whenever they chose, I doubt if they thought twice about these new notions. As it happened they had just been on strike for a few days, forcing the management to surrender. The printers stipulated, if I understood rightly, that they had no objection to new labour-saving machines being introduced so long as none of the existing labour-force were laid off.

It was said that new print-machinery *had* been introduced, but had simply been put under dust-sheets while the labour-force, recently augmented, used it as a table for their tea-mugs, or play cards on. My Luddite soul applauded. I was all for the printers and their shameless defiance of technological progress. Because of it, I liked to see these overalled figures leaning against the front of the *Telegraph* building in off-duty hours, surveying the world with conscious superiority as they had always done. There was a pretentious restaurant opposite the *Telegraph* where journalists and other such people took their meals. One evening a leader-writer who had eaten unwisely was carried out of it as an ambulance came screaming up the road. The lounging printers gave a rousing cheer. So might their brutish ancestors have cheered the writhings of some greedy burgher. They did not know their time was short, that in a few years this kind of life would disappear forever.

If I had been looking for signs I might easily have found them. A certain restlessness began to be apparent. There were continual repairs in the building. Scaffolding appeared for no clear reason; often I had to write my column under difficulties; the noise of hammering, shouting, the howling of pop singers on transistors as Irish faces stared through the windows. Even the 'Lodge' was changed: tasteless and intrusive partitions of plywood now marred the noble symmetry of its mahogany and marble. The cash-desk where I negotiated my preposterously small expense claims was moved from one place to another and back again. It seemed like trivial change for the sake of change, an aimless shifting from one foot to the other while waiting for the really important changes to begin. Lady Hartwell, Lady Pamela Berry as she had been, died. The Hartwells' son, Adrian Berry, became Science Correspondent, a friendly, boyish man and a total believer in conventional science; he may well have agreed with the Russian cosmonaut who blithely announced he had been into space and found no God or Heaven there,

convinced he had thus disposed of all such outmoded super-
stitions. Adrian did not resent my fictitious astronomer who, if
the universe did not fit his theories, rearranged it till it did.
Once, when I had this character give a sound kicking to a white
dwarf he had trapped in his observatory, Adrian told me: 'You
know, if he really did that he'd get the worst of it! It would be
solid diamond.'

Soon there was a new dispensation by which the whole *Telegraph* building, except for Lord Hartwell's own sacrosanct Fifth
Floor, was rearranged. Protesting, I had to leave my squalid
little room on the third floor and move to what was admittedly
a pleasant, civilised room, slightly larger too, on the fifth floor.
It had carpets and press-button telephones. But I kept our
furniture intact, including the sacred symbolic hat stand, and
as far as possible in the same relative positions. There was a
better view out of the window, west instead of north-west, along
Fleet Street to the Strand and the distant top of Nelson's
column. One November evening, as Claudie and I, our day's
routine finished, looked out of the window at sunset at a sky
leaden and overcast, we saw a *sign*. A narrow band of dying
light stole up from the western horizon, gradually suffusing the
dull grey cloud until the whole sky was a solemn elegiac purple.
It was a sky fit for an emperor's funeral, a thing never seen
before or since. There was even a paragraph about it in next
day's paper.

There were other, more mundane signs of change, breaches
in what had seemed the eternal order of things. Mark O'Donnell, the man we called 'the greatest publican of the twentieth
century', retired from the Kings and Keys, whether to take over
some other pub or to engage in the affairs of the great world I
cannot say. He was succeeded by Andrew O'Connor, an excellent landlord but a very different kind of Irishman. Where Mark

had been cheerful and confident, Andrew was melancholy and retiring. If, as occasionally happened, he allowed drinking after hours on the ground that the drinkers were his personal friends, as in a sense they were, he showed signs of nervousness and hesitation at the possible appearance of the police, whereas Mark would have handled them, if they had appeared, with masterful bonhomie.

Andrew combined a certain meanness with fits of almost painful generosity. One day, for instance, appearing to take pity on me for my unvarying diet of corned-beef sandwiches, he offered me a plate of his own Irish stew, muttering its praises in his rapid Kerry accent, and almost reducing me to tears. When he discovered I knew a certain amount of book Irish he became, not unnaturally, extremely suspicious. After all, the new round of Troubles was in full swing, and although the Provisional IRA had planted no bombs in Fleet Street, it was not unusual to find, on my way to work, streets barred by the emergency white tape of the police. I sometimes wondered why the Provisionals did not put a bomb in Lord Hartwell's dining-room on the occasion of the annual staff Christmas luncheon which all 'Heads of Departments', including myself, attended, listening through a haze of alcohol to the statutory speeches and eating the statutory meal of smoked salmon, turkey and plum pudding which, though always the same, seemed to decline subtly in quality through the years. The Provisionals could have made a clean sweep of the staff of the English newspaper they must have thought most hostile to them. Was our immunity due to Peter Utley? Or had they taken note of my own vestigial Irish nationalism? It had led me several times to object to the spelling of Cardinal O'Fiaich's name as 'O'Fee', on the grounds that as well as being incorrect, it was gratuitously discourteous not to spell his name in the way he spelled it himself.

For some reason I never discovered, Weston never forgave O'Donnell for leaving 'his' Kings and Keys and took an immediate dislike to his successor, who perhaps did not protect him with O'Donnell's open-handed injustice. Very soon he swore that he would not enter the pub again while Andrew remained landlord. And so the Theatre of the Absurd, which had given so much innocent amusement to thousands and become famous throughout Fleet Street and beyond, came to an end. In any case, its great days were gone; for some time Weston's genius for insult had been in decline; although he still performed, to diminishing acclaim, a few favourite set pieces, he seemed unable to add to his repertoire and his powers of improvisation were failing. Occasionally there was a reminder of the old fire as he obliged with a bravura performance. Once, in a rare flash of poetry, he denounced Stephen Daneff in a fine, florid passage: 'Daneff! You're superficial! Shallow! Swimming on the surface of life like a – like a water boatman!' and went on to extend this entomological simile in brilliant style, drawing much applause from all who heard him, particularly the victim.

But it was not long before Weston and his one-time sparring partner, Jameson, both of whom had reached the statutory age of 65, retired, Weston to his garden (it was one of the paradoxes of this extraordinary and very gifted man that in his other primary character of urbane and civilised person as opposed to raving lunatic he was a dedicated gardener) and Jameson to his bungalow and precarious boat on an island in the Thames. Both separately swore a vow that they would never again set foot in Fleet Street; and as far as I know they kept that vow. About the same time my friend Stephen, with whom I had enjoyed so many drunken conversations on historical matters, also retired, not for reasons of age but to enjoy a life of leisure, study and writing. He produced one excellent book on 'Foxy' Ferdinand of Bulgaria. I got very drunk with him on his retirement, unusually so for me; and after I had climbed the stairs at Prince of Wales Mansions and fallen into my flat I got up from the floor and immediately fell into the bath, but transversely, so that my legs dangled over the edge and, as I was wearing my good black overcoat of heavy Crombie cloth, I could not get out again for all my struggles. There I remained without hope of rescue, till the wintry light of morning glimmered through the panes. There was still no hope of rescue; I felt like a character in one of Kafka's humorous short stories; but as I grew sober my powers of muscular coordination returned and with a supreme effort and a dexterous twist I was free. Later that morning, when I reached the office with an appalling hangover, I found, as I knew I would, more than one letter congratulating me on being an oasis of sanity and commonsense in a world gone mad.

Would my readers have thought this manner of life disqualified me from having serious opinions about the madness of the world and from attacking, as I tried to do in my column both directly and by irony and fantasy, lying, dishonesty and humbug? Did they imagine I spent my time in grave discussion with my intellectual peers rather than drinking and talking nonsense in a rather low-grade pub? I was disqualified, as I have always been, from any place in what they would have thought of as respectable society by my ambiguous origins, by temperament and by lack of social graces. There had been a time when I resented this; but it had passed; I had long been reconciled to a life of obscurity.

I have always had an instinctive fear of people, a defensive attitude impressed upon me from my earliest years. It may have

245

sprung from my mother's perpetual fear of being exposed as
inferior to those whose society she had entered through an
unequal, even preposterous marriage. For all my dreams of
wealth and fame, perhaps as an inverse reflection of them, my
conviction of necessary failure has never shifted for a moment.
It is possible that if I had been able to overcome this feeling I
might have achieved worldly success and mixed in more elevated
company. But would there have been any point in getting drunk
in the Garrick Club rather than in the Kings and Keys? And
would I then have been able to write my column, which in
some ways was a compensation through consoling fantasy for a
somewhat meagre social life? Would I have been able to write
anything at all if I had been at home in the halls of the mighty
rather than retiring into a corner as I did on such rare occasions
as I was admitted?

Since my third marriage I had had two distinct lives, one
during the working week, when things went between the little
room in Fleet Street and the flat in Prince of Wales Mansions
as I have described, the other at weekends, which I spent in
our cottage in the Chilterns, a pretty spot among beechwoods
very suitable for dog-walking, mild gardening, doing nothing in
particular and thinking about writing a novel, all of these activities except the last being very congenial to me. As for the flat,
it was inevitable that it should grow more squalid through the
years. The roof of my bedroom began to leak in the autumn of
1976 and in spite of the landlord's attempts to repair it was still
leaking five years later. I took a certain amount of masochistic
pleasure in the placing of bowls to catch the drips, sometimes
waking in the night to lie in the darkness calculating the rate
of stillicide on my luminous clock until warned that an overflow
was imminent and emptying and adjustment of the bowls essen-

tial. I knew none of the other flat-dwellers except by sight but was greatly helped by Mr Gates, the caretaker, a remarkable man of whom I grew very fond. Tall, gaunt and then about sixty years old, he was rather dirty, usually unshaven, and wore an assortment of cast-off clothes. He lived in a ground-floor flat in a distant part of the block, an Aladdin's cave of objects he had acquired from all manner of past tenants: broken armchairs, defunct wirelesses, fragments of crockery, mouldering clarinets and other musical instruments, treadles of sewing machines, hammers, rusting saws, parish-hall chairs, melted gramophone records.

In fine weather, or even in a slight drizzle, whatever the time of year, he spent a great deal of his time standing outside his front door on the pavement, 'keeping an eye of things, sir'. He was a great one for calling me 'sir', partly, perhaps, because he had discovered I once had had the rank of lieutenant-colonel, but also because of a genuine rapport and regard we had for each other. He sometimes hinted at a mysterious and important career in Army Intelligence for himself, once even implying, as I thought perhaps mistakenly, that he had spent most of the War in Spain, based in Gibraltar, though when I addressed him in my meagre Spanish he did not reply but spoke of the iniquity of the police, who made no attempt, he complained, to catch the burglars who infested the flats. These burglars, mostly juvenile West Indians in search of a little cash, had twice broken into my flat, but to my humiliation had found nothing worth taking except a gold Mao Tse-tung badge which my friend Richard West had given me on his return from Communist China. 'I saw them, sir', Mr Gates told me. 'I was after them, sir, but they can run like monkeys, and at my time of life, Dr Gollom says, I have to take it easy.'

I often met Mr Gates, as he stood keeping an eye on things,

on my way from my flat to the bus-stop and we always had a short but most enjoyable conversation. He had a fierce attachment to Prince of Wales Mansions, or 'Prince' as lesser people called it. He felt for it rather as an Oxford college porter would feel for his own college above all others. 'Prince' was only one of a series of mansion-blocks running the whole length of the south side of Battersea Park and beyond it to the west into Battersea proper. It was the oldest block but socially by no means the best; York and Overstrand, which had lifts and central heating, were regarded as socially superior and if, as I imagined, these colleges of my fancy, with their college-like staircases complete with nameboards on the ground floor, went in for rowing on the Thames, 'Prince' would most probably have finished up rather badly. But Mr Gates would have none of this. 'Look at our pavement, sir, clean as a whistle', he said when the dustmen's strike left the London pavements piled with stinking rubbish. 'And look at York, their pavement's a disgrace'. Modestly, he did not point out that this was due to his own hard work and defiance of Dr Gollom's orders. But he knew that I knew.

Mr Gates could not repair my leaking ceiling. But he was sympathetic, lending me a plastic baby's bath with a design of rabbits on it out of his treasury to cope with the widening area of stillicide. He was solicitous about the full and correct presence of my name on the board in the entrance-hall of my staircase. The names were made up of separate plastic letters which he got from the menu-board of the canteen at the local branch of the British Legion, where he was highly respected. Pointing out the imperfect state of some of the other names, which were mere approximations like 'A. S. Own' or alarming Maltese-like constructions like 'X. N. Pxemdezgasx', he lamented that some letters were 'in short supply though there are as many spare X's and Z's as you could wish for'.

So it was a much appreciated privilege and mark of esteem to find 'Lt Col M. B. Wharton' on the board, embarrassingly bogus though it may have seemed to those who saw only an old, mackintoshed figure shambling up the stairs. With all his vagaries, Mr Gates was a valued friend and solace in the stylised loneliness and squalor of my life in Battersea which my wife, who disliked the place, was understandably disinclined to share unless she had things to do in London. Jane, though she lived not far away in a house she had bought after moving out of her flat in Gambetta Street and gradually beautified with enterprise and good taste, was even more disinclined to visit me in 'Prince' for similar reasons. But as a psychologist, she understood my attitude: that unless I could live in a magnificent castle I did not much care about my surroundings so long as they were not actually verminous. My old armchair with the springs gone might be uncomfortable, but 'it made a statement'.

It was in the year 1985 that signs of change began to multiply in Fleet Street. 'The new technology', so long anticipated by some, such as Adrian Berry, with rapt excitement, by others, such as myself, with boredom and scepticism, by others again, particularly the printers, I suppose, with nameless dread, was actually beginning to appear. Were the printers, on the other hand, so armoured in complacency, so certain, through years of having their own way with the management, that they were invulnerable, that nothing untoward could possibly happen to them? There were sporadic strikes; for a time I could never be certain that my column would actually appear. Even more annoying, I sometimes had to complete it ahead of time or suffer other changes in the routine which was so important to me. Suddenly all the talk was of the malpractices of the printers, or, even worse, of the workers who made up the papers into bundles in the evening and until the early hours. These were largely casual workers and there were said to be hundreds of them or even thousands, drawing enormous wages for doing nothing merely by signing on. Many of them did not even exist, it was said, except by way of fictitious signatures like 'Mickey Mouse', 'Popeye' or 'Benito Mussolini', but someone drew their wages just the same.

The various malpractices of the printers and manual workers, together with all their hereditary privileges, were collectively known as 'Old Spanish Customs' and the new technological reformers were determined to abolish them. I don't know how soon it dawned on these workers that they were not merely going to be reformed, but done away with altogether as their beautiful presses and hot metal composing machines – all the ancient paraphernalia down on 'the stone' – gave way to electronic word-processors and other gadgets. It all happened very quickly. There was a period of confusion. I still went on writing my column by hand and Claudie still went on typing it and sending appropriate copies of it to the 'printers'. But soon the printers turned into something else and what happened to the column before it appeared in print next day became mysterious, inexplicable and very worrying. My concentration suffered, and something of the general unease began to communicate itself to Michael ffolkes.

He had always been a steady drinker rather than a drunk. Whenever I climbed the steep stairs which led to his studio and entered that room full of confused bric-à-brac and unexpected contrasts I would find him sipping away as he worked and happy to offer as much wine – often champagne – as anyone could want. Now he began to drink more. His second marriage to

Sophie, a small Scotswoman with pale red hair, of the type I have always found irresistible myself, had collapsed in furious quarrels and he took it badly. Sometimes, when he telephoned for orders at the customary time of 1.30, he would be incoherent, or declare he felt incapable of drawing anything; or he would fabricate absurd obstacles, maintaining grandly that he could not draw a council house or the interior of a bus because he had never been in either.

Sometimes I would lose patience and say: 'Oh, just draw anything! Draw a rhinoceros!' He was particularly fond of drawing animals and very good at it. 'I suppose nobody ever notices my drawings anyhow,' he would retort sullenly. He was in financial trouble too, partly from the cost of his impending divorce and second lot of alimony, partly from an investment he had made in the ghoulish world of fashion, inhabited by corrupt grotesques for whom he was an innocent. He went to see 'Bill' Deedes, the editor, about getting more money, but since he strolled into the office in his battered hat, wearing his artist's 'Bohemian' clothes, he made a bad impression on a man who was also eccentric in his way but who, being of an ancient landowning family and holder of a Military Cross, with a different kind of eccentricity. ffolkes, this lovable man who had always been 'difficult', was becoming 'impossible'. Yet it was impossible not to love and forgive him.

I think of one absurd incident, one of the most absurd which ever took place even in the Kings and Keys, as a true sign of the impending collapse of the old order. One hot afternoon in late summer I was drinking 'BGA' and eating a corned-beef sandwich in the pub when a full-grown lioness stalked in. She was accompanied by several young men and women and a photographer. It was, I soon realised, some kind of advertising stunt. Yet it had an unmistakably mythological character. The lioness, who looked thirsty and unhappy, as well she might, was manoeuvred into the far corner of the L-shaped bar where Utley sometimes held court. He was there now with his female attendants, booming away, chain-smoking and oblivious of the animal, which came to a halt just behind him. Did the most comely of his handmaids rest an elegant white hand on the lioness's tawny head or shoulder, completing a picture which might have hung in the Victorian Royal Academy?

I do not know, because at that moment there was a commotion by the door and in came Hugh Westwood, an important member of the *Telegraph*'s management staff, then much preoccupied with 'labour relations'. A portly, youngish man with the air of a pompous waiter – somewhat like one of those cardboard, dinner-jacketed figures which used to be found outside cheap restaurants with 'Today's Special' written on the broad shirt-front – Westwood had probably never before been in this or any other pub in his life. But he had heard of this intrusion on *Telegraph* property and resolved to deal with it himself. 'Get that animal out of here at once!' he shouted. 'You know perfectly well it's against the rules!' What rules? He stalked out, as though unwilling to stay in the same room as a creature which, he may have thought, could not really exist and was therefore extremely undesirable.

But it was not easy to get the animal out. She flopped down at Utley's feet, evidently exhausted. One of his attendants got a bowl of water for her. She drank noisily and deeply and seemed grateful. Then Westwood returned, angrier than ever. 'If that animal is not out of here within five minutes I shall send for the police!' he roared, then stamped out again. A taxi was sent for; somehow the lion was ushered out, manoeuvred into the taxi, a lengthy process, and driven away. It was an incident which made a deep impression on all who beheld it; most of all on me. From that moment on rumours of doom began to proliferate.

For years now, Lord Hartwell had been warning us in his Christmas luncheon speech that times were hard and the papers, both *Daily* and *Sunday*, were losing money, and for years now we had been paying no attention. But that year, just before Christmas, when we should all have had our invitations, came the sudden announcement that *there was to be no Christmas luncheon*. Then we all knew the end was near. Never again would we sit, inwardly groaning, at the board; never again would our eyes stray to the framed historic pages on the walls in their quaint antique type – 'Mafeking Relieved', 'Kaiser Abdicates', 'Hitler Invades Russia' – or to the portraits of the founding fathers of the newspaper, the Burnham and Camrose dynasties, looking down on us so commandingly as we ate our less and less appealing food and talked, boring and bored, to neighbours who seemed to grow more unintelligible every year. Never again would I glimpse, through the tall windows, Lord Hartwell's magic garden which extended in my imagination over vaster and vaster distances and defied ever more outrageously the laws of spatial relations.

In the New Year we heard that Lord Hartwell's annual warning that his newspapers were losing money was only too disastrously true. Amid reports of recriminations, perhaps ill-founded and certainly confused as far as most of the staff were concerned, we heard that a Canadian millionaire, Conrad Black, had taken over control of the company, the only way, it seemed, in which the newspapers could be saved at all, and that henceforth the Berry family would have only a minority interest. Lord Hartwell, not surprisingly, fell ill and went into hospital for an operation. Not long after he came out I had the dreaded experience of descending several floors in the lift with him. The poor man was in agony, which added helpless sympathy to my dread but still did not enable me, to my guilty regret, to think of one single word to say to him.

More changes were on the way. 'Bill' Deedes who, being seventy-two, had been of retiring age anyhow, duly retired and was succeeded, to everyone's surprise, by Max Hastings, the illustrious war correspondent who had been the first man into Port Stanley at the end of the Falklands War. Previous editors had been in their early sixties when they took over. Max was only forty, an amiable, intelligent man with a lot of genuine charm; tall, lanky, black-haired, energetic and physically active, with long limbs he obviously found difficult to accommodate at his desk when they should have been striding over rough mountains, if not under shot and shell then at least with the sound of sporting guns not far away. I took to him at once, though I perhaps had even less in common with him than with previous editors. But he went out of his way to impress on me that the *Telegraph* was anxious to keep my services. As I was now nearly seventy-four, long past the age of retirement, I had been seriously considering it. So a comical period of negotiation began.

I had an offer from Charles Moore, the editor of the *Spectator*, to move my column from the rapidly changing *Telegraph* to the safety of his own weekly in Doughty Street. Moore was then a man of about thirty who to me seemed too good to be true. He was an Etonian of impeccable family, handsome, intelligent, amiable, sufficiently rich, with a handsome, intelligent wife and I imagine, though I never met them, children of equal excellence. So fortunate did this man seem to be that I feared for him; was he not tempting Fate to strike him down, or liable to be the subject of a 'Job-type' experiment? So far, I am glad to say, my fears for him have proved unfounded.

254

I was tempted to accept his offer. But my habitual prudence and self-doubt prevailed. Would the *Telegraph* allow me to transfer their property elsewhere? Was I capable of writing the column in unfamiliar conditions? I was beginning, after thirty years, to tire of it anyhow. So I dithered for months, no doubt infuriating Moore, though typically there was not the slightest modification of his habitual good manners as he several times gave me lunch 'to discuss matters' at the sort of expensive restaurants I would never have thought of going into myself, even though the *Telegraph* would have paid up without a murmur. Eventually caution prevailed. So that matter passed away, and with it my last chance of achieving notice under my own name. I remained at the *Telegraph* to the end, flattered by the blandishments of Max and his determination to retain my column as one part of the paper which would not change, though everything around it was changing moment by moment.

The 'new technology' was now triumphant, though the fierce battles which ensured the total defeat of the printers largely took place elsewhere. On the *Telegraph* they seemed to fade away insensibly as the old machines, with their reassuring rhythmic uproar, gave place to noiseless electronic flickering. Adrian Berry ran courses of instruction in word-processing for all journalists, with the exception of myself, as a known Luddite and relic of the past, and Peregrine Worsthorne, who declared after one lesson that he could not get the hang of the thing and was excused. In any case, in another quite sensational change among all the other changes, this flamboyant figure had now been appointed editor of the *Sunday Telegraph* in succession to the more sober John Thompson. Perry was a great success, and soon became the necessary 'fabulous monster' of the right which the left required. He appeared on television a great deal, often in discussion programmes where, needless to say, he was the only participant who did not subscribe to the 'left-wing package deal' and was therefore, for all his eloquence, at the required disadvantage.

Should I not have been filling this role myself, as a more thoroughgoing reactionary and, moreover, one not constrained by having a responsible position on a newspaper? Yes; but not only did I hate and despise television in itself, as the most evil and superfluous of all inventions, but my own experience of it had not been fortunate. Years before I had been interviewed on a late-night programme by Robert Kee, whom I had met occasionally in the FitzGibbon circle, though we hardly remembered each other. Urged on by my wife and others, I had agreed, most unwillingly, to submit to a fifty-minute programme of questioning, and as the time drew near for the advance filming one afternoon in an independent television studio in London I grew more and more nervous. As well as drinking a good deal of brandy in the company of John Chisholm, I took several pep pills left over from Desmond O'Neill's prescriptions, and when the time came for me to appear before the cameras and the television people had given me more brandy I was literally 'stoned out of my mind'. I was no longer nervous but was scarcely reacting to my surroundings at all.

So when poor Kee, a state-registered melancholiac like myself and suffering from a bad head-cold, asked me questions about my opinions on various subjects, such as the future of the world, I merely answered 'Yes, in a way' or 'I suppose so'. Although I did manage at the end to advise people to 'get on their knees and pray', the conversation was a 'goalless draw'. I am told by friends who saw the film broadcast that it was one of the funniest performances they had ever seen on television. As I stumbled out of the studio into the 'hospitality area' they gave me yet more to drink and in the end found it quite difficult to get rid of me. I was never asked to appear on television again. So yet another road to fame – today the greatest and most instantaneous of all – was closed to me.

Now the mania for change which had destroyed traditional printing methods and introduced the new electronic technology to Fleet Street was taking a further, terminal form – it was destroying Fleet Street itself. One by one the national news-papers – or rather, those who owned and controlled them – began to sell their premises for enormous sums and make their plans to move to cheaper sites and build new offices on them. The *Telegraph* newspapers, which had been the Berry family's chief personal possession but were now merely a part of Conrad Black's international financial empire, were constrained to move with the rest. New kinds of business executives, wearing ident-ical suits and carrying identical document-cases, were to be seen moving in groups about the building; the soft noise of their incessant conferences could be heard coming from behind closed doors. They seemed to look at such aboriginals as myself, who still remained, with blank, unseeing eyes. Rumours of their decisions abounded: the paper was moving to Battersea; it was moving to Kensington; it was not moving anywhere.

But at last, after months of uncertainty, a decision was announced. It was moving to the Isle of Dogs, to a site in the former docks of the East End, where a new glass palace would be built to house it. The move would be complete by September 1987. So now I knew the date of my own retirement. In his kindly efforts to persuade me to move to the Isle of Dogs with the rest, Max put forward many pleasing fancies: I could be taken there each day in a gold-plated Rolls-Royce; each day a special launch could wait for me on the Thames at Battersea and convey me to the Isle of Dogs by water. But for once my mind was made up. Meanwhile Claudie and I continued to produce the column, sticking as far as possible to the old routine.

I was now the oldest journalist on the staff. All my coevals and many of my juniors had retired or taken 'early retirement', that is, been made redundant with some sort of handout. There were a lot of retirement ceremonies, usually painful, at which speeches and presentations were made. Utley left the *Telegraph* and took the post of Chief Obituarist on *The Times*, dying untimely two years afterwards. I spent solitary lunch intervals at the Kings and Keys. Sometimes, as I stood in a state of half-melancholy with my double 'BGA' and corned-beef sandwich, a new friend, the strange, diminutive genius Roy Kerridge, with his plastic bag and interest in many congenial matters from Celtic myths to what Borrow called 'the affairs of Egypt', would materialise beside me in the intervals of his wanderings around the country, drink his moderate 'light and lime' and, after a little conversation which must have baffled any eavesdroppers, set off on his wanderings again. Or the one-eyed Irish Republican journalist and left-wing borough councillor, Gerry Lawless, would pass rapidly behind me as I stood heedless at the bar, whispering to me messages of Irish import, sometimes, triumphantly, 'We're winning' and once, mysteriously, 'Arthur Scargill's mother was Irish'.

Most of my old friends were dead by now: Con FitzGibbon, René Cutforth, 'Jack' Dillon, Colm Brogan; David Thomson, who was getting long-deserved recognition for his books, notably *Woodbrook* and *The People of the Sea*, was growing frail and was soon to die. But Denis Hills, another friend from my Oxford days, would turn up looking worn, watchful but undefeated from a life as varied and adventurous as mine had been the reverse (he had been rescued once by James Callaghan from the dungeons of Idi Amin). One rainy evening, as I searched Fleet Street for a missing bus-stop I came across John Davenport, a ghost from the past if ever there was one, now penniless and spending sad last days at his mother's house in Worthing. Forgetting that he was barred for life from El Vino's, I bought him a drink there; dirty and unshaven as Davenport was, his flies gaping open and his high patrician voice shrunk to a papery whisper, the manager, usually so mercilessly vigilant, may not have had the heart to throw him out.

It was a consolation to visit Keisley now and then, though it was haunted by Ruth, over whose ashes in the garth Jimmy had planted a walnut tree. For a time he stayed on there; and thanks to him we could still spend sunny hours on the narrow terrace in front of his house, drinking and looking at that incomparable prospect. That last summer of 1987, with my wife and our two yellow labrador dogs, Rosie and Daisy, the latter Rosie's puppy by Jimmy's Leo, I carried out a long-planned undertaking: to climb from Outhgill in Mallerstang, near the ruins of Pendragon Castle, King Arthur's reputed birthplace, up the rocky, pathless slopes of High Seat to the source of the River Eden. I have always been fond of tracing the sources of rivers, whether in England, France or Spain; and of all rivers in the world I love the Eden the best.

Back in Fleet Street the last act was now played out. In the 'Lodge' the bronze memorial plaques from the two wars had been unscrewed and removed – where I cannot say. The space on the wall where test match scores had once been shown – part of a lost England and a lost *Daily Telegraph* – was now a mere patch of discoloration; the mahogany fittings at the reception desk where great ones had once loitered had been removed, and 'Inquiries', now few, had to be made at a peep-hole in one corner; the racks of newspapers remained, but it was months since they had been kept up to date. And from everywhere in the great building came the sounds of departure. By mid-August most of the staff had already left for the Isle of Dogs. Soon Claudie and I were the only editorial staff still working in the building, transmitting the column by a new-fangled fax machine whose workings we did not understand to the sub-editor far away in the new glass building in the East End. We had become objects of suspicion. Sometimes, as I worked away at my desk at an intricate paragraph, a face came round the door: 'Still here?' We put a notice on the door: 'This room is still a working area'.

The last day came, a mild, sad day of early autumn. We had burned some of our archives, thrown away most, including Miss Thompson's filing system and many files of old, mouldering letters, in the great refuse bins provided for the purpose; most of the books, too, including a great deal of 'conspiracy' litera-ture, had to go; now the question was: what to do with the furniture? Since none of it was suitable for the ultra-modern open-plan offices of the new glass palace in the Isle of Dogs, the whole building was full of unwanted objects: desks, tables, bookcases, filing cabinets, anglepoise lamps, unwieldy cup-boards full of paper.

A man I had never seen before, evidently a member of the office furnishing department, had come into his own, as some-one must in such moments of crisis, and assumed authority; he had even devised a kind of uniform for himself, with an official-looking peaked cap. It was he who restored order among the dozens of people milling round to see what they could pick up, some of them, perhaps, people who had walked in off the street and had no connection with the *Telegraph*. But for this natural leader of men there might have been scenes of looting and pillage as in the sacking of a great city. He put a fair price on everything and if there was any dispute as to how many desks or chairs any one person could have, he dispensed justice, operating with his minions from a strange headquarters full of swivel chairs and rolled-up maps. He set guards on the doors and handed out chitties and receipts, making sure that the high-piled cars and pick-up trucks speeding from the building contained no loot that he had not himself approved.

Hysteria was mounting as we despatched the last column via the fax machine and prepared to leave the room where so many thousands of words had been written to be turned into ephemeral newsprint. Will any of them survive? At Claudie's suggestion, I took the bottle and glass from the bottom drawer of the filing cabinet and solemnly prepared to drink the meagre half-measure of vodka that remained. Then, as a confused uproar of voices and the crash of furniture mounted from below, I had a better thought, pouring it on the carpet as a libation to the departing tutelary gods. Was smoke rising from a final holocaust? Was that the crackle of statutory flames which came to our ears? No; but it should have been; likewise a pair of ravens should have winged across the tawdry street, and the noisome Fleet River should have risen to engulf this final scene. Where was Lord Hartwell, I wondered, with a rapid shift of scenario. Where was the once all-powerful master of this doomed domain? As we walked down the marble stairs for the last time, noting that with utter rightness all the lifts were out of order, I had a sudden vision of him, poignant and noble, striding up and down his battlemented garden where the grass grew rank among untended, weed-grown borders, on a Fifth Floor emptied of all its grandeur, lashing with his stick at the overblown, already mouldering flowers of Fleet Street's end.